Immigration and Social Capital in the Age of Social Media

Immigration and Social Capital in the Age of Social Media

American Social Institutions and a Korean-American Women's Online Community

Joong-Hwan Oh

LEXINGTON BOOKS
Lanham • Boulder • New York • London

Published by Lexington Books
An imprint of The Rowman & Littlefield Publishing Group, Inc.
4501 Forbes Boulevard, Suite 200, Lanham, Maryland 20706
www.rowman.com

Unit A, Whitacre Mews, 26-34 Stannary Street, London SE11 4AB

British Library Cataloguing in Publication Information Available

Library of Congress Cataloging-in-Publication Data

Names: Oh, Joong-Hwan.
Title: Immigration and social capital in the age of social media : American social institutions and a Korean-American women's online community / Joong-Hwan Oh.
Description: Lanham : Lexington Books, [2016] | Includes bibliographical references and index.
Identifiers: LCCN 2015047496| ISBN 9781498519267 (cloth : alk. paper) | ISBN 9781498519274 (electronic : alk. paper)
Subjects: LCSH: Koreans--Social networks--United States. | Koreans--Cultural assimilation--United States. | Korean American women--Social networks. | Social institutions--United States. | Online social networks--United States. | Internet and immigrants--United States. | Internet and women--United States. | United States--Emigration and immigration--Social aspects.
Classification:LCC E184.K6 O356 2016 | DDC 305.8957/073--dc23 LC record available at http://lccn.loc.gov/2015047496

∞™ The paper used in this publication meets the minimum requirements of American National Standard for Information Sciences Permanence of Paper for Printed Library Materials, ANSI/NISO Z39.48-1992.

Printed in the United States of America

To my mother, Jung-Hwa Kim
And to my family:
Kyung-Hwa Oh Lee,
Jenny Oh,
Janet Oh,
and Justin Oh

Contents

Acknowledgments

Prior to writing this book on *Immigration and Social Capital in the Age of Social Media,* I published almost two dozen scholarly works that appeared in various academic journals in which my research methodologies focused more on a quantitative data analysis for my proposed research questions. On the other hand, whereas I knew that writing a book would require different orientations and skills, it has been four years since I finally made up my mind to write this book. In fact, my decision to write this book would never have materialized without a great deal of support from my two best friends and colleagues, Charles Green and Ruth Sidel, who often encouraged me to write a book and advised me how to write a book many times. This book is the outcome of their warm, strong words of encouragement. I am also grateful to my two other department colleagues, Lynn Chancer and Thomas DeGloma, for sharing the deep knowledge of their scholarship with me and suggesting their thoughts on the focus and direction of this book.

I must express my deepest appreciation to Dae Young Kim at George Mason University. After reading all chapters of this book, he not only provided me with extensive comments and numerous ideas, but also helped me improve its style and content. I also want to thank Mike Owen Benediktsson for organizing the department seminars of digital media and digital communities for almost two years. These seminars were very helpful in developing the key themes of this book. In addition, many other people instilled so much confidence in me during my academic career in sociology. I would like to express my gratitude to them here. They include Seung Kook Kim, Eui Hang Shin, John Skvoretz, Elwood Carlson, Jimy Sanders, Patrick Nolan, Michael Wood, Philip Kasinitz, Daeki Kang, Sung-Chul Lee, Naomi Kroeger, Robert Perinbanayagam, and Marvin Scott.

I have learned a lot about the rules of the American social institutions from those messages posted by many anonymous members of the "MissyUSA" community on its "Life Q&A" message board in which messages are accessible to anyone. I have greatly benefited from their intelligence, expertise, and experiences. I am also indebted to Abigail Kolker and Jenny Oh who assisted with proofreading. I would also like to thank my mother, my elder brother who passed away (Dong-Hwan Oh), my second brother and three sisters, my mother-in-law who passed away (Kwang Seo), and my wife's brothers and sisters. Without their support and tolerance, it would have been impossible for me to become the person I am today.

The editors and staff at Rowman & Littlefield Publishing Group have as always been very supportive. I especially can't thank Brighid Stone, Joseph C. Parry, and Caitlin Bean enough for that. Finally, I couldn't find the words to thank enough my spouse, Kyung-Hwa, and my three children for their support and endless patience.

ONE

Immigration, Social Capital, and New Social Institutions in the Age of Social Media

In his 1972 article of *Insiders and Outsiders*, Sociologist Robert Merton stated that when accessing certain types of knowledge, "some groups have privileged access, with other groups also being able to acquire that knowledge for themselves but a greater risk and cost."[1] To many immigrants—especially new immigrants—it is quite true that acquiring knowledge about their new country's social institutions is not a simple or easy task. In mid-August 1993, my wife and I came to the United States for my graduate studies in sociology. For the first twelve or thirteen years of our lives here, we underwent many hardships in our attempts to complete simple tasks such as attaining our driver's licenses and Social Security numbers, opening and managing our bank accounts, purchasing our different cars and health insurances, reporting our income taxes, going for regular health check-ups for my pregnant wife and our unborn and newborn children at several county health clinics and hospitals, registering my children in school, maintaining our legal status and acquiring our permanent resident status, and leasing and purchasing houses, among others. Just like for my wife and me, understanding and navigating the social institutions of the host country is a huge challenge for many immigrants in their new land. In this book, my approach to the social institutions of the host country is largely in the regulative framework. More specifically, I argue that for many immigrants, different social institutions of the host country represent different rule settings—e.g., different arrays of laws, policies, programs, regulations, guidelines, standards, or conventions. Despite many unpredictable challenges and difficulties in their new land, some immigrants will strive to find ways to enhance their knowledge or understanding about the rules of their new country's social institutions. The social institutions that this book focuses on are American immigration, welfare, education, housing, and financial institutions. Furthermore, my second argument in this book is that ethnic immigrants' online social networks serve as important venues and channels when they attempt to improve their knowledge or understanding about the rules of the host country's social institutions. For that matter, this book shows that for some Korean-American women, their online ethnic networks play as important a role as offline ethnic networks—i.e., kinship, friendship, and other co-ethnic groups or organizations.

In this book, I have chosen a Korean-American women's online network, called the "MissyUSA" community, to examine both of my arguments stressed above. The "MissyUSA" community is widely known as one of the largest Korean-American women's online communities in North America. Moreover, it is the kind of online network where only married Korean-American women who are born in Korea and currently reside in the United States (and recently, Canada) are allowed to join. Although the actual number of its members has not been publicly released in recent years, the estimated total number was more than 13,000 in November 2002, and there are innumerable daily hits to the website; as described below, there are many links on this website.[2] One such link on the "MissyUSA" website is a message board called "Life Q&A," within which its members can request a wide range of information from its other members. For that reason, the "MissyUSA" community is a typical social network that becomes a very valuable source of social resources to some of its members.[3] Therefore, this book stresses that this Korean-American women's online community, in the perspective of the inquirers (information seekers), functions as a great source of their social resources and in particular, an important source of information needed to improve their knowledge or understanding about the rules of the American social institutions.

In this book, the "MissyUSA" community is also viewed as the network of social supporters—that being respondents or information providers—for the inquirers seeking information or advice on it.[4] Indeed, social support for the inquirers seeking information about the rules of the American social institutions is the other form of social capital that is inherent in, and attainable through, the "MissyUSA" community. In this respect, two distinctive patterns of social support are indeed revealed among the "MissyUSA" respondents. First, some of them take on the role as American institutional guiders who inform the inquirers of the rules of American social institutions. Additionally, there are some respondents who offer emotional support to the inquirers (information seekers). By and large, the "MissyUSA" respondents become information guiders and/or emotional supporters, that is, more generally, social supporters, to the inquirers (information seekers). In this book, all the social supporters—respondents (information providers)—are further classified into two broad groups and their respective sub-groups, in accordance with their response patterns towards the inquiry messages about the rules of the American social institutions: instrumental guiders (information describers, analysts, confirmers, and advisors) and emotional supporters (companions, encouragers, and critics). It is this book's basic premise that their messages in response to the inquiry messages are mostly subject to their personal experience, expertise, judgment, or based on hearsay.

Overall, what I want to emphasize in this book is that membership in the "MissyUSA" community can create two distinctive forms of social capital (social resources and social support) among its participating members. The clear implication of this is that some of its members can request information about the rules of the American social institutions (social resources), and in response, some other members provide information seekers with certain kinds of information about the rules of the American social institutions, and/or support them emotionally (social support). More specifically, the first proposition I suggest here is that one group of "MissyUSA" members, who I call "inquirers" or "information seekers," tends to seek information about the rules of the American social institutions through their ethnic online community (see more details below in this chapter's section of Immigration and the Five American Social Institutions). The second proposition that is discussed in detail in the following section is that another group of "MissyUSA" members, who I call "respondents" or "information providers," become a group of social supporters—instrumental guiders or/and emotional supporters—for the inquirers seeking information. In short, in this book, I delve into these two propositions in great detail through the examination of messages posted on the "Life Q&A" message board of the "MissyUSA" community.

THE KOREAN-AMERICAN WOMEN'S ONLINE COMMUNITY AS THE EPITOME OF SOCIAL CAPITAL

Much of sociological research on social capital has been conducted by examining its sources, main characteristics, forms or types, functions, processes, as well as both its positive and negative effects.[5] What these diverse research areas of social capital have in common is their emphasis on the significant role of social networks for social capital. Here, social networks refer to a set of relations or ties among members of the same or different groups.[6] Social networks generally produce two distinctive forms of social capital: "strong ties" or "bonding social capital" versus "weak ties" or "bridging social capital."[7] By and large, "strong ties" or "bonding social capital" are a set of relations developed and maintained among members of a single and relatively small-size group—e.g., kinship, friends, close neighbors, or intimate colleagues in the workplace—and ultimately, it has the potential to support its members in various ways. In contrast, a set of relations formed across members of different groups—e.g., acquaintances, or even unfamiliar persons—can be often called as "weak ties" or "bridging social capital." Similar to "strong ties" or "bonding social capital," the structural position of one group in relation to other groups, characterized by "weak ties" or "bridging social capital," also operates as an important factor affecting its members' access to social resources.

As a whole, social networks of any kind typically produce different degrees of social capital for their members. As a definition, social capital at the individual level can be understood as individual awareness of the properties inherent in his or her social networks.[8] There is one important question related to this definition of social capital: What are the properties inherent in social networks? Essentially, one of the properties inherent in social networks is the resources embedded in, or accessible through, social networks, also called "social resources."[9] According to sociologist Nan Lin, there are two distinctive types of social resources: material goods—e.g., houses, car or money, and symbolic goods—e.g., education, memberships in clubs, reputation, or fame.[10] As the supplement to Lin's social resources, one form of social resources emphasized in this book is information, especially any sort of information about the rules of the American social institutions. According to sociologist James Coleman, who approached the pursuit of personal goals or interests as one of the main drives of people's membership (or participation) in organizations or associations, the inclusion of information as a form of social capital is because sometimes certain types of information can be costly or difficult to obtain without the aid of social networks.[11] For the inquirers seeking certain kinds of information, such information solicited from other members of their social networks, such as the "MissyUSA" community, can be a really critical avenue for them to gain material or symbolic goods, or even both.

From the standpoint of inquirers (information seekers), the concept of social capital in this book is identified as one's awareness of how to access information on the basis of his or her participation in social networks. However, this book takes two different points from Lin's and Coleman's works on the impact of social networks on social capital, namely, the acquisition of information. First, the size and intensity of social networks matter here. In both sociologists' views, the social networks they examined are closure networks (i.e., dense or personal networks), whose memberships are relatively small in size, spatially bounded, and generally acquainted with each other. As a result, these small-scale, sometimes personal networks often make certain types of information difficult for non-members to assess, since this information is only offered to their participating members. Similarly, the "MissyUSA" community analyzed in this book is also a kind of closed network because full membership is only permitted to Korean-born immigrant women in the United States and Canada. However, it cannot be entirely treated as such closed network because full membership is widely open to any Korean-born American and Canadian married women. In fact, it is very large in its membership size and anonymous in the disclosure of its members' personal profiles, and it is also a network beyond space and time. Nevertheless, its online members can seek a wide variety of information, subject to the social support of its unknown co-ethnic members (respondents).

Second, an acquisition of information through closed or personal networks often relies upon members' constant efforts to abide by his or her network norms and expectations, and their willingness to build up mutual trust with their group members over a relatively longer period of time. This is not generally the case on the "MissyUSA" community where its members are somewhat free from their compliance with the network's underlying norms and their buildup of reciprocity and mutual trust among its other online members. The result is that the seeking of information among its online members is always possible on their connections to its website links. Furthermore, what's interesting here is that there is no requirement for the inquirers (information seekers) of the "Missy USA" community to compensate respondents in return for the acquisition of information they wanted. Overall, this "MissyUSA" community of married Korean-American women may be a type of Castells' "specialized communities" where individuals join networks with low entry barriers and low opportunity costs.[12] More importantly, however, it is an essential feature of the "MissyUSA" community in which both sides of its information seekers and providers feel comfortable or committed, even before they post the messages seeking information or providing the information sought. This is because this Korean-American women's online community is indeed predicated on a great sense of "we"-ness among its anonymous members.

Social support is another vital property embedded in social networks and available to their members. If no response message took place after the online posts seeking certain information, the "MissyUSA" community loses its function as a provider of social capital in the perspective of information seekers. A social network like the "MissyUSA" community requires its other members to provide social support for its information seekers. In this book, I approach this aspect of social capital from the position of respondents (information providers). For them, social capital comes through their actions which support network members—here, the postings of their messages in response to the inquiry messages. As a matter of fact, for the information providers of the "MissyUSA" community, the sense of we-ness, or connection, with other anonymous online members is the foundation of why many of them are inclined to post their response messages that consist of not only information, but also sometimes of emotional support for inquirers; the disclosure of information and expressions of emotional support are two general aspects of social support that are voluntarily offered to the inquirers (see details below).

The question that follows is from where the sense of we-ness shared by both the inquirers and their respondents of the "MissyUSA" community originated. In general, the creation of a sense of we-ness among members of co-ethnic groups is connected to the sense of their "imagined community"—that is, their retention of certain group values, identity, and images of the past widely spread in their homeland,[13] or their similar mental world, both of which arose under the common language, shared cultural traits, and life experiences.[14] In turn, the ethnic group membership serves as the main source of its members' sense of we-ness what Sociologist Milton Gordon called "the locus of the sense of intimate peoplehood."[15] Before emigration to the United States, many Korean-American women grew up in Korea, a nation that is highly homogeneous racially, unitary in language, and has a very collective in cultural orientation (group goals, norms, and identity) rather than having an individualistic cultural orientation (personal goals, needs, and identity). Even in the chronological trend of residential settlement among Koreans in the United States, a great number of them have lived in large gateway cities such as Los Angeles, New York, San Francisco, Chicago, Honolulu, and so on.[16] This geographically selective concentration of Korean-Americans in such large American cities for a long time is very well reflected in their higher-level economic activities in Korean ethnic enclaves, adjacent residence in the same local areas, and ongoing social interactions with each other through their cultural institutions such as religious organizations, mostly Korean-American churches.

Along with these commonly shared backgrounds which includes ethnicity, language, homeland, and immigration experiences, their shared gender, marital, and parental statuses as married Korean-American women can also be an important contributing factor for constructing or maintaining a sense of we-ness among its anonymous online members. Likewise, one other factor contributing to a sense of we-ness among them could conceivably be the possibility of their regular access to local Korean language media, which are mostly stationed in their large gateway cities—i.e., daily Korean newspapers in both printed and electronic forms, locally aired Korean televisions or radios, or weekly Korean magazines or periodicals. Through these ethnic media outlets, many Korean-Americans have a better chance of learning the news related to Korean-American communities, information useful for their adjustment into American society, and perceptions and evaluations of non-Korean Americans to Korean-Americans, which reveal to new immigrants their relative racial and class position in American society. Thus, as a result, immigrants' connection into their local ethnic media operating in the host society can strengthen their sense of collective identity among group members by creating boundaries for inclusion and exclusion.[17] Moreover, the rapid development of computer-mediated communications or information technology—e.g., cable networking, electronic transmissions of text, voice, and video by the Internet—has made it possible for a greater number of Korean-Americans regularly to hear the latest happenings and events occurring in contemporary Korean society, and to watch up-to-date Korean programs such as Korean TV dramas, reality shows, sports, and so on. The fact of the matter is that this continuous connectivity with their homeland through the Internet has the potential to create and maintain a sense of we-ness among anonymous Korean-American women participating in the "MissyUSA" community. To put it simply, the base of their collective sense of identity makes it possible for the "MissyUSA" community's anonymous members to request or provide information by posting their inquiry or response messages on the website.

In personal networks like small-scale ethnic networks, generally, social support is offered or given by family members, friends, neighbors, or colleagues in the workplace in the form of small services, large services, financial aid, emotional aid, and companionship.[18] In the "MissyUSA" community, as stressed above, social support for its information seekers is voluntarily initiated and provided by some of its anonymous members through their messages in response to the posts seeking information. At this point, one important question that needs to be addressed here is in what general and specific ways these respondents support the inquirers (information seekers). To answer this question, this book suggests two broad groups of "MissyUSA" respondents who all act as social supporters for the inquirers seeking information on the rules of the American social institutions. The first group of respondents is instrumental guiders. These instrumental guiders can be further divided into four subgroups; information describers, analysts, confirmers, and advisors. The major role of information describers is to provide simple or straightforward information (facts or short descriptions), or to provide information that has little or nothing to do with the inquiry. Explanations, logical thoughts, or suggestions are completely absent in the contents of their response messages. Information analysts are another subgroup of instrumental guiders. They take on the role of explaining, interpreting or evaluating the background, causes, or nature of the key issues contained in the inquiry messages, without including their advice or suggestions in the text.

Information confirmers are the third subgroup of instrumental guiders. Their principal role is to give reassurance or confirmation to those "MissyUSA" inquirers who want to make sure whether the information they wrote in the text is accurate or proper on the issue, or whether they are on the right track. The fourth and last subgroup of instrumental guiders is information advisors. Their main role focuses on advice, correction, or suggestions. Thus, they are inclined to post their messages that give advice, suggest some ideas or options, correct misinformation, or project what will happen next (outcomes) on the grounds of their own past or present experiences, their expertise in the area of the request for information, or their accounts of someone else with whom they were acquainted. In some cases, the messages of some respondents also contain specific instructions that include necessary steps, procedures, or ways to tackle the issues raised by their inquirers. Taken together, some instrumental guiders will belong to more than two of its four subgroups, while some others will only belong to one of them.

In the "MissyUSA" community, the second group of these respondents is composed of emotional supporters. What their response messages have in common is the presentation of their inner feelings or emotions in the message. More specifically, this kind of social support group can be further divided into three subgroups: companions, encouragers, and critics. In their messages in response to the postings of inquiry, companions are those who express their sympathy, warmth, or empathy to the inquirers. In the "MissyUSA" community, their close companionship to the inquirers was often demonstrated in their postings of expressing agreement to the inquirers' points, or revealing their own past or current experiences or stories similar, or identical, to the inquirers'. Thus, sharing the feelings of the inquirers such as anxiety or fear is the main role of these companions. Similarly, encouragers tend to support the information seekers facing difficult situations by stressing their personal worth, which is often expressed through a positive comment or praise, by encouraging them to continue to give a little more effort, and/or by convincing them that at last, their efforts will come to fruition. As the third subgroup of emotional support, critics admonish the information seekers' misjudgment, poor knowledge, effortlessness, or negligence, and sometimes attempt to turn them towards the right direction by providing appropriate instructions or information. By and large, the respondents of the first two subgroups of emotional supporters (companions and encouragers) become anonymous consolers especially for those information seekers who feel stressed due to little or no understanding about the rules of the American social institutions.

For some respondents, their role as the instrumental guiders to the inquirers will take primacy over that of emotional supporters. However, the converse is also true. Moreover, it is also possible that some respondents will conduct joint roles, namely, those of both information guiders and emotional supporters. In short, in the perspective of respondents (or information providers), the "MissyUSA" community becomes a social support network for the information seekers (social support).

IMMIGRATION AND THE FIVE AMERICAN SOCIAL INSTITUTIONS

Many immigrants struggle to comprehend how their new country's social institutions work. The first sign of how difficult this is for them arises often when they find each of the social institutions of their host country to be totally unfamiliar to them. Their troubles can become more intensified when they do not know what to do during their encounter with its wide array of legal and unwritten rules, procedures, and various types of organizational units in each individual social institution. However, even under this troublesome situation, some immigrants are inclined to exert their own efforts to understand each of them or their certain elements—e.g., in the American immigration institution, a legal policy and procedure about citizenship through naturalization, or the stated rules of home finance or the related policies on the eligibility criteria in the American housing institution. Sociologist Milton Gordon described this aspect of immigrants' approach toward American social institutions as "an unquestioning reverence for existing American institutions."[19] In one sense, his statement alludes to immigrants' own dispositions to learn for themselves how American social institutions work. In turn, immigrants' admiration for the social institutions of their host country signifies their growing sense of the importance of these social institutions for their new settlement.

In this book, my reasoning on why some "MissyUSA" members called inquirers (or information seekers) post the messages requesting information about American social institutions is that knowing and understanding them is a basic prerequisite of their lives to better adjust themselves into their new social environment, regardless of whether or not they pay reverence to American social institutions. Since the lack of knowledge about American social institutions often creates a lot of inconvenience for them and some losses (financial costs, emotional stress) during their settlement process, the expectation is that they will have some plan of action to meet their concerns.[20] To put it another way, their willingness to learn American social institutions reflects one aspect of their mentality to reduce the costs, material and emotional, that can occur during the adjustment period to their new life, or otherwise to gain some tangible or intangible benefits on the basis of such learned knowledge. In this respect, the actions of some "MissyUSA" members (inquirers)—the postings of messages requesting information on American social institutions—can be considered part of their planned, purposive (rational) actions seeking help to cope with their personal or family issues related directly or indirectly to the American social institutions.

My perspective on the social institutions of the host country is largely in the regulative framework.[21] Basically, one of my arguments stressed in this book is that different social institutions are really different rule setting entities. In other words, to many immigrants, a typical social institution of their host country can be seen as an amassed entity of the rules, especially legal and formal written rules, which were generated institution-wide as well as at its individual organizational level.[22] The categories of institutions—which I call social institutions—that this book covers are American immigration, welfare, education, housing, and financial institutions at the national, state, and local levels. The range and types of organizations that this book focuses on are all the organizational bodies that form and structure a typical social institution. For example, the American financial institution at the organizational level, which is introduced in the sixth chapter of this book, encompasses all the public-sector organizations (U.S. Congress, the U.S. Supreme Court, state or local assemblies, state or municipal legislatures, state courts, and all the finance, insurance, and taxation departments and regulatory agencies at the federal, state, and local levels), and all the related private-sector ones (i.e., commercial banks, savings and loans associations, credit unions, investment banks, insurance companies at the federal, state, and local levels). From that point on, this book, however, avoids further discussion on whether and how the various organizations of the social institution are associated with each other.[23]

The economic historian Douglas North defined the terms "institutions and organizations" very concisely. He defines institutions as "the rules of the game" which consist of written or formal rules (laws, statutes, contracts) as well as unwritten or informal rules (conventions, codes of conduct, norms of behavior).[24] From this definition we can conclude that a set of choices available for the general public is indeed bounded by the realm of "the rules of games." Then, he further characterized various groups of organizations—i.e., political (political parties, a regulatory agency), economic (firms, trade unions), social (churches, clubs), and educational (schools, universities)—as not only just "players" heavily constrained by these rules of the game, and also as "agents of institutional change."[25] Overall, one important point this book takes from North's approach to institutions and organizations is that "both what organizations come into existence and how they evolve are fundamentally influenced by the institutional framework."[26] Furthermore, this book also draws much attention to some other points that were of little interest in North's study of institutions and organizations. The first is that there are different sources that create institution-wide rules. The second is that some organizations are not only enactors of institution-wide rules, but also creators of their own rules. Thirdly, the questions of whether and the extent to which institution-wide rules influence organizational rules within the institution also need to be addressed to some extent here.

At first, American public (legislative or judicial) authorities—e.g., U.S. Congress, state or local assemblies, federal or state supreme courts—have legal powers to enact institution-wide rules (laws, statutes, decrees, or ordinances). A clear example of this, at the federal level, is all the laws and rulings enacted by U.S. Congress (i.e., common laws) or the U.S. Supreme Court (i.e., case laws). In the following chapters of this book, some of the vital laws of the American social institutions at the federal level are briefly summarized. For example, the second chapter of this book will introduce the key laws of the American immigration institution, such as the 1952 Immigration and Nationality Act (INA), also known as the McCarran-Walter Act, and its 1965, 1976, and 1978 amendments passed by U.S. Congress. At the state level, for example, individual states (state assemblies), under the federal banking laws such as the McCarran-Ferguson Act of 1945 and the Gramm-Leach-Bliley Act of 1999, also have had legal powers to issue and enact their own state insurance laws that allow them to determine insurance company licensing and producer licensing (insurance agents and brokers) in the state, as well as to approve or prohibit the sale of certain insurance products (life and annuities, property and accidents, health) and terms (policy premiums, policyholders' coverage or benefits)—see the sixth chapter of this book.

At the state or local levels, other forms of institution-wide rules were also initiated and enacted by state or local legislative or state judicial organizations (state or local assemblies, state supreme courts) in the past. For example, U.S. Congress, in 1972, passed the Uniform Residential Landlord and Tenant Act (URLTA) that enunciates the uniform terms and conditions of the rental agreement between a tenant and a landlord—see the fifth chapter of this book. Then, to those states adopting the URLTA not entirely (i.e., California and New Jersey), their own tenant-landlord laws were, or can be further, initiated not only by state legislatures (statutes) and state Supreme Courts (case laws), but also by local jurisdictions (ordinances) within a state—i.e., city, county, or town. As another example, in the sixth chapter of this book, taxation is dealt with as a distinct sector of the American financial institution. As a whole, American tax laws are a good example for the case that reflects the interests of all federal, state, and local governments. Indeed, U.S. Congress, under the Sixteenth Amendment to the U.S. Constitution, codified and re-codified federal tax laws, broadly named as the Internal Revenue Code (IRC) by which the Internal Revenue Service (IRS), as a bureau of the Department of the Treasury, is responsible for collecting taxes on the four main sources (income, employment, estate or gift, and excise taxes). In the same way, state and many local assemblies (e.g., the New York State Assembly, the New York Council) also created, or can enact their own tax laws or codes to collect taxes from these four sources.

Under the protection of institution-wide rules, some public or private organizations also have legal powers to introduce their own organizational rules (managerial or regulatory guidelines or standards, policies, or programs). In fact, it seems that in general, private-sector organizations (mostly for-profit organizations), relative to public-sector (government-sector) ones, are much more interested in having their own organizational rules, albeit under the confines of their institution-wide rules of course. For example, under the laws and formal regulations of national, state, and local housing and community development, home finance, and real estate, individual mortgage lenders (banks) can set up their own organizational rules, namely, their own home loan terms and conditions—i.e., mortgage packages (conventional or Federal Housing Administration loans), mortgage types (fixed- or adjustable rate mortgages), interest rates, and payment periods (15 or 30 years)—see the fifth chapter of this book. As evidence for the existence of public-sector organizational rules, some of them were often explicated in their formal written policies or guidelines for the applications (required documents, methods to prepare application forms or submission) and for the following procedures after submitting the applications—e.g., fingerprinting and interviewing for citizenship (see the second chapter of this book), weekly claims for unemployment insurance (see the third chapter of this book).

Along with the formal written rules, many different kinds of unwritten and informal rules—e.g., conventions, norms, codes of behavior, customs, or practices—exist in a typical social institution. But, these sorts of rules are not easy for people outside of its organizations to detect. For the immigrants planning to apply for citizenship through naturalization, for example, the completion of their application form with integrity (ethics) is not only a legal rule, but also an unwritten convention emphasized by the United States Citizenship and Immigration Services (USCIS), also known as a component of the United States Department of Homeland Security (DHS). As another example, in the United States, the primary responsibility for public education is granted to individual state (state legislature, governor, state-level board of education, and state education department or agency)—see the fourth chapter of this book. Although states set formal policies on educational standards for their public schools, it is still our belief that local educational units (district superintendents, principals, and teachers) should have more of a right to develop course curriculums and classroom instructions for local students. As another example, in a typical home-buying process that is elaborated on in the fifth chapter of this book (the American housing institution), both a home inspection of the property and the application of a mortgage on the property are required. But, the steps between them are not formally outlined. Nonetheless, as a general rule, a mortgage application tends to precede the home inspection of the property.

In a social institution, do its institution-wide rules affect its organizational-level rules?[27] As this book demonstrates, the answer to this question is not simple. Nonetheless, in this book, it is my premise that in a typical social institution, its institution-wide rules shape its organizational-level rules to varying degrees. Although this book has no interest in research on the impact of extant institution-wide rules on the creation or transformation of organizational rules within a social institution, the fact that three different types of relationships exist between them cannot be completely ignored. The first type of their relationships is a strong hierarchical (or coercive) one.[28] For example, in the American immigration institution, the United States Citizenship and Immigration Services (USCIS) and the National Visa Center (NVC) in the Department of State take charge of the main body of work on immigration petitions (i.e., family-based or employment-sponsored immigration) under the annual limits of immigration visas mandated in the Immigration and Nationality Act (INA) of 1952 and its amendments. In the area of public primary and secondary education, some U.S. states or municipal governments (e.g., New York City) have stringent assessment rules in evaluating the performance of the public schools in their jurisdiction—see the fourth chapter of this book. A result can be cuts in school funding, or in an extreme situation, school closings due to poor graduation rates and students' academic performance. The second type is a moderate hierarchical (or coercive) relationship between the institution-wide rules and the organizational-level rules. In this case, institutional rules grant within-institutional organizations a legal authority in the creation and action of their own organizational rules. Thus, this type of relationship takes place when the central goals or missions of a social institution are, to a great degree, ingrained in those of their organizational bodies. To tackle public health conditions, employment insecurity, or the shortage of affordable housing units, some individual state or local agencies, under both federal and state legal rules, have introduced their own organizational rules (eligibility and coverage guidelines) to run Medicaid, Unemployment Insurance (UI), and public housing programs. The third type of their relationship is a weak hierarchical (or coercive) one. One of such cases can be found in the American educational institution. It is well-known that a city school district's board of education should comply with both state and city educational measures. At the same time, these district boards of education can apply their own educational rules or policies to the public elementary and secondary education schools in their jurisdiction. Thus, district boards of education also have their own latitude somewhat in the creation and operation of their own educational policies or codes that explicate the interests of their community constituents, the approval of district employee hiring, the evaluation of superintendents, the contract negotiation with teachers or a teacher union, and the oversight of curriculum.

In discussing the American social institutions in this book, it is also assumed that the goals of a social institution legitimate the creation, maintenance, amendment or revision, or revocation of both its institution-wide rules and its organizational-level rules; then, discussions of the sources of its goals are the topic beyond the scope of this book. For example, earlier immigration laws, such as the Immigration and Nationality Act (INA) of 1952 and its 1965, 1976, and 1978 amendments, were unquestionably enacted to meet those goals of the reunification of American citizens' families abroad, American economic prosperity, the promotion of human rights for refugees and American population diversity. Thereafter, specific procedural and administrative rules (application guidelines or instruction) were systematized through the United States Citizenship and Immigration Services (USCIS), and the National Visa Center (NVC) and the U.S. embassies or consulates in the Department of State. Likewise, the goal for improvements to homeownership rates among American working- and middle-class families was reflected in earlier national housing legislations that established the FHA (Federal Housing Administration) loan program by the National Housing Act of 1937, the Veterans Administration (VA) loan program by the Servicemen's Readjustment Act of 1944, the regulation of housing and mortgage discrimination on the basis of race, color, country of origin, and religion by the Fair Housing Act of 1968 and its following amendments, as well as others. Moreover, all the U.S. private banks' and credit associations' own mortgage policies and business rules are also to some degree in compliance with this goal that lies behind some federal-level housing and financial laws.

Overall, in this book, a social institution is broadly defined as the composite of all of its organizations (both public and private sectors) that are primarily oriented to achieve its institution-wide goals (for national purposes, in the public sector and mostly, for economic profits in the private sector), or at the micro level, to complete its organizational mission through administration, oversight, and/or enforcement, under both its institution-wide and within-institution organizational rules (laws, policies, programs, or organizational procedures, guidelines, or conventions). Indeed, a large group of "MissyUSA" members (inquirers or information seekers) tend to post messages seeking information on both or either institution-wide or within-institution organizational rules from each of the five afore-mentioned social institutions, respectively. As a matter of fact, what is really driving them to post their inquiry messages on the "MissyUSA" community is the desire to learn these institutions' general or specific rules. In short, from the standpoint of the inquirers (or information seekers), the "MissyUSA" community ultimately becomes an important network and source of information about the rules of the American social institutions (social resources).

A STUDY FROM THE "MISSYUSA" COMMUNITY

The history of Korean immigration to the United States dates back to almost 110 years ago. The size of the Korean populations in the United States was relatively small until 1970, when it consisted of a little less than 70,000 people. Since then, it has grown in number substantially from more than 350,000 in 1980 to almost 800,000 in 1990, and then to more than 1.4 million in 2010.[29] Sociologist Min explained this rapid growth of Korean-Americans over the last three decades in the four key reasons; changes in the difference of economic and educational opportunities between Korea and the United States, the U.S. Immigration Act of 1965 that opened the doors to Asians, the arrival of both Korean wives of U.S. servicemen stationed in Korea and Korean orphans, and the movement of labor from Korea to the United States due to the close economic ties between both countries.[30] According to immigration status, the Korean populations in the United States are, by and large, made up into three distinctive groups: family-sponsored preference immigrants, employment-sponsored immigrants, and temporary residents—e.g., Korean international students, trainees, exchange scholars, temporary workers, visitors, and undocumented immigrants. In any case, there is no doubt that their accessibility to a wide variety of information on American society and the Korean-American community—i.e., employment or business, housing, community, or children's schools—will help alleviate the burden of new Korean settlement in the United States. Wherever Korean immigrants reside in the United States, similarly, many of them also strive to access information about their homeland (Korea)—i.e., news, entertainment, culture, and so on.

For those matters, both local and transnational Korean media outlets in the United States—e.g., newspapers, cable televisions, and radios—exert a pivotal role in providing valuable information to many information- or advice-seeking Korean-Americans. Thus, these Korean media housed in the United States tend to report up-to-date news and provide them information about both of the nation-wide American society and local American community, the Korean-American community, and contemporary Korean society. Before the Internet, the majority of Korean-language newspapers issued in the United States were, unfortunately, unreachable to those Koreans living outside of Korean-American gateway cities or communities. As a result, the unavailability of the Korean-language print media, coupled with the immigrants' limited proficiency in English, made it difficult for them to obtain the information critical for their adjustment in the new land, as well as knowledge about what was happening in Korean society. However, the recent development of computer-mediated communications, also known as the Internet, has made it possible for Korean media stationed in both the United States and Korea to publish their content online and to reach Korean audiences without geographical barriers. Nowadays, most Korean-Americans can easily assess news and information about "here" (the United States and the Korean-American society) and "there" (Korea) through online Korean media. In fact, the two major Korean newspapers issued in the United States, *Korea Daily* and *The Korea Times*, perform such dissemination of local, national, and transnational happenings, information, and entertainment through their online platforms. Moreover, in print or online, there are many other locally based Korean newspapers, magazines, and periodicals that provide updates on a wide range of information about local communities for those locally settled Korean-Americans. In general, any type of Korean-language media in the United States, in print or online, stands as the critical source of social capital (information) among many Korean-Americans.

However, these types of media generally become less effective when certain groups of Korean-Americans seek case-specific or more in-depth information in order to meet their own personal needs or concerns. This being the case, some of them will turn to some members of their ethnic networks, for example, those people in the family circle, tight-knit groups of co-ethnic friends or neighbors, Korean-American churches, or from various other kinds of not-for-profit or for profit Korean-American community organizations or associations (i.e., Korean-run community services, family counseling centers, senior service centers, real estate business firms, law firms, banks, cram schools) as their major sources of information. Moreover, some others will also turn more attention to certain Korean-language digital media (the websites on the Internet) to acquire such case-specific and/or in-depth information in pursuit of their particular interests.

South Korea (Korea hereafter) is recognized as the leading Internet nation of the world.[31] Since the early 1980s, the tremendous investment of the Korean government and larger Korean IT industries in the basic computer and telecommunication networks have made Korea the leading nation in the development of broadband Internet and other information infrastructures.[32] Consequently, 97.5 percent of all Korean households, for instance, were broadband service subscribers, as of 2010.[33] As a result, the majority of the general public in Korea nowadays consists of Internet users who regularly do online shopping, banking, or café, and assess Internet-based news, entertainment, game sites, or other websites. Moreover, such diffusion and popularity of the Internet in Korea has also led the greater number of Korean Americans' participation in various Korean-run online communities. By far, some of the most well-known Korean-American websites are "HeyKorean" (heykorean.com), "MissyUSA" (missyusa.com), "Mizville" (mizville.org), and "Korean Community of US" (there are also 10 local websites—e.g., lakorean.com, sfkorean.com, newyorkkorean.com). A common feature of these four Korean American websites is the operation of many message boards (links), in which members post messages on a wide range of topics in order to request, transmit, or share certain information to or with their online members.

To serve all members who have diverse interests or demands, these four websites run those message boards that individually focus on the specialized themes relating to employment, immigration and law, family, house, finance, health, education, language, location, moving, technology, and so on. For those Korean-Americans who want to know Korean cultural practices or the current news of their homeland and the United States, for instance, these websites run the message boards that cover topics, such as food and cooking, motherhood, Korean popular culture (TV dramas, entertainment programs, music), and the message boards relating to social and political affairs that recently took place in Korea and the United States. What is important here is the fact that the message boards of these four websites can be used to exchange a wide variety of information anytime among their online members (social resources). More importantly, such function of these message boards will work only when members—here, respondents or information providers, respond to the messages seeking information or advice. Thus, as stated earlier, these respondents are instrumental guiders and/or emotional supporters for the information seekers. In other words, some members (respondents) through the message boards of these four websites commonly provide information seekers information and/or emotional support (social support).

Of these four Korean-American websites, on the website of "MissyUSA" (missyusa.com), the message board "Life Q&A" has been selected to illustrate a great number of both inquiry and response messages posted regarding the rules of the American social institutions with the aim of evaluating them in the conceptual framework of two distinctive forms of social capital (social resources and social support). In November 2000, this "MissyUSA" website was established by the wife of a Korean international student in the United States.[34] Above all, the "MissyUSA" website is known as the largest Korean-American women's online community; full membership is permitted only to married Korean-American women and, recently, married Korean-Canadian women. To join the "MissyUSA" community as a full member, she needs to receive approval from its website manager after sending her personal information that includes current American home address, contact number, birthdate, family members, the reasons to come to the United States (or Canada), and so on. Like most online communities, any full members of this "MissyUSA" community can freely post messages and read and comment on the postings of others. The homepage of the "MissyUSA" website offers a list of links for married Korean-American women, such as talk lounge, health and beauty, home and food, motherhood, life information, commerce, missy writer, and missy shopping. In this book, the messages posted on the "Life Q&A" message board are examined in detail under two distinctive forms of social capital (social resources and social support). The "Life Q&A" message board is a link in the talk lounge page that also runs other message boards such as secret talk, hot issues/society/politics, household management, and others. Interestingly, all the messages (inquiries and responses) posted on the "Life Q&A" message board can be accessed by its associate members, such as Korean-American men,

Koreans in any region of the world, and non-Koreans.[35] However, these associate members are banned from posting their own messages, nor are they allowed to make comments on the postings of others.

On a daily basis, there have been a lot of postings on the "Life Q&A" message board. For instance, the total number of posts from January 1, 2012, to December 31, 2012, on this link was 121,297, and that is only counting the initial messages seeking information; on average, there were 332 posts per day. Faced with too many daily postings, only those postings of more than 100 views, within the first ten days of each month from January 2012 to December 2012, were selected. This selection method does not mean that those initial messages of less than 100 views are of less importance. Then, a challenge that ensues is the systematic classification of all the initial postings seeking information or advice. First, as this book's analytical strategy, all of the selected postings have been divided into two groups: one for any inquiries on one of the aforementioned five American social institutions and one for all other inquiries. In total, there were 2,050 postings (inquiries) that are directly or indirectly related to the five American social institutions. Second, all of the inquiries in each of the five American social institutions have been further divided into two components: for example, in the American immigration institution, one subsection was for any inquiries about the legal immigration status (legal permanent resident status or citizenship through naturalization), and the other one for all other inquiries under the arena of the American immigration institution. In the third step, these messages of inquiry in each of the five American social institutions were sorted by general dimensions (or themes) and topics. Taken together, these three steps of the classification of inquiries have been based upon the most important theme, argument, or idea contained in the text of each message, rather than upon its words, phrases, or separate sentences. Table 1.1 briefly presents the broad classifications of these five types of American social institutions and their accompanying dimensions and topics.

Table 1.1. The Classification of the Five American Social Institutions by Their Major Dimensions and General Topics

Social Institutions	*Dimensions*	*General Topics*
Immigration	Legal permanent resident status	Application documents, petition types, fingerprint, duration of approval, sponsorship, renewal, investment for green card, temporary green card, re-entry permit, and interview

Social Institutions	*Dimensions*	*General Topics*
	Naturalization	Application documents, qualifications, interview, exam, oath-taking ceremony, dismissal, and duration of stay outside of the U.S.
Welfare	Unemployment	Qualifications, documents, duration, payment cycle and methods, and amounts
	Social security	Eligibility, benefits, and scores
	Medicaid	Qualifications, coverage, benefits, and providers
	Food assistance	Qualifications, documents, and items
	Public housing	Qualifications and documents
Education	Public elementary schools	Registration, school programs, school absence, course selection, and class textbooks
	Public middle schools	Regulation, course selection or curriculum, school programs, volunteer, and school lunch
	Public high schools	Tests, AP courses, music/band, sports, dress code, textbooks, and counseling for college
	Colleges/universities	College applications, college grade, transfer, majors, tuitions, scholarships, and loans
Housing	Home finance	Mortgage types, periods, payments, interest rates, mortgage insurance, and legal status
	A home-buying process	Home inspection, title insurance, the hiring of real estate lawyers, and the closing costs
	Homeowners' options	Refinancing, house sales or short sales,

Social Institutions	*Dimensions*	*General Topics*
		foreclosures, and property tax
	Rental housing	Lease contract or re-contract, security deposit, and late payment penalty
Finance	Banking	Checking or credit card accounts (monthly, transfer, interest, late payment charges)
	Insurance	Coverage, benefits, payments or costs (copayment, deductible), and providers
	Taxation	Filing status, tax credits/ exemptions/deductions, filing extension, and tax penalty

Source: The "Life Q&A" Message Board of the "MissyUSA" Community.

In addition, this book's analytical strategy also classifies all the postings in response to the messages seeking information by instrumental guiders (information describers, analysts, confirmers, and advisors) and emotional supporters (companions, encouragers, and critics), as stressed earlier. In the following chapters, two different types of posts (inquiries and responses) are introduced according to the key dimensions (or themes) and topics of the individual social institutions, one for inquiries on the rules of the American social institutions and the other for responses on them. Otherwise, the former signals the "MissyUSA" community as a source of social resources (information), whereas the latter indicates it as a community of social support. Finally, almost all postings are written in Korean; there are some posts in English, however they are very rare. All postings written in Korean were translated into English by an expert who is bilingual in Korean and English.

ORGANIZATION OF THE BOOK

As stated above, this chapter introduced the key rationales and major questions of the book, and included an extensive literature review on ethnic online communities, social capital, and social institutions. Additionally, it also summarized the key features of the "MissyUSA" community.

Chapter 2 begins by stressing the importance of the American immigration institution, especially for those seeking the legalization of their residence status (lawful permanent residency and citizenship through naturalization) in the United States. It follows an overview of the major characteristics of the American immigration institution, which includes its goals, foremost important laws, policies, and its key governing bodies in modern American history. Thereafter, this chapter points to historical trends in the number of Korean immigrant populations in the United States over time, and the role of their ethnic social networks in seeking information about the rules of the American immigration institution. Then, the chapter introduces many online postings in inquiry and response forms that relate to the rules of the American immigration institution, from the "Life Q&A" message board of the "MissyUSA" community, analyzing them under the aforementioned two distinctive approaches to social capital (social resources and social support).

In the United States, social welfare programs are key public services, especially for socially vulnerable, economically insecure and needy people, a group in which many immigrants are included. Chapter 3 overviews the five main social programs of the American welfare institution in terms of its individual underlying goals, the backgrounds of legal authorization, formal laws, policies or guidelines, and their governing bodies in modern American history; two in social programs (Unemployment Insurance and Social Security), one in health care assistance programs (Medicaid and children's health insurance), one in nutrition assistance programs for low-income families (i.e., the Supplemental Nutrition Assistance Program), and one in housing assistance programs (two public rental assistance programs). The section that follows is the discussion about how valuable various social networks available to Korean immigrants or in the Korean-American community are in the pursuit of information about the rules of the American welfare institution. The main focus of this chapter is on the introduction of many online messages related to the rules of the American welfare institution in the framework of two distinctive forms of social capital (social resources and social support).

Most Korean parents living in the United States believe that better education should be offered to children. Chapter 4 overviews the American educational institution in modern American history in terms of its key goals, laws, formal and informal policies and programs, different governing bodies, and school systems. Here, the school systems of the American educational institution discussed in this chapter range from public school education from Kindergarten to twelfth grade to higher education, including both public and private colleges and universities. The following section sums up the impact of social networks on the Korean-American community in terms of information gathering about children's education and schooling. By incorporating social resources with social support in the concept of social capital, this chapter explores many inquiry and response messages in detail under a set of themes and topics involving the rules of the American educational institution.

For many immigrants in their host country, purchasing or renting a house requires proper knowledge of the terms and conditions of home finance (mortgage loans) or rental agreement. Similarly, their continued dwelling in or moving out of a house purchased or leased also demands their understanding about their host country's rules and regulations on payments of mortgage, property tax, home insurance, refinancing, the cancelation of the rental contract, the renewal contract for their rented house, and so on. Chapter 5 deals with this topic of the rules of the American housing institution that is further divided into four broad categories: the financing of homeownership, the home-buying process, homeowners' options and burdens, and rental housing. In this section, a literature review will focus on the major goals, landmark laws, policies, programs, and key governing bodies in modern American history. The next section pursues the potential impact of Korean immigrants' social networks and their ethnic community on their access to information about the rules of the American housing institution. The final section of this chapter introduces a wide range of themes and topics related to the rules of the American housing institution; they are depicted in great detail by some selected inquiry and response messages and analyzed through the application of two forms of social capital: social resources and social support.

Obtaining good financial standing is an important goal that immigrants of different racial and ethnic backgrounds want to achieve in their new country. To that end, they need better knowledge of how each sector of the American financial institution works. Chapter 6 puts into focus the rules of the American financial institution, specifically exploring three areas: banking (deposits, savings, loans, and money transactions), insurance (life/annuities, accident, health, and property/casualty) and taxation (income, employment, estate or gift, and excise taxes). All three of these sectors of the American financial institution are separately reviewed according to their main goals, laws, policies, programs, and their governing bodies in modern American history. The following section discusses the impact of Korean immigrants' social networks and their ethnic community on their ability to gather information about the rules of the American financial institution. Then, this chapter introduces many inquiry and response postings about the rules of the American financial institution, analyzing them with two forms of social capital (social resources and social support).

Chapter 7 begins by readdressing this book's two main arguments: the first argument proposed in this book is that one group of "MissyUSA" members (inquirers or information seekers) has a propensity to post messages seeking information mostly on institution-wide or within-institution organizational rules of the American social institutions; and the second is that another group of "MissyUSA" members (respondents or information providers) is in the positions of instrumental guiders or/and emotional supporters for information seekers. In the following section, both arguments will be demonstrated through a summary of the key findings revealed after the analyses of all five American social institutions. Then, the remaining sections of this chapter will evaluate the importance of the "MissyUSA" community in both contexts of the American social institutions and social capital. Here, there will be much discussion about such topics as the character and content of online social capital (social resources), immigrants' approach to the host country's social institutions as different rule setting institutions, and the role of co-ethnic social support groups.

NOTES

1. Robert K. Merton, "Insiders and Outsiders: A Chapter in the Sociology of Knowledge," *American Journal of Sociology* 70 (1972): 11.

2. "Social Bonds among Korean American Mothers," *The Chosun Ilbo*, July 23, 2003; and "The Popularity of the 'MissyUSA.com' among Korean American Women," *The Korea Times*, March 20, 2005. Then, as of 2013, the total number of its full members was projected to be more than 300,000 (see the article entitled "MissyUSA as a Reliable Source of Information," *The Chosun Ilbo*, May 10, 2013).

3. James Coleman, *Foundations of Social Theory* (Cambridge, MA: Harvard University Press, 1994); Nan Lin, *Social Capital: A Theory of Social Structure and Action* (Port Chester, NY: Cambridge University Press, 2001); and Barry Wellman, "Physical Place and Cyber-Place," *International Journal for Urban and Regional Research* 25 (2001): 227–252.

4. Howard Rheingold, *The Virtual Community* (Cambridge, MA: MIT Press, 2000); Wellman, "Physical Place and Cyber-Place"; and Barry Wellman, Janet Salaff, Dimitrina Dimitrova, Laura Garton, Milena Gulia, and Caroline Haythornthwaite, "Computer Networks as Social Networks: Collaborative Work, Telework, and Virtual Community," *Annual Review of Sociology* 22 (1996): 213–238.

5. Pierre Bourdieu, "The Forms of Capital," in *Handbook of Theory and Research for the Sociology of Education*, ed. Richardson John (New York: Greenwood, 1986), 241–258; James Coleman, *Foundations of Social Theory*; Mark Granovetter, "The Strength of Weak Ties," *American Journal of Sociology* 78 (1973): 1360–1380; Mark Granovetter, "Economic Action and Social Structure: The Problem of Embeddedness," *American Journal of Sociology* 91 (1985): 481–510; Nan Lin, *Social Capital*; and Alejandro Portes and Julia Sensenbrenner, "Embeddedness and Immigration: Notes on the Social Determinants of Economic Behavior," *American Journal of Sociology* 98 (1993): 1320–1350.

6. Stanley Wasserman and Katherine Faust, *Social Network Analysis: Methods and Applications* (New York: Cambridge University Press, 1994), 20.

7. Mark Granovetter, "The Strength of Weak Ties"; Robert Putnam, "Bowling Alone: America's Declining Social Capital," *Journal of Democracy* 6 (1995): 65–78; and Robert Putnam, *Bowling Alone: The Collapse and Revival of American Community* (New York: Simon & Schuster, 2000), 24–26.

8. James Coleman, *Foundations of Social Theory*; Portes and Sensenbrenner, "Embeddedness and Immigration."

9. Nan Lin, "Social Resources and Instrumental Action," in *Social Structure and Network Analysis*, eds. Peter V. Marsden and Nan Lin (Beverly Hills, CA: Sage, 1982), 131–145; and Nan Lin, *Social Capital*.

10. Nan Lin, *Social Capital*, 43.

11. James Coleman, *Foundations of Social Theory*, 310.
12. Manuel Castells, *The Internet Galaxy* (New York: Oxford University Press, 2001), 132.
13. Benedict Anderson, *Imagined Communities: Reflections on the Origin and Spread of Nationalism* (New York: Verso, 1991).
14. Mary Chayko, *Connecting: How We Form Social Bonds and Communities in the Internet Age* (New York: State University of New York Press, 2002); and Samuel M. Wilson and Leighton C. Peterson, "The Anthropology of Online Communities," *Annual Review of Anthropology* 31 (2002): 449–467.
15. Milton M. Gordon, *Assimilation in American Life: The Role of Race, Religion, and National Origins* (New York: Oxford University Press, 1964), 38.
16. Pyong Gap Min, "The Immigration of Koreans to the United States: A Review of 45 Year (1965-2009) Trends," *Development and Society* 40 (2011): 195–223.
17. Lenie Brouwer, "Dutch Moroccan Websites: A Transnational Imagery?" *Journal of Ethnic and Migration Studies* 32 (2006): 1153–1168; Mirca Madianou, "Contested Communicative Spaces: Rethinking Identities, Boundaries and the Role of the Media among Turkish Speakers in Greece," *Journal of Ethnic and Migration Studies* 31 (2005): 521–541; Anastasia N. Panagakos, "Downloading New Identities: Ethnicity, Technology, and Media in the Global Greek Village," *Identities: Global Studies in Culture and Power* 10 (2003): 201–219; and Emily Skop and Paul C. Adams, "Creating and Inhabiting Virtual Places: Indian Immigrants in Cyberspace," *National Identities* 11 (2009): 127–147.
18. Barton J. Hirsch, "Natural Support Systems and Coping with Major Life Changes," *American Journal of Community Psychology* 8 (1980): 159–172; James S. House, *Work Stress and Social Support* (Reading, MA: Addison-Wesley, 1981); Alan Vaux, *Social Support: Theory, Research, and Intervention* (New York: Praeger, 1988); Barry Wellman and Scot Wortley, "Different Strokes from Different Folks: Community Ties and Social Support," *American Journal of Sociology* 96 (1990): 558–588; Carolyn E. Cutrona and Julie A. Suhr, "Controllability of Stressful Events and Satisfaction with Spouse Support Behaviors," *Communication Research* 19 (1992): 154–174; and Kevin Wright, "Perceptions of On-line Support Providers: An Examination of Perceived Homophily, Source Credibility, Communication and Social Support Within On-line Support Groups," *Communication Quarterly* 48 (2000): 44–59.
19. Milton M. Gordon, *Assimilation in American Life*, 104.
20. Richard Alba and Victor Nee, *Remaking the American Mainstream: Assimilation and Contemporary Immigration* (Cambridge, MA: Harvard University Press, 2003), 41–42; Richard Alba, and Victor Nee. 1997. "Rethinking Assimilation Theory for a New Era of Immigration." *International Migration Review* 31 (4): 826–874.
21. To characterize what institutions are, many scholars in different academic disciplines attempted to define the term institutions. For an excellent, detailed review of the definitions of institutions, see W. Richard Scott's *Institutions and Organizations: Ideas and Interests* (Sage: Los Angeles, 2008).
22. A social institution defined in this book differs from the concept of "institutional rules" (Meyer and Rowan, 1977) by which adoption organizations can " increase their resources and survival capabilities" and acquire the normative legitimacy of their organizational activities from their outsiders (regulatory agencies, the general public or consumers, their collaborating or competing organizations). To these scholars, institutional rules emerge and are legitimated "by public opinions, by the views of important constituents, by knowledge legitimated through the educational system, by social prestige, by the laws, and by the definitions of negligence and prudence used by the courts" (p. 343). Then, institutional rules are here understood as "rational myths" (or macro cultural logics or ideas) strong enough to make the organizations become homogeneous to each other in their forms and structures. Thus, organizations tend to conform to their environment for legitimacy or survival in a way that rearranges their forms and structure similarly to each other, with or without introducing their own organizational rules (see John W. Meyer and Brian Rowan, "Institutionalized Organ-

izations: Formal Structure as Myth and Ceremony," *American Journal of Sociology* 83 (1977): 340–363.

23. DiMaggio and Powell (1983: 148) introduced the concept of an "organizational field" to feature organizational homogeneity and organizational interactions in "a recognized area of institutional life" and further specified the types of its participating organizations as "key suppliers, resource and product consumers, regulatory agencies, and other organizations that produce similar products and services." Following this, for example, all the types of inter-organizational relationships, in a certain economic sector, can include all the transactions of goods and services (production, distribution, and retailing), personal and resource exchanges, or governance arrangements (regulations) between the regulatory agencies and the regulated (for the detailed argument, see Paul DiMaggio and Water Powell's "The Iron Cage Revisited: Institutional Isomorphism and Collective Rationality in Organizational Fields," *American Sociological Review* 48 (1983): 147–160.

24. Douglass C. North, *Institutions, Institutional Change and Economic Performance,* 3-6.

25. Douglass C. North, *Institutions, Institutional Change and Economic Performance,* 4.

26. Douglass C. North, *Institutions, Institutional Change and Economic Performance,* 5.

27. This book has no intention to address a research topic about whether and the extent to which organizations and their actors or rules transform extant institutional rules, or have an influence to create new types of institutional rules. An underlying assumption that this book starts with is that there exist already written institutional and organizational rules in a social institution. There is some sociological research on the transformations of extant institution-wide laws or rules by the roles of the key actors or agents (managers or specialists) who lead the introduction of new organizational policies or practices in response to the complexity or ambiguity of institution-wide laws. See Frank Dobbin and John R. Sutton, "The Strength of a Weak State: The Rights Revolution and the Rise of Human Resources Management Divisions," *American Journal of Sociology* 104 (1998): 441–476; Lauren Edelman, "Legal Ambiguity and Symbolic Structures: Organizational Mediation of Civil Rights Law," *American Journal of Sociology* 97 (1992): 1531–1576; Lauren Edelman, Christopher Uggen, and Howard S. Erlanger, "The Endogeneity of Legal Regulation: Grievance Procedures as Rational Myth," *American Journal of Sociology* 105 (1999): 406–454; Erin L. Kelly, "The Strange History of Employer-Sponsored Child Care: Interested Actors, Uncertainty, and the Transformation of Law in Organizational Fields," *American Journal of Sociology* 109 (2003): 606–649; and Douglass C. North, *Institutions, Institutional Change and Economic Performance.*

28. This is similar to the approach that "the regulative pillar of the institutional environment" like formal rules, regulations, or sanctions constrains organizational behavior totally (Scott, 2008: 52–54).

29. Pyong Gap Min, *Growth and Settlement Patterns of Korean Americans,* Report No. 4 (The Research Center for Korean Community Queens College of the CUNY, 2012).

30. Min, "The Immigration of Koreans to the United States," 197–199.

31. Kim, Pyungho, "Is Korea a Strong Internet Nation?" *The Information Society* 22 (2006): 41–44.

32. Chon, Kilnam, Hyun Je Park, Jin Ho Hur, and Kyungran Kang, "A History of Computer Networking and the Internet in Korea," *IEEE Communications Magazine,* February 2013, 10–15; and Sangmoon Park and Soo-Hyeon Yoon, "Separating Early-Adopters from the Majority: The Case of Broadband Internet Access in Korea," *Technological Forecasting & Social Change* 72 (2005): 301–325.

33. Organization for Economic Co-operation and Development, *OECD Broadband Statistics* (Paris, France: OECD, 2011). See the link of its websites: http://oecd.org/sti/ict/broadband.

34. See *The Chosun Ilbo,* 23 July, 2003.

35. I, as a Korean American man and an associate member, can also access all the inquiry and response messages posted on this message board of "Life Q&A," but I am not allowed to post my own.

TWO

The American Immigration Institution on the "MissyUSA" Community

To many noncitizens pursuing permanent resident status or citizenship status through naturalization in the United States, the American immigration institution may stand firm as an incomprehensible entity particularly at the time when they begin to prepare for their application materials for either of them, or while they are waiting for its approval after application. However, the complexity of the American immigration institution in their eyes is unlikely to discourage their efforts to understand its core characteristics and in particular, to identify the legal requirements and specific procedures appropriate for their own petition cases. To be sure, seeking information for the acquisition of their legal status from diverse sources can be part of their efforts. Nowadays, ethnic online communities are an efficient, very easily accessible source of information for some noncitizens who attempt to seek general or specific information about what to prepare or the steps for the acquisition of their permanent resident status or citizenship status through naturalization. This chapter posits that the Korean-American women's online community, known as the "MissyUSA" community, is an important source and channel of information for some of its members seeking a wide range of information or knowledge about the rules of the American immigration institution in times of their pursuit of their permanent resident status or citizenship status through naturalization in the United States.

For example, there are several important reasons, at the individual and family levels, why undocumented immigrants or those with temporary legal status are very eager to pursue permanent legal status in their new land. First, not having the status of lawful permanent residency is a constant cause of their anxiety or stress. Therefore, hearing news of the approval of their petition for it is a huge emotional relief for them. Thereafter, they no longer are burdened with feelings of uncertainty about the waiting time, application procedures, or all the hassles of file for renewals of existing permits or new permits. Most importantly, they are eventually more secure in their own and their family's future in their new land. Indeed, constant uneasiness caused by lack of documentation on lawful permanent residency in their new country is particularly intense for those noncitizens who are at the end of their legal stay period, or who have already overstayed their visas. Unfortunately, once their legal permits for stay expire, they often feel frustrated or helpless due to ever-present possibility of deportation as the result of civil immigration violations—e.g., undocumented status by overstay.[1] The point stressed here is that the sense of security is the key factor behind their rush to file petitions for lawful permanent residency. Second, there is an instrumental, practical value that comes with lawful permanent residency. Thus, this new status can bring many opportunities for noncitizens to stabilize their personal or family life in their host country. Like legal permanent residents or naturalized citizens, holders of temporary work or family visas are typically allowed to open bank accounts, have a driver license, register their children at schools, lease or buy a house, work at their sponsoring companies, among other things. However, their legal rights in the host country are substantially restricted at times when they want to change their employment from one company to another, to buy their homes through a bank or a mortgage company, to apply for government-sponsored financial aid for college, and so on.[2] Without doubt, legal permanent residents and especially naturalized citizens also have great advantages over temporary or undocumented residents in the case of the eligibility rules for welfare benefits available from the public institutions of the host countries. In the United States, the Personal Responsibility and Work Opportunity Reconciliation Act of 1996 (PRWORA) includes the provision that temporary or undocumented residents are lawfully ineligible for many federal- and state-level welfare benefits, such as cash assistance (Temporary Aid for Needy Families, or TANF), Supplementary Security Income (SSI), Medicaid, food stamps, child care, foster care, public housing, and others.[3] Additionally, their status of lawful permanent residency, as compared to those holders of temporary or undocumented immigration status, will make their international trips much easier, and they also will meet less legal hurdle in receiving their Social Security checks, pension checks, or other public benefits after retirement from work.

Whatever the reasons for the pursuit of permanent resident status or naturalized citizenship status among many noncitizens in the United States are, one thing that is generally clear here is that understanding the rules of the American immigration institution is an important matter for most of the non-citizens in the United States, especially those who are proceeding now with the application for either of them. Then, preparing a formal application for it cannot be an easy task for some applicants who have little or insufficient knowledge about the rules of the American immigration institution. For that matter, the Korean-American women's online community is the kind of social network that offers some of its members willing to seek, or currently pursuing, either permanent legal resident status or naturalized citizenship status in the United States a great source of information, especially information relating to their own or their family members' immigration petition cases. In their perspective, this Korean-American women's online community can be also regarded as a critical network of social resources that is, in this book, known to be a form of social capital, and in particular, an important source of information for its members seeking knowledge about their personal or family application cases for the acquisition of either permanent resident status or naturalized citizenship status in the United States.

In this Korean-American women's online community, the acquisition of such information on case-sensitive immigration petitions is made possible through its other members' social support that emerge in the forms of conveying relevant information, correcting misinformation, clarifying unclear information, giving advice, or eliciting emotional encouragement. Typically, these information providers (respondents) can be broadly classified into two groups in accordance with patterns of their social support: instrumental guiders and emotional supporters. Instrumental guiders are further classified into four subgroups: information describers, analysts, confirmers, and advisors. Likewise, emotional supporters can be also divided into three subgroups: companions, encouragers, and critics. In general, this Korean-American women's online community, from the position of information providers (respondents), is a network of social supporters that is, in this book, regarded as another important form of social capital.

This chapter begins by briefly overviewing the major characteristics of the American immigration institution in terms of its core goals, laws, policies or programs, and its governing bodies in modern American history. Then, it will go over a close nexus between the history of Korean immigrants in the United States and that of changing American immigration laws and policies, as well as the importance of social capital in their efforts to seek information about the rules of the American immigration institution. Lastly, the remaining part of this chapter introduces some messages about the rules of the American immigration institution, which were posted on the "Life Q&A" message board of the "MissyUSA" community. More specifically, this section will in detail examine some inquiry and response messages that address matters involving the acquisition of permanent resident status or citizenship status through naturalization. Through this way, this section will prove that this "MissyUSA" community functions as the source of social capital to its information seekers (social resources), as well as a network of social supporters by its information providers for information seekers (social support).

THE AMERICAN IMMIGRATION INSTITUTION: HISTORY, LAWS, AND ORGANIZATIONS

A social institution is, in this book, referred to as an amassed entity of the rules, especially legal and formal rules that were (or are) generated at either institution-wide or intra-institutional (organizational) levels. Following this broad scope of definition, a social institution is composed of all the formal (public or private) organizations which stretch and operate from national, through state, to local levels, and which primarily aim to introduce its certain laws, policies or programs (or preferences), and then, administer the accompanying rules, regulations, and procedures in order to accomplish its defining goals or missions. In a society, the more the legitimacy of any social institution is enhanced rather than challenged, the greater its longevity is as long as its manifest goals embrace much of the dominant values, thoughts, and interests widely accepted from the majority of its social members. Undoubtedly, the form and structure of social institutions will undergo changes throughout history so that modifications of some of their defined goals will also be expected to occur afterward.

This is quite true of the case of the American immigration institution. Despite this fact, there are some major underlying goals of the American immigration institution that have persisted over quite long periods of time.[4] These are (1) family reunification, (2) American economic interests or prosperity (or employment-based immigration), (3) the promotion of human rights for refugees,[5] (4) the support of diversity in the composition of American population,[6] and (5) the restriction of undocumented immigrants and terrorists for national security.[7] These five main goals of the American immigration institution have been, implicitly or explicitly, contained in the passages of the old and new immigration legislations passed by the U.S. Congress. Once the proposed immigration laws and policies are enacted by the U.S. Congress, the designated administrative branches of the federal government that are obliged to administer and enforce them by additionally introducing their own specified organizational rules or guidelines, programs, and procedures. This far-reaching and complicated role of administering and enforcing immigration laws and policies, over a century in the history of the American immigration institution, has been, individually or jointly, conducted by many administrative branches and their designated agencies of the federal government, which include the Department of Labor, the Department of State, the Department of Justice, the Department of Homeland Security, the Department of Health and Human Services, the Department of Treasury, the Department of Commerce, and others. So far, then the majority of Koreans admitted legally in the United States have been through the acquisition of immigrant visas based upon family reunification and employment. Therefore, below is a brief description about these two critical goals of the American immigration institution in line with its major immigration laws and policies and the main roles and functions of its federal administrative branches or agencies.

First, one of the major laws of family reunification enacted by the U.S. Congress was the 1952 Immigration and Nationality Act (INA), also known as the MaCarran-Water Act.[8] Family reunification was also the keystone of the 1965 amendment to the INA, commonly called the Hart-Cellar Act: To this day, family reunification is still in the absolutely pivotal part of American immigration laws and policies. According to this 1965 immigration legislation, for example, an annual limit of 170,000 immigrant visas was established for the Eastern Hemisphere (Asia, Europe, Africa, and Oceania), with per-country limits of 20,000 visas, and an annual limit of 120,000 immigrant visas was allotted to the Western Hemisphere (North, Central, and South Americas), with no per-country limits; the 1976 amendments to the INA set per-country limits of 20,000 visas for the Western Hemisphere.[9] More importantly, its key provisions on family reunification were well manifested on the basis of the creation of classes of admissions preferences that were applied to only those immigrants from the Eastern Hemisphere; this system of admissions preferences was extended to the Western Hemisphere by the 1976 amendments to the INA. Of the total number of annual visas for the Eastern Hemisphere, for example, 125,800 visas (74 percent) were set aside for family-based immigrants.[10] This family-based immigration policy especially gave its preferences (or priorities) to unmarried sons and daughters of U.S. citizens, spouse and unmarried children of legal permanent residents, followed by married sons and daughters of U.S. citizens and siblings of U.S. citizens. This 1965 immigration law, like the 1952 INA, also permitted immediate family members of U.S. citizens—spouses and unmarried minor children—to immigrate into the United States without legal restrictions from the extant family-preference system; however, the minimum number allotted to immediate relatives of U.S. citizens was set to 239,000 visas in the 1990 Immigration Act.[11] Since March 1, 2003, the newly created U.S. Citizenship and Immigration Services (USCIS) in the Department of Homeland Security, which replaced the former Immigration and Naturalization Service (INS) in the Department of Justice, has managed the early immigration petition process that allows current U.S. citizens and legal permanent residents to bring their family members abroad into the United States.[12] After their immigration petitions are approved by the USCIS, the next step is that the National Visa Center (NVC) in the Department of State administers the immigration visa application process by collecting the affidavit of support forms and fees from the petitioners in the United States, and immigration visa application forms and fees from the applicants, or the applicants' designated agents.[13] The step that follows next is that after receiving the interview schedules noticed by the NVC, the applicants will be interviewed at the U.S. Department of State's embassies or consulates in their home countries to determine their eligibility to immigrate to the United States. Finally, they can enter the United States, with their approved immigration visas issued by the U.S. embassies or consulates and other document checks from the Department of Homeland Security's Customs and Border Protection (CBP) at a U.S. port of entry.

Second, bringing or enhancing greater prosperity in the American economy is another important goal of the American immigration institution. The timely and adequate supply of the workforce, in response to shifting national economic structures and productivity over time, is one of the key preconditions for national economic prosperity. Prior to the mid-twentieth century, the intermittent demand of the foreign labor force in the United States was well reflected in such immigration laws as the 1864 Contract Labor Act, the 1885 Alien Contract Labor Act, the 1924 Immigration Act, and the 1942 Bracero Program.[14] At last, more comprehensive employment-based immigration rules and policies unfolded through the 1952 Immigration and Nationality Act (INA). In particular, this 1952 immigration legislation placed the highest priority on a skills-based immigration, and therefore, in the immigration visa process, it favored foreign nationals in professional or highly skilled occupations and their spouses and children. Thereafter, this immigration law ultimately becomes a principal barometer of the post-1952 U.S. immigration laws on employment-based immigration. In the 1965 amendments to the INA, a preference system for immigration visa was introduced for the Eastern Hemisphere within which employment-based immigration was assigned as the third and sixth preferences (or categories). Here, the third preference was for foreign professionals of exceptional ability and their spouses and children, with the allocation of 17,000 visas, while another 17,000 visas were granted to the sixth-preference applicants, such as foreign workers in skilled or unskilled occupations and their spouses and children.[15] This system of two-category employment preference remained unchanged until the 1976 and 1978 amendments to Immigration and Nationality Act (INA).

At this time, the U.S. employment-based immigration policies are essentially based upon the 1990 Immigration Act that extended the number of employment-based visas from 34,000 in 1965 to 54,000 in both 1976 and 1978 to 140,000 in 1990: This immigration legislation raised the annual ceiling on immigration numbers to 461,000, from 270,000 in both 1976 and 1978.[16] This immigration law of 1990 also created the system of five employment-based immigration visa preferences (categories).[17] In the first preference, 40,000 employment visas are reserved for foreign nationals of "extraordinary ability" in sciences, arts, education, business, or athletes, outstanding professors and researchers, and multinational executives and managers. In the second preference, another 40,000 employment visas are reserved for foreign professionals with advanced degrees or for foreign persons with "extraordinary ability" in the arts, sciences, or business. In the third preference, an additional 40,000 employment visas are reserved for foreign professionals, skilled workers, and other workers, including unskilled workers whose annual visas are limited to 10,000. Its fourth preference provides 10,000 visas to "special immigrants," such as certain religious workers, employees of U.S. foreign-service posts, retired employees of international organizations, and others. Finally, its fifth preference provides 10,000 visas to foreign business investors who invest $1 million or $500,000 and employ at least ten full-time U.S. workers.[18]

The approval process of the employment-based permanent visas passes through various administrative branches and their designated agencies of the federal government. If foreign workers fall into either of the second and third preferences, the U.S employer must obtain labor certification from the U.S. Department of Labor (DOL). The labor certificate approved by the DOL verifies that there are not sufficient U.S. workers "able, willing, qualified, and available" to fill the positions being offered, and that the foreign workers' employment will not adversely affect the prevailing wages and working conditions of U.S. workers in the same employment sectors.[19] Those in the other three employment-based preferences are exempt from the requirement to receive the DOL labor certification. The employer, as the sponsor of a foreign worker, is required to file "an immigration petition for alien worker" (Form I-140) to the U.S. Citizenship and Immigration Services (USCIS); business investors can file "an immigration petition for alien entrepreneur" (Form I-526) on their own behalf. If the employer's petition (I-140) has been approved, and an immigrant visa is currently available, the foreign worker who is already in the United States can file "an application to register permanent residency or adjust status" (Form I-485) to the USCIS often called "concurrent filing."[20] Thereafter, the granting of permanent residency by the USCIS comes after the completion of all I-485 application processes, including criminal background checks, an interview, and other eligibility requirements. However, the foreign worker outside the United States takes different steps to earn a U.S. legal permanent resident status. In his or her case, the USCIS sends the approved petition (I-140) to the National Visa Center (NVC) in the Department of State. When an immigration visa number is finally available, the applicant, here the foreign worker, will be interviewed at the consular office of the U.S. embassy or consulate in his or her home country, and be granted an immigrant visa if all required conditions of eligibility are met. After being admitted from the Department of Homeland Security's Customs and Border Protection (CBP) at a

U.S. port of entry, the foreign worker can live and work permanently in the United States.[21]

Individuals can obtain American citizenship based upon their birth on American soil (*jus soli*), or based upon both parents' or one parent's American citizenship if they were born in foreign countries, on the condition that they apply for citizenship before the age of eighteen (*jus sanguinis*). Naturalization is another path to acquire American citizenship. Thus, it is a lawful way for legal permanent residents in the United States to become American citizens. However, it was not until the mid-twentieth century that individuals from certain countries eventually became eligible for American citizenship through naturalization. For example, the 1943 Naturalization Act made it possible for Chinese individuals in the United States to naturalize, and the 1946 Naturalization Act provided an opportunity for Filipinos and Asian Indians in the United States to become American citizens through naturalization.[22] Thereafter, the 1952 Immigration and Nationality Act (INA) removed all the racial or national origins of immigrants as a legal barrier to their naturalization. These days, most American citizenship policies and requirements for foreign citizens' naturalization have stemmed from this 1952 immigration law. In general, those foreign-born applicants for American citizenship are required to be eighteen years old or over, to be a legal permanent resident for at least five years of residence in the United States, and for at least three months, they should have residence in the state or district in which they are applying.[23] There are also additional eligibility requirements for citizenship. For example, the applicant for American citizenship must demonstrate good moral character (i.e., no felony crimes), support of the U.S. Constitution, knowledge of the U.S. government and history, and a willingness to take an oath of allegiance to the United States, and revoke one's former national citizenship. The applicant also must to be able to read, write, speak, and understand basic-level English.[24] The Department of Homeland Security's U.S. Citizenship and Immigration Services (USCIS), as an agency of the federal government, now enforces these eligibility requirements for American citizenship by administering the applicant's security and criminal background checks, reviewing his or her application documents, conducting an in-person interview with oral and written testimony, proctoring English, history, and civics tests, overseeing the applicant's oath of allegiance, and determining the naturalization application.

KOREAN IMMIGRANTS IN THE UNITED STATES

Legal Status

Table 2.1 presents the numbers of Koreans who obtained the lawful permanent resident status of the United States (or green card), from 1940 to 2011.

Table 2.1. The Numbers of Koreans Who Obtained U.S. Legal Permanent Resident Status, 1940-2011

Period	*Number*
1940-1949	83
1950-1959	4,845
1960-1969	27,048
1970-1979	241,192
1980-1989	322,708
1990-1999	179,770
2000-2009	209,758
2010	22,022
2011	22,748

Source: Office of Immigration Statistics, U.S. Department of Homeland Security.

Until 1969, not many Koreans acquired the permanent resident status of the United States. However, during the 1970s, the number of Koreans who received American green-cards increased almost nine-fold from the 1960s. From 1970 to 1979, this rapid rise in the number of Koreans' acquisition of legal permanent resident status in the United States also indicated that they started to immigrate en masse to the United States during the decade. The 1980s was the peak period in the total number of their U.S. legal permanent resident status. Then, the total number for it dropped rapidly during the 1990s, and once again bounded back during the 2000s. In 2011, for example, the annual number of Koreans who obtained the legal permanent resident status of the United States was over 22,000. In short, more than 270,000 immigrants obtained the legal permanent resident status of the United States between 1940 and 1979, and about 760,000 Koreans became American lawful permanent residents between 1980 and 2011.

Table 2.2 shows the numbers of Koreans' legal permanent resident status in the United States by classes of admission in the three separate years of 1997, 2005, and 2011. In 1997, the category of immediate relatives of U.S. citizens—e.g., spouses and unmarried minor children of U.S. citizens—was the highest number (almost 5,400) and percent (roughly 38) for obtaining a U.S. legal permanent resident status among Koreans. In the same year, the category of employment-based immigration was the second highest (33 percent), and the category of four family preferences comprised nearly 29 percent of all the Korean U.S. green-card recipients. In both years of 2005 and 2011, more than 50 percent of all the Korean U.S. green-card recipients came from the category of employment-based immigration (60 percent and 55 percent, respectively).

Table 2.2. The Koreans of the U.S. Legal Permanent Resident Status by Broad Class of Admission: 1997, 2005, and 2011

	1997		*2005*		*2011*	
	Number	*Percent*	*Number*	*Percent*	*Number*	*Percent*
Total	14,239	100.00	26,562	100.00	22,824	100.00
Family-sponsored preferences	4,086	28.70	1,997	7.52	2,503	10.97
Immediate relatives of U.S. citizens	5,381	37.79	8,598	32.37	7,637	33.46
Employment-based preferences	4,710	33.08	15,929	59.97	12,593	55.17
Diversity	6	0.04	8	0.03	10	0.04
Refugees and asylees	3	0.02	7	0.08	10	0.04
Other	53	0.37	23	0.09	71	0.31

Source: Office of Immigration Statistics, U.S. Department of Homeland Security.

Such high-growth rates of the Korean U.S. employment-based immigration in recent years can be the result of their modifications in legal immigration status among some of them who were initially admitted in the United States as non-immigrant visa holders. For example, many international students and temporary workers later accepted job offers from American academia, enterprises, or public sectors, which had led them to employment-based immigration under the sponsorship of their U.S. employer. The next largest category (more than 30 percent in these three different years) came from those who immigrated through the category of immediate relatives of U.S. citizens. Additionally, the category of four family preferences comprised almost 7.5 percent in 2005, and almost 11 percent in 2011. Reviewing this recent two-year pattern of how Koreans acquired legal permanent resident status in the United States, new employment in the United States, rather than family reunification, became the main reason for main Koreans to immigrate to the United States.

Table 2.3 reports changes in the annual numbers of Koreans who naturalized as American citizens for over two decades between 1990 and 2012. Except for 1992 and 1993, more than 10,000 Koreans became naturalized American citizens yearly since 1990. In particular, on an annual basis, more than 20,000 Koreans acquired American citizenship through the naturalization process in 1990, 1996, 2000, and 2008. For whatever reason, if Korean citizens in the United States want to naturalize, it is a lawful requirement that they should revoke their Korean citizenship to become naturalized American citizens.

Table 2.3. The Numbers of Koreans Who Obtained the U.S. Citizenship Status, 1940- 2011

Year	*Number*
1990	21,988
1991	12,538
1992	8,330
1993	9,681
1994	12,367
1995	15,709
1996	27,969
1997	16,056
1998	10,305
1999	17,738
2000	23,858
2001	18,053
2002	17,252
2003	15,928
2004	17,184
2005	19,223
2006	17,668
2007	17,628
2008	22,759
2009	17,576
2010	11,170
2011	12,664
2012	13,790

Source: Office of Immigration Statistics, U.S. Department of Homeland Security.
Note: Data for South Korea prior to Fiscal Year 2009 included a small number of cases from North Korea.

Annually, many Koreans come to the United States on a temporary basis for the purposes of studying, working, living, or traveling. As usual, they come to the United States on non-immigrant admissions visas, which are also known as temporary visas for admission into the United States. In general, individuals holding such non-immigrant visas include temporary workers, trainees, academic or vocational students, scholars, artists or entertainers, foreign government officers or employees, visitors, their spouses and children, or spouses and/or children of the U.S. citizens or lawful permanent residents under pending visas. Table 2.4 shows the total number of admitted Koreans into the United States in the broad category of non-immigrant visas, as of 2011.

Almost 1.5 million Koreans came to the United States in 2011 through various types of non-immigrant visas. Temporary tourists constituted nearly 83 percent in this category. Students and visiting scholars, along with their spouses and children, constituted almost 11 percent, and nearly 6 percent of them were composed of temporary workers and their spouses and children.

Table 2.4. The Numbers of Nonimmigrant Admissions into the United States by Selected Category of Admission from South Korea, 2000

	Number	*Percent*
Total[a]	1,460,972	100
Students and exchange visitors[b]	159,218	10.90
Temporary workers and families[c]	83,080	5.69
Diplomats and other representatives[d]	6,266	0.43
Tourists and business travelers:	1,208,626	82.73
Visa waiver[e]	863,116	
Other[f]	345,510	
All other classes	2,134	0.15
Unknown	1,648	0.11

Source: Office of Immigration Statistics, U.S. Department of Homeland Security.
[a]The number of I-94 admissions in 2010 and 2011 greatly exceeded totals reported in previous years due to a more complete count of land admissions.
[b]It includes principals, spouses, and children (F1, F2, J1, J2, M1, and M2 admissions).
[c]It includes principals, spouses, and children (E1 to E3, H1B, H1B1, H1C, H2A, H2B, H2R, H3, H4, I1, L1, L2, O1 to O3, P1 to P4, Q1, R1, R2, TD and TN admissions).
[d]It includes principals, spouses, and children (A1 to A3, G1 to G5, and N1 to N7 admissions).
[e]It includes GMB, GMT, WB, and WT admissions.
[f]It includes B1, B2, and a limited number of Border Crossing Card (BCC) admissions.

SOCIAL CAPITAL AND LEGAL STATUS

In the immigration history of Koreans toward the United States, family-sponsored immigration has been one of the driving forces behind their population growth, as shown in Table 2.2. By making the best use of the U.S. immigration policies which uphold the family reunification of American citizens or lawful permanent residents, many of the previously settled Korean immigrants who had already obtained either their American citizenship status or their permanent resident status in the United States brought their kin and relatives in Korea into the United States. Likewise, the subsequent acquisition of citizenship or permanent resident status in the United States among these newly settled Korean immigrants has also made it possible for them to invite their other close family members and relatives in Korea into the United States. Consequently, this chain migration from Korea to the United States has produced extended family networks among some Korean immigrants in the United States whose members often become the primary sources of both social resources and social support to each other and in particular, for their newly arrived family members.

By and large, some key elements of the social resources available through their family-centered networks in the United States are composed of information, monetary capital, credit, training, or services that are often very valuable for their resource-seeking family members. For example, preparing the application of petitions for a U.S. permanent resident status or citizenship through naturalization can be much easier for its applicants who can obtain a reliable source of information through his/her family members who are knowledgeable about such specific information as its timing, eligibility, required documents, and anticipated procedures. Because many applicants for permanent legal immigration toward their countries of destination often suffer from feelings of severe anxiety or stress during the preparation of the application, the waiting period after submission, or after its decision, their family members also play the role of their emotional supporters by sharing one's own experiences or tribulations, by revealing his/her personal care, concern and optimism, or by expressing his/her joy with the news of approval or his/her new hope with news of denial.

As presented in Table 2.5, Korean immigrants have been historically concentrated high in their ethnic gateway cities or their surrounding suburban areas—e.g., Los Angeles, New York, Chicago, and Atlanta.

Table 2.5. The Numbers of Korean-Americans and Growth Rates in the 10 Largest Korean Population Areas, in 1990, 2000, and 2010 U.S. Censuses

Metropolitan Area	*1990*		*2000*		*2010*	
	Number	*Percent*	*Number*	*Percent*	*Number*	*Percent*
Los Angeles CMSA[a]	194,437	24.34	257,975	23.96	324,586	19.02
New York CMSA[b]	118,096	14.78	170,509	15.83	221,705	12.99
Washington D.C. CMSA[c]	39,850	4.99	74,454	6.91	90,157	5.28
Seattle CMSA[d]	23,901	2.99	41,189	3.82	64,771	3.79
Chicago CMSA[e]	36,952	4.63	46,256	4.30	61,229	3.59
San Francisco CMSA[f]	42,277	5.29	57,386	5.33	50,867	2.98
Atlanta CMSA[g]	10,120	1.27	22,317	2.07	48,788	2.86
Honolulu CMSA[h]	22,646	2.83	21,681	2.01	41,689	2.44
Philadelphia CMSA[i]	24,568	3.08	29,309	2.72	40,292	2.36
Dallas CMSA[j]	11,041	1.38	18,123	1.68	33,593	1.97
Total in the 10 Largest Metropolitan Areas	523,888	65.58	739,199	68.64	977,677	57.28

Metropolitan Area	*1990*		*2000*		*2010*	
	Number	*Percent*	*Number*	*Percent*	*Number*	*Percent*
Total in the United States	798,849	100.00	1,076,872	100.00	1,706,822	100.00

Source: Adapted from Pyong Gap Min's Report (2012).

Note: Ten metropolitan areas with more than 10,000 Korean Americans, excluding multi-racial cases (children of interracially married parents), in the 1990 Census were selected.

*Multi-racial Koreans composed 12 percent (151,555 out of 1,077,000) in 2000 and 17 percent (160,033 out of 1,706,822) in 2010.

**The names of the metropolitan areas follow the 2010 definitions:

[a]Los Angeles-Long Beach-Riverside, CA CMSA

[b]New York-Newark-Bridgeport, NY-NJ-CT-PA CMSA

[c]Washington-Baltimore-Northern Virginia, DC-MD-VA-WV CMSA

[d]San Jose-San Francisco-Oakland, CA CMSA

[e]Chicago-Naperville-Michigan City, IL-IN-WI CMSA

[f]Seattle-Tacoma-Olympia, WA CMSA

[g]Philadelphia-Camden-Vineland, PA-NJ-DE-MD CMSA

[h]Atlanta-Sandy Springs-Gainesville, GA-AL CMSA

[i]Honolulu, HI MSA

[j]Dallas-Fort Worth, TX CMSA

***In the 1990 and 2000 censuses, San Jose, San Francisco, and Oakland were included in the San Francisco CMSA. In the 2010 census, San Jose was excluded from the San Francisco-Oakland CMSA.

Settled there, many of them tend to participate in local Korean economic sectors and social and cultural organizations or associations. At a small-scale level, they are also affiliated with various types of their other ethnic networks, such as tight-knit cliques of co-ethnic friends, workers, business owners, or neighbors. This is no exception to many Korean temporary or permanent legal workers at American companies and their spouses. They often reside in either local Korean communities or these adjacent areas that are relatively much convenient for them to assess their ethnic goods and services. They also tend to participate in some other co-ethnic organizations or associations, and/or small-scale ethnic gatherings. To many of them, these types of ethnic networks are indeed a very important source of information in a time of the preparation, or during the process, of their legal immigration petitions for either a U.S. permanent resident status or a U.S. citizenship. Faced with limited proficiency in English and their difficulty in understanding some complicated rules of the American immigration institution, some Korean immigrants in or near their gateway metropolitan areas can also rely on their co-ethnic immigration lawyers there as another option available for themselves to cope with their plights during their application process for acquiring a U.S. permanent resident status or its citizenship status.

Moreover, in the same locations, assistance on legal immigration issues can be also offered to them by their non-profit, ethnic-oriented, organizations with free or low-cost services. For example, like private-run immigration offices, some non-profit organizations—e.g., Korean Immigration Service of NY, Korean-American Community Center of NY—provide various immigration services that include workshops on immigration laws, personal eligibility counseling for the acquisition of a U.S. citizenship or permanent resident status, preparation of the required documents for its petitions, and consultation on interview or civics exam. Another advantage living in or near larger Korean immigrant gateway metropolitan areas, especially their cities, is their relatively easier accessibility to Korean language media, such as local Korean television or radio stations, or daily Korean newspapers, weekly magazines, or periodicals. For example, the broadcast of NY Radio Korea, a Korean language radio, covers the large areas of North Eastern states, including NY, NJ, CT, DE, and PA. Its regular program coverage focuses on the news about the United States and Korea, as well as the news pertaining to the local New York areas and the local Korean communities in these states. In particular, news on immigration laws, provisions, and policies is one of its important broadcasting items on U.S. news program. The information and the experts' insights on all kinds of legal immigration issues are also disseminated through the broadcasting of its other regular weekday programs.

In the territories of North Eastern states, there are also two well-known Korean language newspapers—*The Korea Times* and *The Korea Daily*—which also cover this kind of news with great concern. Because the news on legal immigration and any other matters of immigration are frequently reported in the headlines of these two ethnic newspapers and regularly dealt with in one of their pages, their Korean readers have much opportunity to learn information about broad or updated U.S. immigration laws, policies, and programs. In addition to print versions, these two NYC-based Korean newspapers also publish them on their online websites, alike. Their online publications can now reach most Korean immigrants in the United States regardless of their residential location, thus enabling them to improve their knowledge about the rules of the American immigration institution. More importantly, these Korean language media, like Korean immigrants' family and ethnic networks, function as an important resource for those who seek the information needed for a legal status of their permanent residence in the United States.

Table 2.5 also reveals another interesting pattern and trend of Korean immigrants' settlement or resettlement in the United States. There has been a recent substantial drop in the concentration of Korean immigrants in the top ten largest gateway metropolitan areas, decreasing from almost 69 percent in 2000 to over 57 percent in 2010. In turn, almost 43 percent of the Korean population in the United States in 2010 lived in non-gateway metropolitan areas or nonmetropolitan areas. Obviously, Korean immigrants in these geographical areas are still expected to participate in some clusters of their local family and ethnic networks and some relatively small-scale Korean organizations or associations, which have the potential to circulate some information helpful to obtain their legal status for permanent residency in the United States. Moreover, it is not any more difficult for them to access online Korean language newspapers published in larger Korean gateway cities from which they can have an opportunity to learn some valuable information on legal immigration, such as information on various types of legal proceedings for permanent residency and their individual legal requirements in eligibility. As already well known, immigration petitions for a U.S. permanent resident status or a U.S. citizenship status through naturalization must be an urgent and important matter for many immigrant families in the United States. These days, many Korean immigrant women, whether working or staying home, play a key role in collecting and analyzing all the information necessary to secure their own and their family's legal status for permanent residency in the United States. However, it is an undeniable fact that for some of them, their spatial isolation or distance from ethnic gateway communities limits not only the number and scope of ethnic networks or organizations they can join, but also the ethnic resources—e.g., ethnic language media—which they can utilize. It especially affects Korean immigrant wives there who are fully committed to taking care of their home and family members.

In this respect, the Korean-American women's online community here called the "MissyUSA" community is an important network for some of its members who seek information for the acquisition of a U.S. permanent resident status or its citizenship status through naturalization. In other words, it is also possible that their residential location and local ethnic networks would have little to do with their participation in this ethnic, married-women oriented online community. Likewise, even Korean immigrant women living in their gateway metropolitan areas can resort to the "Life Q&A" message board of the "MissyUSA" community because it provides them rich information and trustworthy responses about all kinds of rules of the American immigration institution.

LEGAL PERMANENT RESIDENT STATUS

The "Life Q&A" message board of the "MissyUSA" community is a valuable link or source for its members to assess social resources—specifically, a wide array of information for obtaining the legal permanent resident status of the United States. Thus, it is an online ethnic community and information outlet for some of its Korean-speaking members who seek or request certain information for their lawful permanent residency in the United States. Therefore, at first, this section sorts out the main types or general themes of information they look for through it in this section of legal permanent resident status. Then, its "Life Q&A" message board can be also seen by its respondents as an online ethnic network or channel of social support for its information seekers in their perspective. In turn, the revelation of their social support follows the posting of those messages seeking certain information through its message board. More importantly, their response messages comply with various sorts of social support for its information seekers, but more broadly, there exist two social support groups: instrumental guiders (information describers, analysts, confirmers, and advisors) and emotional supporters (companions, encouragers, and critics).

Qualifications

Prior to, or after, the submission of the applications for acquiring a U.S. legal permanent resident status at the USCIS, some "MissyUSA" members requested certain kinds of information or advice on it to their other online members by posting their inquiry messages. They often asked questions, such as what qualifications are required for their personal immigration petitions, whether their conditions are qualified for their immigration petitions, or what to do next if they are or are not qualified. In this broad theme of qualifications for a legal permanent resident status in the United States, there were many different sets of inquiry messages. More specifically, these include the qualifications associated with timing, family immigration, undocumented status, investment, criminal records, marriage, divorce, and so on. Below, these different sets of information inquiries about its qualifications illuminate the two aspects of social capital online, namely, social resources and social support. The first set of information inquiries involves the eligibility requirements and immigration procedures for family members of U.S. citizens or legal permanent residents. Most of the posted messages of this kind cover information inquiries about the qualifications related to those cases of immigration petitions for spouses, unmarried or married sons or daughters under or over the age of twenty-one, parents, non-immigrant spouse's parents, and brothers and sisters of U.S. citizens over the age of twenty-one. As an illustration, a member posted a message on its message board on January 4, 2012, through which she asked for some information about the eligibility and other important requirements in the immigration petition case of a Korean mother and sister of a U.S. citizen. There were seven response messages for the posting of this inquiry message:

> Q: I live alone in the United States. My mother and younger sister now live in South Korea. I am a naturalized American citizen, but they hold Korean nationality. I want to live with them here. I think that my mother's acquisition of legal permanent resident status will take six months to one year without much difficulty. The problem comes from my 16-year-old sister. I don't know what to do for her. Someone told me that it would take at least 10 years to bring her to the United States. But, I must bring both of them together into the United States. I really need your information or advice to cope with this problem. . . . Also, do I need an affidavit of support for my mother's application?
>
> A1: You are certainly right about both the separate applications for them and your prediction of their approval periods. They can come together, but your younger sister needs to apply for a non-immigrant student visa [F1 visa] to stay in the United States. Then, your younger sister will be expected to obtain her U.S. legal permanent resident status in two or three years after your mother's immigration petition for her.
>
> A2: Before you file the application for your mother, check whether your sister can obtain a non-immigrant student visa. Aside from that, file separate petitions for your mother and sister. You must file an affidavit of support with a copy of your fiscal-year filed tax report as evidence of your financial support to your mother.
>
> A3: A faster route for it seems to be that your sister can immigrate 5 years later after your mother files the immigration petition for your sister by means of a change in her legal status from lawful permanent residency to citizenship through naturalization.

A4: I agree.
A1: I am the person who commented first. Your mother as a green-card holder can file the petition for your sister. In case your financial qualifications are unmet, you should file another person's separate affidavit of support with yours to sponsor your mother financially.
A5: The processing time of immigration admissions is much faster for their unmarried sons and daughters than that of lawful immigration petitions through the family preference category of unmarried sons and daughters of U.S. citizens.
A6: Obtaining your mother's legal permanent resident status should be given the priority. Then file your sister's application through your mother as her petitioner and sponsor. . . . Your sister will be over the age of 21 at the time when your mother as a naturalized American citizen files the immigration petition for your sister.

All of these six respondents take on the broad role of instrumental guiders to the person who posted the message about the qualifications in immigration petitions for the Korean mother and sister of a U.S. citizen. One of the common points in their responses features the conveying of information that could be useful to handle the problem faced by the inquirer. Thus, most of them belong to information analysts as a subgroup of instrumental guiders, except for Respondent 4 (A4) who agreed to the account of Respondent 3 (A3). That role is well depicted in the messages of two respondents (A5 and A6) who explained the different processing times by immigration admissions. Information confirmers are another subgroup of instrumental guiders. Respondent 1 (A1) fits into this subgroup because she verified the accuracy of the inquirer's description about the separate applications for her mother and sister. Information advisors are the fourth subgroup of instrumental guiders. Five respondents, except for Respondent 4 (A4), also belong to the subgroup of information advisors for the inquirer by posting their suggestions or new ideas in their response messages.[25]

The second set of questions about the preconditions for the acquisition of a U.S. legal permanent resident status concerns the recipients' illegal immigration status. The prevailing inquiries here were about the qualifications for the cases of immigration petition that relate to an illegal immigrant's marriage to a U.S. citizen, a U.S. citizen's patronage to her undocumented, unmarried adult son, or an adult U.S. citizen's patronage to her undocumented parents. There was one specific message of this kind that was posted on the message board on March 9, 2012. This inquiry message received the five response messages, and three additional messages were further posted by the inquirer.

Q: I came to the United States as a non-immigrant student visa [F1 visa]. After its expiration, I have now been in the state of an illegal immigration status for almost ten years. But I have a social security number. Sooner or later, I am intended to marry my fiancé holding

American citizenship. Does it matter my illegal stay when filing for my U.S. legal permanent resident status? If this is so important, do I have to hire an immigrant lawyer? I need your advice, particularly from those folks of such experience. After filing my immigration petition, how long does it take to receive my conditional permanent resident card?
A1: It will take about 6 months to receive your conditional permanent resident card. There will be generally no problem. However, you need to hire an immigration lawyer because of your long stay in illegal immigration status. I hope everything turns out okay. I also wish you to be happily married. For the last 10 years, you did a good job enduring hardship.
Q: I really appreciate your advice. Your words of comfort make me feel so relieved.
A2: You had a really hard time. Congratulate heartily. I advise you to hire a good immigration lawyer. The pleasant life is waiting for you.
Q: Thank you. Thank you.
A3: Congratulations! Be happy!
A4: Congratulations! You need to hire a low-cost immigration lawyer.
A5: I know one of my friends who stayed illegally but later obtained her legal permanent resident status. She prepared for the petition herself without hiring an immigration lawyer. Congratulations!
Q: I feel full of energy and very pleased. Thanks to you for supporting me.

In general, two respondents (A1 and A5) take on the role of information describers to the inquirer as they posted their knowledge or information very shortly upon the inquirer's request. The role of information advisors can be observed in those messages posted by three respondents (A1, A2, and A4). Two of them (A1 and A2) also belong to the subgroup of companions for the inquirer. Besides, Respondent 5 (A5) is in the position of encouraging the inquirer. Notwithstanding their lack of personal connection with the inquirer, all of them sent congratulatory messages for her upcoming marriage. In several replies, the inquirer posted her heartfelt gratitude to her respondents. Though it might have been temporary and online, the respondents' touching expressions and the inquirer's feedback unveiled a sense of friendliness and amity to each other.

Under this topic of the qualifications, the third set of inquiry messages is about the influence of divorce from the spouse holding American citizenship status on the eligibility to receive a U.S. legal permanent resident status. One specific example on this matter was posted on the message board on August 9, 2012, and there were four messages in response to this initial post:

Q: Almost three months ago, I filed an application for legal permanent resident status through marriage and received a notice letter of my legal resident status. If I plan to get a divorce in this juncture by mutual agreement, please inform me of what and how I should do it.

A1: Why don't you decide to get a divorce after receiving your legal permanent resident card?
A2: That letter is the notice of one-year legal residence being received in the middle of the change in legal status from conditional residence to permanent residence. I expect you to receive your legal permanent resident card in about the next six months without interview. It is not too late to get a divorce at that time.
A3: If you filed your application at the USCIS's Vermont Service Center, the processing time will take ten to twelve months. Also, you might have an interview with the USCIS officer. I am very tired of waiting for the approval, but I still didn't hear any news yet. If you are going to begin processing your divorce now, the USCIS will request additional documents from both you and your husband to review your petition. Whenever there is evidence that your marriage is at risk due to your spouse's violence or abuse against you, your case can be easily approved.
A4: Your question is a little bit unclear to me. As far as I know, it is possible to file a petition for a U.S. legal permanent resident status after two years of conditional permanent residence through marriage.

Of instrumental guiders, two respondents (A2 andA3) take on both roles of information analysts and information advisors for the inquirer because they referred to the proceedings of the application based upon their own experiences and also advised the inquirer about what to prepare for after filing the petition for a U.S. permanent resident status. Respondent 1 (A1) became an information advisor to the inquirer on the ground of her role suggesting the postponement of the divorce. Respondent 4 (A4) seems to have trouble understanding the core content of the message posted by the inquirer. Nonetheless, she is also likely to be in a position to take on the role of an information advisor for the inquirer because she wrote the timing of status alteration for conditional residence through marriage.

Application Package

Before filing a petition for legal permanent resident status, preparing the full package of the required documents is quite a difficult task for many of its applicants. Some "MissyUSA" members and their family members can fortunately avoid facing this hassle somewhat by obtaining information relevant to their cases through the help of its other online members. Indeed, in the message board of "Life Q&A," there have been a wide variety of messages requesting information about the application package for a U.S. legal permanent resident status. The whole application packages for it generally include filing fees, all the required application forms, and other supporting materials, such as proof of employment, birth certificate, marriage certificate, medical check-ups, copies of income tax reports, passport, visa, and diplomas, and so forth. Two specific examples for this topic are introduced below. First, on April 10, 2012, a member posted a message seeking information about the preparation of the documents verifying legal marriage amid the proceeding of a petition for a U.S. permanent resident status. This inquiry message received two response messages:

> Q: Greetings! My two-year conditional permanent residence through marriage ended so that I have filed the application for my legal permanent resident status. I hired an immigration lawyer to handle my case for this conditional permanent residence before. This time, my husband and I have filed the application for my permanent resident status without the help of an immigration lawyer. I finished taking my fingerprints and have been waiting for the approval of my legal permanent resident status. Then the USCIS sent me a mail noticing the submission of more documents proving my legal marriage. I am set to visit Korea at the end of May, but this notice letter ruins my plan. Can you share your experiences with me? And what documents do I have to prepare for further? Can you also share the processing time of your cases like mine?
> A1: This time last year, my husband and I prepared and filed my application for a U.S. legal permanent resident status. Upon request from the USCIS, I also mailed additional materials that demonstrate my legal marriage. My return mail included the copies of my and my husband's bank statements, credit card bills, wedding pictures, vehicle registration and insurance cards, and three-year income tax reports. Both of our names and home address were only available in the letter of car insurance policy. In my mail package to the USCIS, I also included a letter explaining why one of my cars was registered in the address of my parent's house. After sending my mail, I expected another mail from the USCIS, which would notice the schedule of my interview date. But the letter I received stated that I would obtain my legal permanent resident card within the next two weeks. I was very happy to have that without interview. Sending any materials proving your residence with your husband can lead to a good result like my case.
> A2: The best proof of your legal marriage is to send the copy of your joint income tax reports. With the cover letter, send it with any other important materials all together.

Respondent 1 (A1) takes on the multiple roles for the inquirer, such as those of an information analyst, advisor, and an emotional companion. Like Respondent 1 (A1), Respondent 2 (A2) also belongs to the subgroup of information advisors to the inquirer on account of her suggestion for the filing of joint income tax reports.

As another example, one member wrote a message requesting opinions about a record of an application form on March 4, 2012. It followed with twenty-five response messages and five additional messages from the inquirer. Of these twenty-five response messages, the first six responses are introduced below, along with two more messages from the inquirer below:

> Q: I have hired an immigration lawyer to handle my application for legal permanent resident status. I came to the United States with a non-immigrant student visa and thereafter, I have stayed unlawfully. Then, my lawyer asked me to write everything I have done during the period of my undocumented status, including my illegal jobs, wages, and no reports on income taxes. My lawyer said to me that such information will demonstrate what I have done in America. But, I worry about some penalty like the denial of my immigration petition at the time when I admit my illegal employment and tax evasion. I am very confused about what I am supposed to do. I need your advice.
> A1: Don't write about that. If your income was tax deducted, it is fine to write it. If that is not case, both you and your employer might be punished.
> Q: I am worried about that point.
> A2: Don't write it. I don't think that your lawyer is sane. Don't mention your employment at all during the period of your non-immigrant student and undocumented statuses.
> A3: You violated immigration laws. If you admit your illegal employment, you might be deported. Instead, you need to write the fact that you have lived with your parents' financial support. There are so many immigration lawyers devoid of expertise and experiences.
> A4: If your parents really supported you financially during the period of your undocumented status, you need proof of the bank statements your parents sent money to you by wire transfer from Korea . . .
> A5: Don't write it. You don't have to prove anything about how you have lived here. Your application can be denied when you admit your past illegal employment.
> Q: Some "MissyUSA" members recommended my current lawyer at another "MissyUSA" message board. I will call my lawyer not to write about it.
> A6: That's just common sense. Not only have you stayed illegally, but also evaded taxes. Both violations can result in the denial of your case.

In the message posted by the inquirer, she requested advice about whether or not to write about illegal employment and a history of tax evasion to anonymous "MissyUSA" members. In general, all of her six respondents agreed with her by expressing their own thoughts, suggesting solutions in her dilemma, and/or predicting future results. Therefore, all of them belong to the subgroup of information advisors to the inquirer. At the same time, four of them (A1, A43, A4, and A6) also take on a role of information analysts for her because they attempted to make sense of the key points of the question raised by their inquirer. Additionally, none of them are emotional supporters because they gave no indication as to whether they sympathize or encourage the inquirer. Nonetheless, it is quite interesting to observe that two respondents (A2 and A3) criticized the misjudgment or incapability of her lawyer.

Sponsorship

Immigration petitioners are usually U.S. citizens, permanent resident aliens, or U.S. companies (employers), who act as sponsors by filing immigration applications at the USCIS for their relatives (spouses, children, parents, brothers, or sisters), friends, or non-immigrant workers. For example, immigration laws require a petitioner filing for the immigration of his relatives to demonstrate the proof that his or her own income is at or above 125 percent of the federal poverty level. This requirement of a petitioner's financial support for the beneficiaries aims to prevent their use of public benefits for needy families, such as food stamps, Medicaid, supplementary security income (SSI), and temporary assistance. Therefore, income verification is critical to their approval or denial of family-based immigration petitions. As a result of their sponsorship, their beneficiaries can immigrate to the United States to live and work permanently. Under this topic of sponsorship, the inquiry messages posted on the "Life Q&A" message board included requests for information or advice about how to financially support parents, brothers, sisters, and friends, and how to find those companies that are willing to sponsor non-immigrants workers who wish to file petitions through employment for their lawful permanent residency in the United States. There were also some inquiry messages about which of them—e.g., the company or the non-immigrant workers—are primarily responsible for the preparation of the paperwork, the checking of their cases' progress, and the payment of all filing fees in employment-based petitions. Below, two specific illustrations are introduced. First, a message requesting information about a financial supporter was posted on March 6, 2012. Four members responded to this post:

> Q: For many years, the U.S. citizen has been unemployed so that he didn't file income tax for those years. His spouse has been living illegally, but she continued to report her income tax. In this case, is she as the beneficiary, instead of the petitioner, possible to become the financial sponsor?
> A1: No, she is unqualified. She needs to find another person to support her financially.
> A2: Another person should be her financial sponsor.
> A3: In my case, I worked legally and reported my income tax consecutively. In the application for my permanent resident status in the United States, I filed my own affidavit of support in consultation with my lawyer, and then, my case was approved without any problem. When you read the instructions of affidavit of support [Form I-864] available at the USCIS website, you can learn the threshold of minimum income level in the case of joint sponsors. I think that you would meet the financial qualifications, if the combined income of you and your husband is more than $30,000.

A4: It is a better idea to consult with your immigration lawyer, rather than your communication in this online message board.

Because all these four respondents offered suggestions and guidance about what the inquirer should do next, they all belong to the subgroup of information advisors for the inquirer. In addition to the role of an information advisor, Respondent 3 (A3) also takes on both roles of an information analyst and an encourager for the inquirer.

One message of who should be in charge of immigration petitions for non-immigrant workers was posted on December 5, 2012. Three messages were posted as responses to it:

Q: In an immigration petition on the basis of employment, I am not sure about who should pay for all the costs, such as all the filing fees, the expense of job advertisement for recruitment, and legal fees. In some companies, all of these costs were paid by them. But, I also learned that such responsibility of the U.S. employers is not always true in some other companies. Is there an official rule for this matter?
A1: In case foreign workers are hired in American companies, it is true that their employers take full responsibility for their immigration petitions. This is completely a different story for small-scale Korean-own companies in the United States whose employers sometimes request the handling of all the processing fees on their own. There is no choice for these workers.
A2: The filing fees and the expense of job advertisement should be paid by the employer. But, the payment of legal fees by the employer is optional, not compulsory. Besides, the costs of "an application to register permanent residency or adjust status" (Form I-485) are often unsupported by the employers. Then, the larger American companies pay for all the costs of their foreign workers' permanent resident status applications.
A3: Before you consult with your company's lawyer, I advise you to meet an immigration lawyer first because your company's lawyer might specialize only in commercial laws, not immigration laws.

The first two respondents (A1 and A2) belong to the subgroup of information analysts for the inquirer because both explained the immigration policies and the requirements for the immigration petitions filed by typical American employers. Respondent 1 (A1) further added the text that there exists the discrepancy between immigration regulations and the employers' practices—e.g., small-scale Korean companies in the United States. In this short thread of response messages, Respondent 3 (A3) serves as an information advisor for the inquirer because she suggested that the inquirer should set up an early meeting with an immigration lawyer and a later meeting with her company's lawyer.

Fingerprinting and Interview

Taking fingerprints is a legal requirement after filing for immigration adjustment for their lawful permanent residency in the United States. Their fingerprints are taken at a designated USCIS office and are sent to the Federal Bureau of Investigation (FBI) for a criminal background check. Some "MissyUSA" members posted the messages requesting information about what to do (i.e., which forms to fill out, how to prepare to meet with USCIS officers), or what documents they should bring at the time of their fingerprinting appointment (i.e., passport, driver license, Social Security card, an appointment letter). After the applicant's criminal background check is finally cleared, the USCIS schedules an interview by sending a letter that notifies the date, time, and location of one's interviewing. Like their fingerprinting appointment, some "MissyUSA" members posted the messages requesting information about how to prepare for their interviews with a USCIS officer, or what to do during their interview time. Below, two specific examples are illustrated under this topic of fingerprinting and interviewing. One message posted on October 2, 2012, raised a question about what types of personal identification one should bring to the USCIS office for fingerprinting. Two members responded to this post:

> Q: I am a naturalized American citizen, and an application for lawful permanent residency was already filed for my husband. He received an appointment letter from the USCIS to take his fingerprints. However, his valid IDs, like passport and driver license, have expired in the past. Is there any other way to prove his identification in his meeting with a USCIS officer?
>
> A1: Renew either his passport or driver license, and then visit the USCIS for his fingerprinting. If he has no valid ID, he cannot take his fingerprints.
>
> A2: I carried my two-year passed passport for my fingerprinting. I finished taking my fingerprinting there without difficulty. By seeing it, the USCIS officer will only check the correct identification and facial appearance of the applicant. That's it.

Both respondents (A1 and A2) posted their suggestions so that they belonged to the subgroup of information advisors to the inquirer. Respondent 2 (A2) also became an information analyst for the inquirer because she explained a general happening before taking fingerprints in a USCIS office. Besides, there is an indication that Respondent 2 (A2) also takes on the role of an encourager to the inquirer by sharing her past experience similar to that of the inquirer's husband.

On February 6, 2012, the posting of an inquiry message in content was about language concerns regarding her interview with a USCIS officer. This post received three response messages along with an additional message from the inquirer:

Q: During my interview with a USCIS officer, I can speak to him or her in my basic-level English when his or her questions are simple or very clear, like the questions related to my marriage and family. My husband speaks fluently in English. Do you think that I should bring my husband as a translator [an interpreter] in my interview?
A1: In your interview, a USCIS officer will ask most of questions to your husband. He or she may ask you some simple questions like your name and home address.
A2: If you have stayed legally in the U.S. and your husband speaks English fluently, you don't have to go to the office with your immigration lawyer for your interview. Being asked the absence of your lawyer, tell him or her that your lawyer charges $500 for his coming . . .
A3: In my case, the USCIS officer asked the questions to me, though my English-speaking husband was present there with me. I was poor in my English skills, but the officer asked me really the basic questions I could understand. Go to the interview alone!
Q: Thank you.

All three respondents can be classified as the subgroup of information analysts for the inquirer because they explained what usually happens during the USCIS interviews. Furthermore, the role of an information advisor to the inquirer can be detected from the messages of two respondents (A2 and A3). Respondent 3 (A3) can be also regarded as the encourager for the inquirer because she provided strong encouragement to the inquirer in her response message.

While Waiting for the Decision

After filing an application for the legal permanent resident status of the United States and completing the fingerprinting and interview, its beneficiary will wait for the final decision for his or her immigration petition from the USCIS. In some cases, it will take a few weeks or months. But, in some other cases, it will take a year or more. When his or her case is pending for a long time, he or she may feel very anxious, stressed, and even frustrated. Some "MissyUSA" members posted the messages requesting information about the average length of time it takes for immigration petitions through family reunification (i.e., spouses, children, relatives of a U.S. citizen or a permanent resident alien), and through employment-based preferences (i.e., second and third preferences). For example, an inquiry message about general processing time in immigration petitions for legal permanent residency in the United States was posted on the "Life Q&A" message board on February 2, 2012. Seven members responded to this post:

Q: I have been waiting for my case approval for over the last five years. I am raising children and holding a non-immigrant student visa by attending a school. I am very mad about nothing I can do. What is worse, I have recently heard that a limit of per-country family-spon-

sored and employment-based preferences will be eliminated soon. If this new immigration legislation is passed in Congress, one of my friends told me that my case would be processed with the delay of two years or more. Tired of waiting for the decision, some of my acquaintances returned to Korea, or reapplied their petitions through investment. I also wanted to come back to Korea, but my husband disagreed on that. I feel heavy with worries. Indeed, I have no idea of when I can receive my green card.
A1: I have lived in the United States for almost 10 years. The priority date for my petition through employment-based immigration was in May 2007. I have no hope for the future.[26]
A2: I started in the beginning of 2010. I think that I have to wait more . . .
A3: I guess the average of the proceeding times is 10 years. The applications of petitions for spouses of U.S. citizens will take much less time.
A4: My priority date was in October, 2006. I expected to receive my green card this year. Unfortunately, this new bill of the elimination of per-country limit will further delay the processing time of my case, maybe two or three years more. I wanted to come back to Korea. But it is not easy for my family to start a new life there so that I am waiting for my approval letter . . .
A5: My priority date was in April 2007. I also expected to receive my green card within a year. If this new legislation is passed, I will feel completely frustrated.
A6: In case this bill is passed, its enactment will begin after three years.
A7: No, that's not true. My priority date was in September 2006. The processing time of my case will have one year more as the result of the approval of this immigration bill.

Except for two respondents (A3 and A6), the other five respondents exchanged the priority dates of their applications. For that reason, they overall belong to the subgroup of information describers to the inquirer. Likewise, these five respondents also take on the role of information confirmers because they indicate that their cases are pending just like that of the inquirer. Three respondents (A3, A4, and A7) appear to be in the position of information analysts for the inquirer as they attempted to evaluate the processing times in the immigration petitions that were given the priority dates. In part of the inquirer's message, she expressed her emotional suffering because she has yet to receive an approval letter from the USCIS. Nonetheless, none of her respondents offered any encouragement to the inquirer. However, most of them, except Respondent 6 (A6), appear to share a sense of affinity with her by signifying their emotional insecurity and dissatisfaction in their response messages (companions).

After Approval

Once a permanent resident card (a green card) is issued, all permanent residents have the legal right to live and work in the United States.

They can also use their green card to apply for their Social Security card at the U.S. Social Security Administration (SSA) and their driver's license at their state's Motor Vehicle Agency (MVA) that is no longer temporary. Moreover, their possession of a green card makes their international trips much easier, and likewise, makes it possible for them to stay longer in other countries.[27] However, they must renew their ten-year green card ahead of its expiration date in order to live and work legally in the United States, unless, after five years of permanent residency in the United States, they are planning to file for American citizenship through naturalization. Two specific examples of this topic are extracted from the "Life Q&A" message board and are introduced below. On December 10, 2012, one member posted a message requesting information about her maximum duration of stay in Korea as a U.S. green card holder. Three members responded to this post and the inquirer added another message:

> Q: In January this year, I received my permanent resident card. I returned to America after my two-month stay from last September in Korea. I have my sick sister living in Korea. I am thinking of staying there for a longer time to take care of my sister. In my case, how long can I stay in Korea?
> A1: Legal permanent residents should live in the United States more than six months per year. In your case, you can stay in Korea for another six months.
> Q: Thank you for responding to my message . . .
> A2: When you have a reentry permit after applying for it and taking your fingerprinting, you can stay in Korea for two years. Visit the United States before the end of your five- or six-month stay in Korea to maintain your permanent resident status.
> A3: It really depends on the immigration officials' judgments at a U.S. port of entry. Your stay in Korea for over six months can be excused when you prove your homeownership in the United States and your tax reports at the IRS. Also, show other evidences like your long-term medical or hospital treatment in Korea. Two times, one of my friends as a green card holder stayed in Korea for three or four months. Her reentry was not easy each time because her immigration officials in the airport examined her very thoroughly.

All three respondents belong to the subgroup of information analysts for the inquirer because they provided their own explanations about the question she raised. Two of them (A2 and A3) also take on the role of information advisors to the inquirer by suggesting to her their own ideas of how she could maintain her U.S. permanent resident status.

On April 2, 2012, another member posted a message requesting information about the renewal of a green card. Five response messages followed this post:

> Q: My green card expires in March next year. When can I start to renew my green card?

A1: You will receive a notice letter from the USCIS.
A2: I didn't receive that before.
A3: Three months before its expiration.
A4: You can renew it six months before the expiration. A half a month ago, I applied to replace my permanent resident card.
A5: Please do it three months before its expiration . . .

Four respondents (A1, A3, A4, and A5) belong to the subgroup of information describers to the inquirer because they answered her question very briefly without further explanation. To some degree, four of them can also be regarded as the subgroup of information advisors to the inquirer. Then, Respondent 2 (A2) disagreed with the comment posted by Respondent 1 (A1) without any direct response on the message posted by the inquiry message.

NATURALIZATION

For its members who are currently pursuing, or considering pursuing, American citizenship status through naturalization, the Korean-American women's online community, here specifically the "Life Q&A" message board of the "MissyUSA" community, becomes an important source of information for it. At the same time, some of the other "MissyUSA" members (respondents) become their social supporters by guiding and/or supporting them in various ways.

Qualifications

Before submitting applications for naturalized American citizenship status, some members posted the messages requesting information about whether or not they are eligible to file for it. In most cases, some of the other "MissyUSA" members responded to such information inquiries by posting their messages that contain information, knowledge, experiences, suggestions, and/or emotional support for the inquirers. Under this subject of qualifications, the frequently posted questions on the "Life Q&A" message board include the applicants' (or their parents') current legal status, length of residence in or outside the United States or the USCIS district or state, age (under eighteen), marital status (currently married or divorced), criminal records, traffic violations, bad credit standing, employment (unemployment), and others. Below, three specific examples of such kind are in great detail illustrated. First, the requirement of the permanent residents' length of residence in the United States was asked by one member on October 8, 2012. There were four response messages and an additional message from the inquirer:

Q: After a permanent resident card is issued, when is it the time to apply for naturalization?

A1: 46 months later.
A2: If she has been married to a U.S. citizen, it is possible to apply for it after 2 years and 9 months?
A3: As far as I know, they can apply for American citizenship after 5 years. Also, three-year continuous residence in the United States is further required.
Q: If I visit Korea a week every year, do I have to delay my naturalization application?
A4: No, you don't have to. When you are supposed to have your stay in Korea for over 6 month, at that time, you should recount the date you are eligible to apply for naturalization.

Because Respondent 1 (A1) posted her very short message like a phrase, she becomes an information describer to the inquirer. In general, three other respondents (A2, A3, and A4) belong to the subgroup of information analysts for the inquirer.

On January 3, 2012, another member posted a message requesting information about how a past traffic violation might affect eligibility for citizenship. The five response messages followed it:

Q: In the past, I received a speeding ticket from the police. I think that it won't affect the decision for my naturalization application. What do you think?
A1: It doesn't matter at all.
A2: However, you should report all your offenses in your application form [Form N-400].
A3: I didn't report my past traffic violations, but without it, my application for naturalization was approved. When people were arrested by drunk driving or an alcohol-related traffic incident, they should report it in the N-400.
A4: It doesn't matter at all. If a fine of your traffic violation is less than $500, you don't have to report it.
A5: Don't lie about any offenses you committed after the issue date of your permanent resident card.

Two respondents (A1 and A4) belong to the subgroup of information confirmers because they reassured the issue raised by the inquirer. Two respondents (A3 and A4) are in the subgroup of information analysts for the inquirer because of their role that involves explaining the conditions about the report of a past traffic violation. Additionally, two other respondents (A2 and A5) take on the role of information advisors because they instructed the inquirer about what to do when applying for naturalization.

A message questioning the influence of divorce on the naturalization process was posted on January 1, 2012. There were two messages in response to it:

Q: I lived with my husband holding a U.S. citizenship for the last seven years, but recently I was divorced. I obtained my permanent resident

> card through marriage several years ago. I am planning to apply for my naturalization soon . . . I wonder if my divorce will become a negative factor in the acquisition of my citizenship status.
> A1: If your green card is obtained by your marriage with a U.S. citizen, you are eligible to apply for naturalization after three years. Generally, lawful permanent residents can petition for naturalization after five years.
> A2: You can apply for naturalization after three years. Your divorce has nothing to do with the decision on the approval of your naturalization. I was divorced, too. After checking the issue date of my permanent resident card and applying for naturalization four years and nine months later, I received my certificate of naturalization. In the package of your naturalization application, you should include all the documents that proved the termination of your marriage. Besides, tell the truth during your interview. Don't worry. I am sure everything will be just fine.

Both respondents (A1 and A2) belong to the subgroup of information analysts for the inquirer. It is because they explained the timetable of eligibility for naturalization. Both respondents also take on the role of information advisors to the inquirer. Moreover, the message of Respondent 2 (A2) reveals her additional role as the encourager for the inquirer.

Application Package

The application package for citizenship status through naturalization generally includes the filled out and signed form(s), filing fees, and the required supporting documents. The specific application packages for naturalization differ from individual to individual. For instance, the application package for naturalization on the basis of marriage to a U.S. citizen should include the applicants' current marriage certificate and all the documents proving the termination of all prior marriages (if applicable), the documents of their and their spouse's tax returns, bank accounts, leases, or mortgages. For those lawful permanent residents who have stayed outside of the United States for six months or more, their application package should include the documents of their tax return, lease or mortgage payments, and pay stubs. In the "Life Q&A" message board, some "MissyUSA" members asked for a wide range of information related to the application package for naturalization. These were, for instance, about the preparation of the naturalization application form, filing fees, legal name, divorce, tax return, and so on. Below, two specific cases for this topic of application package are introduced. First, one member posted a message requesting information about a supporting document in the application for naturalization on July 2, 2012. In response, there were two messages for it:

> Q: Do I have to fill out Form U-400? I was divorced. So, do I have to include the original of my divorce degree in the application? I don't have it now because it was held by my divorced husband who died. What can I do?
> A1: The application form for naturalization is not U-400, but N-400. I advise you to read its instruction, Form M-476 [a guide to naturalization].
> A2: Send your N-400 with a copy of your divorce degree. In your interview, you should bring its original. You can order its certified copy in your divorce court.

Both respondents (A1 and A2) belong to the subgroup of information advisors to the inquirer in considering their corrections on the misspelling of the form, or their instructions for what to do next.

On January 4, 2012, another member posted a message requesting information about which one of her names (maiden or married) to write on the naturalization form. Two response messages followed it:

> Q: The last name in my social security card is my married name. But my maiden name was printed in my Korean passport and my U.S. permanent resident card. I am now filling in my application form for naturalization. Which last name is used to fill in its column of last name?
> A1: Write the last name on your permanent resident card!
> A2: The last name in your permanent resident card and social security card should be the same. You should have changed it before. Because your naturalization application is based upon your permanent resident status, you need to use the last name on your permanent resident card.

The role of information advisors to the inquirer was performed by both respondents. In addition, Respondent 2 (A2) seems to condemn the inquirer not to match her last names on her legal papers to some degree. Hence, Respondent 2 (A2) can be regarded as the critic to the inquirer.

Name Change

In Korea, any married Korean woman can keep her last name rather than adopting her husband's surname. But, in the United States, many immigrant women from Korea have learned that changing their last names into their new husbands' surname is common in American society. Moreover, many of them are willing to change their first names into English first names because they recognize that their English-speaking friends or acquaintances have difficulty pronouncing their Korean first names. While preparing for their naturalization application, some "MissyUSA" members posted messages involving this topic of name change. For example, one member posted a message on this topic on December 4, 2012. Five members responded to it:

> Q: When filing a naturalization application, is it a good idea to change the last name? Frankly speaking, I didn't experience much inconvenience for the last eight years. If it is changed, do I have to change the last name on my bank accounts and driver's license? How about the name on the property title deeds? Can you share your experiences?
> A1: Don't be too nervous about what people say. It's a matter of personal preference.
> A2: Although it really depends on your personal preference, the change of your name will bother you for one or two weeks. For instance, you should change your names on bank accounts, driver's license, and even [airline] mileage cards.
> A3: I changed my last name into my husband's one, with advice from my friend who experienced some inconveniences caused by the differences in her and her husband's last names.
> A4: When I petitioned for my naturalization, I changed my last name. . . . Now, I am very comfortable with my changed last name.
> A5: When you have school children, I think that the same last names are much convenient. . . . I didn't change my last name for my first ten years here. But I realized that the school teachers and parents of my children's school friends were confused about the different last names between my children and me. . . . I believe that it is a matter of personal choice.

All the respondents take on the role of information advisors to the inquirer. The reason is that they all expressed their personal thoughts or judgments on this issue of name change, with or without the sharing of their own experiences. Two of them (A3 and A5) also belong to the subgroup of information analysts for the inquirer, whereas Respondent 4 (A4) is placed as the encourager to her.

Processing Time

Some applicants for citizenship status through naturalization will want to know how long the process for it will take. The period of time from the application submission to the receipt of naturalization certificate will vary from case to case. In general, they would like to know the expected time to complete their naturalization process. For some, the relatively long waiting time makes them feel nervous or even upset, especially if they need the certificate of naturalization right away for some reason. Therefore, some "MissyUSA" members posted messages requesting information about the average duration of time for naturalization. One such case was posted on April 7, 2012. Three response messages followed it:

> Q: I filed my naturalization application in late last January. In this late May, I am planning to visit Korea and stay for five or six weeks there. When can I expect to receive my notice from the USCIS? If I cannot hear any notice until that time, I am not sure what to do . . .

A1: In my case, it took a total of six months.
A2: I took my fingerprints three months after the filing of my application. And my interview was done after another three months.
A3: It took me four months from the filing of the application to the naturalization ceremony.

All three respondents shared their experiences with the inquirer in their short messages that replied to her question. In this regard, they belong to the subgroup of information describers to the inquirer.

Fingerprinting, Interview, and Tests

After the submission of the naturalization application, the USCIS will send the appointment notice for fingerprinting to the applicant, which will be used by the Federal Bureau of Investigation (FBI) in order to check his or her criminal background. After the fingerprint requirement is done, he or she will have an interview with a USCIS officer to verify his or her application materials. The applicant will also take the English and civics (U.S. history and government) tests. Some "MissyUSA" members posted messages requesting information about what documents to bring out at the time of fingerprinting or interview (i.e., appointment letter, green card, passport, marriage certificate, wedding picture, driver license, or re-entry permits), how to prepare for their English or civics tests, or how to act during their naturalization interview with a USCIS officer. Below, two specific cases are introduced. First, one member posted a message requesting information about the required documents necessary for the naturalization interview on September 9, 2012. Two members responded to this post:

Q: I filed my application for naturalization and completed biometrics, as well. Now, I am waiting to receive the appointment notice for my interview. What documents do I need to take with me?
A1: You need to carry your appointment letter, driver license, green card, and passport.
A2: I carried my wedding pictures, marriage certificate, and tax return copies. In fact, my wedding pictures and marriage certificate were very useful during the interview.

Because both respondents briefly referred to and suggested the preparation of some documents for the naturalization interview, they belong to not only the subgroup of information describers, but also that of information advisors for the inquirer.

On June 6, 2012, another member posted a message regarding her naturalization test. Four response messages followed it:

Q: I have waited a long time for my naturalization test. I am very worried about whether I can pass it. Can you suggest your ideas about my post?

A1: When you visit a USCIS office to take your fingerprints, you will receive a booklet that helps prepare for your reading, writing, and civics tests. Just memorize 100 civics questions and answers.
A2: Check the link of the naturalization test at the USCIS website. Then, memorize all the vocabularies, questions, and those answers posted on it.
A3: Use an audio CD attached to the booklet. When I drove my car, I listened to it many times to prepare for my naturalization test.
A4: At your naturalization interview, your basic communication skill in English shouldn't be ignored.

All four respondents belong to the subgroup of information advisors to the inquirer because they provided her their own advice as to how to cope with the naturalization interview and tests.

After Approval

The legal process for the acquisition of American citizenship status through naturalization is completed after taking the Oath of Allegiance at a naturalization ceremony. After taking the Oath of Allegiance, a certificate of naturalization granted is as proof of becoming a U.S. citizen. To apply for a U.S. passport and to update a Social Security card are the next steps for a newly naturalized American citizen. Some "MissyUSA" members posted messages about the naturalization ceremony, U.S. passport applications, and Social Security card applications. In addition, they posted messages requesting information about a name change after divorce, loss of naturalization certificate, the crimes committed by naturalized U.S. citizens, and so on. Introduced below are two specific examples posted on the "Life Q&A" message board. First, one member posted the message asking a couple of questions related to her schedule of naturalization ceremony on March 5, 2012. Six members responded to this post:

Q: My naturalization interview was completed, now I am waiting to receive a schedule for my naturalization ceremony. If I am not attending that ceremony, is it that my reapplication for naturalization is likely denied? Is it possible to reschedule the date of my naturalization ceremony?
A1: You should know that once you take the Oath of Allegiance, you can immediately apply for the U.S. passport.
A2: So, you don't want be a U.S. citizen, right?
A3: You can reschedule your attendance at a naturalization ceremony. But you should explain why you cannot come to the scheduled naturalization ceremony . . .
A4: In advance, call the USCIS office to reschedule your ceremony.
A5: Because of my visit to Korea, I had to reschedule the date of my naturalization ceremony. With advance notice to your local USCIS office, it is no problem at all.

> A6: If you do not attend on that day, you won't become a U.S. citizen as you don't receive your certificate of naturalization.

Four of these six respondents 2 (A1, A3, A4, and A6) belong to the subgroup of information advisors because they suggested what she should do next or what would happen as a result. Two respondents (A3 and A5) take on the role of information confirmers to the inquirer. Additionally, Respondent 5 (A5) also takes on both roles of an information analyst and a companion to the inquirer. Then, Respondent 2 (A2) posted a short message with derision to the inquirer. This expression of Respondent 2 (A2) puts her position as a critic to the inquirer.

On February 3, 2012, another member posted a message questioning the possibility of deportation as the result of criminal offenses. There were three messages in response to this post:

> Q: If a naturalized U.S. citizen committed a felony crime, is this person unquestionably deported? How about his or her misdemeanor?
> A1: I remember a local Korean newspaper's article that dealt with this issue before. That article indicated that naturalized U.S. citizens can be deported in consequence of their felony offenses.
> A2: Treason of nation and arrest on tax evasion are the factors affecting their deportation.
> A3: My friend's son was a naturalized U.S. citizen, but he was deported to Korea where he is now serving in the military. I have no idea of what happened to him here.

Two of these respondents (A1 and A2) belong to the subgroup of information analysts to the inquirer. Respondent 1 (A1) also takes on the role of an information confirmer to the inquirer. In general, the message posted by Respondent 3 (A3) placed her position as an information describer to the inquirer.

SUMMARY

One of the main arguments proposed in this book was that ethnic immigrants' online social networks have the potential for their participating members to create two distinctive forms of social capital (social resources and social support). This suggests that some of their members seek information (social resources) about the rules of their new country's social institutions, and in response, some of their other members help provide its information seekers a wide range of information about the rules of their new country's social institutions, and/or support them emotionally (social support), through the platforms of their ethnic online communities. In this chapter, some members of the "MissyUSA" community posted their messages requesting or providing information about the rules of the American immigration institution that are, directly or indirectly, associated with their legal permanent resident status or citizenship status through naturalization in the United States. As shown above, some of their posts in the forms of inquiry and response messages have been illustrated and evaluated on the basis of two distinctive forms of social capital—social resources (information) and social support—by taking into account the "MissyUSA" community as both the important source of social resources (information) and the network of social support.

Focusing on the notion that the "MissyUSA" community can be understood as the important source of social resources (information) to some of its members—here, inquirers or information seekers, this chapter generally provided evidence that its information seekers (inquirers) had a propensity to view the American immigration institution as a composite entity of all the immigration rules at both institution-wide and intra-institutional (or organizational) levels. Thus, most of their inquiries on the American immigration institution involved seeking information on some formal immigration laws, policies, regulations, or procedures in pursuit of either their or their family members' U.S. legal permanent resident status or American citizenship status through naturalization. More specifically, most of their inquiry messages in content focused on the topics of qualifications, sponsorship, required documents for applications (or a full application package), and other accompanying procedures upon submission of application. Under the topic of qualifications, for example, some "MissyUSA" members (inquirers) looked for information on the qualifications associated with timing, family immigration, undocumented status, investment, criminal records, marriage, divorce, and others. In the topic of the application package for naturalization, for example, the focus of their inquiries was mostly on which specific documents are required for it—e.g., marriage certificate, all the documents demonstrating the termination of all prior marriages (if applicable), the documents of you and your spouse's tax returns, bank accounts, leases, or mortgages.

In this book, the "MissyUSA" community was also understood as the network of social supporters (information providers or respondents) for the information seekers. Indeed, social support to the seekers (inquirers) of information regarding the rules of the American immigration institution is the other aspect of social capital that is inherent in, and attainable through, the "MissyUSA" community. Then, it only emerges in response to the inquiry messages posted on its "Life Q&A" message board. This also means that patterns of social support are heavily constrained in the message contents, types, or contexts its information seekers looked for. Nonetheless, there was a great diversity of messages posted by its respondents (information providers). According to a general analysis of their messages in response to the posts seeking information, at first, its respondents were broadly classified into two broad groups of social support: instrumental guiders (information describers, analysts, confirmers, and advisors), and emotional supporters (companions, encouragers, and critics). In fact, the most overwhelming subgroups of instrumental guiders were both subgroups of information analysts and information advisors for the inquirers who were directed to seek information on the rules of the American immigration institution. By and large, information analysts wrote the texts that explain, interpret, or evaluate the backgrounds, conditions, essential issues or major features, reasons, processes, or even outcomes. In comparison, information advisors posted their messages that contain advice, suggest some general or specific ideas or options, or that provide their thoughts regarding what to do now or what will happen next on the basis of their past experiences, expertise, hearsay, or guesswork. Even some of the messages from information advisors included such specific instructions as necessary steps, procedures, or ways to handle the issues associated with the rules of the American immigration institution. Then, in this group of instrumental guiders, some respondents took on a single role, while some others took on multiple roles across their four subgroups.

Relative to social support for the inquirers by instrumental guiders—information describers, analysts, confirmers, and advisors, the messages of respondents overall carried less of emotional support for the inquirers. But, there were some cases where some of its respondents expressed their companionship to the inquirers by sharing their own experiences similar, or identical, to the inquirers'. Besides, there were also some other respondents who took on the role of encouragers to the inquirers through their expressions of praise about the inquirers' past efforts, or through encouragement for the inquirers' further efforts. Interestingly enough, the joint roles of both information guiders and emotional supporters to the inquirers were also revealed in the messages posted by some of its respondents. In short, this chapter showed that the "MissyUSA" community is the online space to create social capital (social resources and social support) for both information seekers and respondents in the realm of the rules of the American immigration institution.

NOTES

1. Cecilia Menjívar, "Liminal Legality: Salvadoran and Guatemalan Immigrants' Lives in the United States," *American Journal of Sociology* 111 (2006): 999–1037; and Nicholas P. De Genova, "Migrant 'Illegality' and Deportability in Everyday Life," *Annual Review of Anthropology* 31 (2002): 419–447.

2. Shannon Gleeson and Roberto Z. Gonzales, "When Do Papers Matter? An Institutional Analysis of Undocumented Life in the United States," *International Migration* 50 (2012): 1–19.

3. Greta Gilbertson and Audrey Singer, "The Emergence of Protective Citizenship in the USA: Naturalization among Dominican Immigrants in the Post-1996 Welfare Reform Era," *Ethnic and Racial Studies* 26 (2003): 25–51; Jennifer Van Hook, Susan K. Brown, and Frank D. Bean, "For Love or Money? Welfare Reform and Immigrant Naturalization," *Social Forces* 85 (2006): 643-666; and Monica W. Varsanyi, "Rescaling

the 'Alien,' Rescaling Personhood: Neoliberalism, Immigration, and the State," *Annals of the Association of American Geographers* 98 (2008): 877–896.

4. Peters D. Salins, *Assimilation, American Style: An Impassioned Defense of Immigration and Assimilation as the Foundation of American Greatness and the American Dream* (New York: Basic Books, 1997); and The Congress of the United States, *Immigration Policy in the United States: An Update* (Washington, DC: Congressional Budget Office, 2010).

5. Refugees are "generally people outside of their country who are unable or unwilling to return home" because of persecution, or fear of persecution, based on "race, religion, nationality, and/or membership in a particular social group or political opinion." (For more information, see the USCIS website: http://www.uscis.gov/humanitarian/refugees-asylum/refugees.) Prior to the currently effective *1980 Refugee Act*, only refugees from the Middle East or Communist countries were admitted to the United States. Their admission was authorized by such major refugee laws and policies as the *1948 Displacement Persons Act* (which allowed for the immigration of over 200,000 people displaced during World War II), *the 1953 Refugee Relief Act* (which allowed for the immigration of over 200,000 refugees), and *the 1965 Immigration and Nationality Act* (INA) (which allowed over 10,000 refugee immigration visas through its seventh preference, specifically for those fleeing from Communist countries or the Middle East). However, this 1980 immigration law removed the seventh preference category for refugees from the 1965 preference system, and set a maximum of 50,000 admissions visas for refugees annually; the actual total number of refugee admissions into the United States was annually determined by the president in consultation with the Congress. Moreover, this legislation included those fleeing from persecution based on race, religion, or nationality in any country, rather than only from Communist countries or the Middle East. Some U.S. governmental branches and their agencies have been assigned to manage the process of receiving, adjudicating, or checking refugee status both overseas and in the United States. For example, applications for refugee status in the United States are being handled by U.S. embassies or consulates abroad, as well as the Department of Homeland Security's (DHS) USCIS, which is responsible for determining applications for refugee status. After refugee status was granted, the DHS's Security's Customs and Border Protection (CBP) at a U.S. port of entry administers an immigration check for refugees.

6. Before the *1965 Immigration and Nationality Act* (INA), the national and racial compositions of immigrant population were less diverse because the pre-1965 immigration laws and policies preferred immigrants from Western or Northern European countries over Southern or Eastern European countries, and secondly, preferred immigration from Southern or Eastern European countries over Asian countries. These preferences were evident in such major immigration laws as *the 1884 Chinese Exclusion Act, the 1917 Immigration Act, the 1924 Immigration Act,* and *the 1952 Immigration and Nationality Act* (INA). However, the 1965 immigration law abolished the national origins quota system that favored immigration from Western or Northern European countries; it generally established an equal immigration policy regardless of race and country of birth. As a result of this immigration law, for example, immigration from Asia grew from 5.4 percent (135,844 out of 2,499,268) in the 1950s (1950 to 1959) to nearly 34 percent in the ten years of the 2000s (2000 to 2009). Likewise, immigration from Mexico, Central America, South America, and the Caribbean increased from 20 percent (508,335 out of 2,499,268) in the 1950s to almost 41 percent in the 2000s, according to Office of Immigration Statistics in the DHS. Moreover, the creation of the diversity immigrant visa program (DV) under *the 1990 Immigration Act* provided for 55,000 visas annually to persons from countries with historically low rates of immigration since 1965; for fiscal year 2013, 50,000 diversity visas are available. The U.S. Department of State administers the diversity immigrant visa program (visa lottery) for DV entrants by managing their applications, checks on their eligibility and required documents, and conducts interviews at the consular office of a U.S. embassy or consulate.

7. Under the name of national security, many immigration laws were created by Congress to reinforce border control and restrict, monitor, arrest, or deport undocumented immigrants and terrorists. Some of these laws were *the 1798 Alien and Sedition Act, the 1918 Entry and Departure Controls Act, the 1924 Appropriations Act, the 1940 Alien Registration Act, the 1950 Internal Security Act, the 1986 Immigration Reform and Control Act, the 1996 Illegal Immigration Reform and Immigration Responsibility Act* (IIRIRA), *the 2001 Patriot Act, the 2002 Enhanced Border Security and Visa Entry Reform Act* (EBSVERA), *the 2005 REAL ID Act*, and *the 2006 Secure Fence Act*. For a specific review of these afore-mentioned immigration laws, see Debra L. DeLaet, *U.S. Immigration Policy in an Age of Rights* (Westport, CT: Praeger, 2000); Mae M. Ngai, *Impossible Subjects: Illegal Aliens and the Making of Modern America* (Princeton, NJ: Princeton University Press, 2004); and Christopher Rudolph, *National Security and Immigration: Policy Development in the United States and Western Europe Since 1945* (Stanford, CA: Stanford University Press, 2006). Since the passing for the Homeland Security Act in 2002, the Department of Homeland Security (DHS) and its two agencies – the Customs and Border Protection (CBP) and the Immigration and Customs Enforcement (ICE) now take charge of enforcing penalties for immigration violations and controlling the border. For a discussion about the role of some state or local law enforcement agencies in the regulation of undocumented immigrants or the reinforcement of border control, see Mathew Coleman, "What Counts as the Politics and Practice of Security, and Where? Devolution and Immigrant Insecurity after 9/11," *Annals of the Association of American Geographers* 99 (2009): 904–913; Liette Gilbert, "Immigration as Local Politics: Re-Bordering Immigration and Multiculturalism through Deterrence and Incapacitation," *International Journal of Urban and Regional Research* 33 (2009): 26–42; Monica W. Varsanyi, "Neoliberalism and Nativism: Local Anti-Immigrant Policy Activism and an Emerging Politics of Scale," *International Journal of Urban and Regional Research* 35 (2011): 295–311; and Miriam J. Wells, 2004. "The Grassroots Reconfiguration of U.S. Immigration Policy," *International Migration Review* 38 (2004): 1308–1347.

8. *The Immigration and Nationality Act of 1952*, also called *the McCarran-Walter Act*, retained key provisions of *the Immigration and Nationality Act of 1924*, which established the numerical ceiling of 154,277 per year and allowed national quotas at 2 percent of a nationality's population in the United States in 1890. However, the 1952 Act eliminated the legal barrier to Asian individuals' admissions to the United States and their citizenship through naturalization, but it created an "Asian Pacific Triangle" that set a national quota of 100 per country and the ceiling of 2,000 for persons of this area of Asian Pacific Triangle per year. Another provision of the 1952 Act included the creation of a system of preferences for immigrants. Under the quota, first preference visas of up to 50 percent were given to highly skilled immigrants with skills in short supply in the United States. Second preference visas of up to 30 percent and third preference visas of up to 20 percent were allotted for parents of adult U.S. citizens and spouses and children of legal permanent residents, respectively. If some quotas for these three preferences were unused, the remaining visas were given to siblings and married children of U.S. citizens or other qualified immigrants. For a detailed review of the 1952 Act, see Debra L. DeLaet, *U.S. Immigration Policy in an Age of Rights*; Arun P. Lobo and Joseph J. Salvo, "Changing U.S. Immigration Law and the Occupational Selectivity of Asian Immigrants," *International Migration Review* 32 (1998): 737–760; and Susan F. Martin, *A Nation of Immigrants* (New York: Cambridge University Press, 2011). In addition, a brief summary of *the Immigration and Nationality Act of 1952* is also available at the link in the website of the U.S. Department of State's Office of the Historian–http://history.state.gov/milestones/1945-1952/immigration-act.

9. Debra L. DeLaet, *U.S. Immigration Policy in an Age of Rights*; Lobo and Salvo, "Changing U.S. Immigration Law and the Occupational Selectivity of Asian Immigrants"; and Susan F. Martin, *A Nation of Immigrants*.

10. Ibid.

11. Ibid.

12. A brief history of U.S. Citizenship and Immigration Services (USCIS), as one component of the Department of Homeland Security, is available at the link in the website of the U.S. Citizenship and Immigration Services (USCIS): http://www.uscis.gov/about-us/our-history. Two other components of the USCIS are U.S. Customs and Border Protection (CBP) and U.S. Immigration and Customs Enforcement (ICE).

13. Those citizens or lawful permanent residents of the United States can sponsor their foreign relatives who are willing to come to the United States. Their qualifications and specific steps to bring their relative(s) into the United States are posted on the website of the U.S. Citizenship and Immigration Services (USCIS); for U.S. citizens, see http://www.uscis.gov/sites/default/files/USCIS/Resources/A1en.pdf, and for U.S. permanent residents, see http://www.uscis.gov/sites/default/files/USCIS/Resources/B1en.pdf.

14. Mae M. Ngai, *Impossible Subjects.*

15. Debra L. DeLaet, *U.S. Immigration Policy in an Age of Rights*; Lobo and Salvo, "Changing U.S. Immigration Law and the Occupational Selectivity of Asian Immigrants"; and Susan F. Martin, *A Nation of Immigrants.*

16. Ibid.

17. Ibid.

18. According to the 2010 report of the Congress of the United States, 144,000 of them (13 percent) of the total legal permanent residents (1,131,000) admitted in 2009 were under employment-based preferences. In the same year, 748,000 of them (66 percent) became U.S. legal permanent residents under family-based preferences (immediate relatives of U.S. citizens or family-sponsored preferences); the remaining admissions were through humanitarian (191,000 or 17 percent) and diversity (48,000 or 4 percent) programs. As for patterns of admissions of legal permanent residents between 2004 and 2009 by major categories, region of birth, and method of admission (first-time entry or change of status in the United States), see http://www.cbo.gov/sites/default/files/cbofiles/ftpdocs/119xx/doc11959/12-03-immigration_chartbook.pdf. Besides, the numbers of legal permanent residents by major categories and region of birth between 2010 and 2011 are also available at the 2012 report of Office of Immigration Statistics in the U.S. Department of Homeland Security: see https://www.dhs.gov/xlibrary/assets/statistics/publications/lpr_fr_2011.pdf.

19. A brief description about foreign labor certification policies and regulations is available at the link in the website of the United States Department of Labor: see http://www.foreignlaborcert.doleta.gov/reg.cfm.

20. The available immigrant visas for family- and employment-based preferences are set in number, but that is not the case for immediate family members of U.S. citizens – e.g., their spouses and unmarried minor children. Immigrant visa numbers are assigned by the Department of State based upon the priority date, the date the receipt of the applications was confirmed for either labor certification to the Department of Labor (DOL) or immigration petition to the U.S. Citizenship and Immigration Services (USCIS). When visa numbers are available (or current), applicants finally can file "an application to register permanent residency or adjust status" (Form I-485) to the USCIS for their permanent resident status in the United States.

21. For information about specific steps to become U.S. permanent residents while living outside the United States, see http://www.uscis.gov/green-card/green-card-processes-and-procedures/consular-processing.

22. Debra L. DeLaet, *U.S. Immigration Policy in an Age of Rights*; and Mae M. Ngai, *Impossible Subjects.*

23. Irene Bloemraad, *Becoming a Citizen: Incorporating Immigrants and Refugees in the United States and Canada* (Berkeley, CA: University of California Press, 2006). After permanent resident cards are issued, applicants are ineligible to apply for naturalization if they spent more than one year outside of American soil without an approved "application to preserve residence for naturalization purposes" (Form N-470). The spouses of American citizens can apply citizenship after three years of residence in the United States. The orderly steps for naturalization are briefly summarized at the link

in the website of the U.S. Citizenship and Immigration Services (USCIS): see http://www.uscis.gov/sites/default/files/files/article/chapter5.pdf.

24. Some exceptions are made when applicants are over fifty years old with at least twenty years of lawful permanent residency in the United States, over fifty-five years old with at least fifteen years of lawful permanent residency in the United States, or have a medical proof of a disability.

25. Respondent 3's (A3's) comment conflicts with the accounts of the other three respondents—A1, A5, and A6. In this case, there is no way to know how the inquirer evaluates her respondents' conflicting answers.

26. As for family-sponsored immigration petitions, the priority date is the date that the USCIS received all required application materials (all the forms signed, filing fees, and supporting documents) from its petitioners. For employment-based immigration petitions, the priority date is either the date that the USCIS received all required applications from its petitioners (U.S. employers), or the date that the Department of Labor received the labor certification application from its petitioners on behalf of their foreign workers in the second or third category of employment preferences (see more information, check http://www.uscis.gov).

27. If their foreign trip lasts longer than one year, they need to obtain the reentry permit [Form I-131] from the USCIS for readmission into the United States.

THREE

The American Welfare Institution on the "MissyUSA" Community

Most human beings in society pursue some degree of economic security that is a basic human desire. The main reason for it is that they need to support themselves and their families, if they have their own families. In other words, the lack of economic security has many negative outcomes. Thus, their growing financial challenges have a close connection with their and their families' food and health insecurities, not to mention those risks of losing their homes, disintegrating their families, and damaging their children's education and plans for the future, among others. For many people in the United States, however, their economic security becomes increasingly out of their control. Even some people in a relatively better economic position in the United States also tend to exert every effort to maintain their economic security. Ultimately, one of the underlying goals of the American social welfare institution is to help support all of their social members in need by offering them a wide variety of social programs. Indeed, the social welfare institution of any society is one of the key mechanisms designed to support people in its socially vulnerable, economically insecure, and relatively disadvantaged groups. The total number of the Korean population in the United States grew from nearly 1.1 million in 2000 to over 1.4 million in 2010, and that is counting only those people who reported Korean as their single race in response to the race question of Census.[1] Among these Korean-Americans, there are a large number of people with socially vulnerable and economically unassisted conditions. Moreover, one noticeable thing here is that the majority of them come from certain population groups. Thus, the most socially vulnerable groups of Korean-Americans tend to be children, the elderly, the disabled, those in single-parent families, those without citizenship, and those with less education.

More detailed descriptions of the population distributions of these select Korean-American groups can be possible through an analysis of the 2000 U.S. census data.[2] For example, in looking into age distributions, 24 percent of the Koreans in the United States were under the age of eighteen, and about 6 percent of them were aged sixty-five and over. With regard to marital status, tabulated from the Koreans aged fifteen and older, 10 percent of the population was separated, widowed, or divorced.[3] In the category of household type, more than 9 percent of Korean-American households were female-headed households with no husband present.[4] In citizenship status, 38 percent of Koreans in the United States were noncitizens, over 37 percent of whom were recent immigrants who settled in the United States between 1990 and 2000. In classifying the level of the educational attainment of the Korean-Americans aged twenty-five and older, more than 35 percent of them had a high school education and less. Under the assumption that an important measure of certain population groups' economic insecurity level is their overall poverty rate, the poverty rate of Korean-Americans was nearly 15 percent in 1999, which is about 165,000 people, according to the 2000 census data.[5] Recently, their poverty rate reached 16 percent, according to the combined 2007-2011 American Community Survey (ACS) data.[6] In fact, the estimated number of the total Korean population in the United States between 2007 and 2011 was more than 1.6 million, and of them, approximately, 260,000 were living in poverty. In addition to the poverty rate, their overall unemployment rate can also be another important indicator of their economic hardships. This five-year ACS data also revealed that almost 6 percent of the Korean-Americans aged twenty-five to sixty-four were unemployed.[7]

Indeed, some groups of Korean populations in the United States are exposed to the harsh reality of economic insecurity and its accompanying problems (i.e., malnutrition, the lack of affordable housing, poor health) as the results that come after no employment, the loss of employment or retirement, the breakdown of family, aging, disability, the lack of education, or other factors. Therefore, it seems predictable that some of these Koreans in the United States will turn to the U.S. social welfare programs to provide a variety of different kinds of support for both themselves and their families. However, making use of certain U.S. social welfare programs that are fit for them is not an easy task for many of them. One of their big challenges may be closely linked to their lack of knowledge or information about which types of the social welfare programs they are eligible for, what specific rules and policies each of these programs are, what benefits these programs offer for them, what documents are required for them to access specific types of public benefits, where to file the applications, and so on. Faced with such challenges, some of them will make attempts to gain information about the American welfare institution and its particular programs through reliable sources within their reach, such as their social networks.

For this matter, the Korean-American women's online community, known as the "MissyUSA" community, is a large-scale online social network many Korean-American women participate in, as well as one of the reliable sources of information for its members who seek information about the American welfare institution. In particular, this Korean-American women's online community becomes a source of social resources—a form of social capital—for some of its members seeking information about the rules of the American welfare institution. Indeed, their posts on its "Life Q&A" message board reflect their expectations to improve their knowledge, or to obtain information, about the rules of some American welfare programs that they themselves are very much concerned about, or interested in.

In this chapter of the American welfare institution, the focus is given to the five social programs of the American welfare institution. Two of its social programs are the Unemployment Insurance (UI) and Social Security (mostly retirement) programs: these two are income support programs largely based upon recipients' past employment. The other two social programs are health care assistance programs for low-income people (i.e., Medicaid and children's health insurance) and nutrition assistance programs for low-income families (i.e., the Supplemental Nutrition Assistance Program). Both programs are also called means-tested public programs because one's eligibility is mainly determined by need, not by employment. The fifth type of social programs explored in this chapter is housing assistance programs, especially public rental assistance programs. Since these five types of social programs in the American welfare institution received more information inquiries on its "Life Q&A" message board than the other important types of social programs—e.g., Supplemental Security Income (SSI), Temporary Assistance to Needy Families (TANF), workers' compensation, or Medicare, this chapter will mainly focus on the introduction of various themes and their specific topics some of its members raised in their inquiry messages, as well as that of certain patterns of the response messages posted by some other members, from each of these five social programs, respectively.

This Korean-American women's online community—the "MissyUSA" community—becomes not only a network of social resources for its information seekers, but also a platform where its respondents can support their inquirers by transmitting knowledge, advice, or offering emotional support. In this respect the "MissyUSA" community produces social support for its information seekers who consider it as a source of social resources (information). As stressed earlier, its respondents have been classified into two broad groups for the purpose of identifying the patterns of their social support offered to information seekers. The first group is called "instrumental guiders" (information describers, analysts, confirmers, and advisors). The other group is known as "emotional supporters" (companions, encouragers, and critics). Here, most respondents are inclined to post their response messages based upon their expertise, knowledge, experiences, or suggestions with or without expressions of their emotions. Overall, this chapter begins by outlining the brief definition, history, and core principles of the American welfare institution. The following is the brief summary of key characteristics and governing bodies about each of these five social programs in the American welfare institution in modern American history. Second, the relationship between social capital and social services is briefly summarized in the context of the Korean-American community. Lastly, each of these five social programs will be, individually and in detail, examined through the analysis of some related messages posted on the "Life Q&A" message board of the "MissyUSA" community, under the framework of social capital (social resources and social support).

THE AMERICAN WELFARE INSTITUTION: HISTORY, LAWS, AND ORGANIZATIONS

The American welfare institution can be broadly defined as a collectivity of all the national, state, and local organizations (mostly, public units and some private agencies receiving government funding) with the aims of maintaining the well-being of American citizens and qualified non-citizens, and particularly improving economic insecurity and its related problems (health, nutrition, shelter, unemployment) for people in need by introducing and administering certain laws, policies, programs, and so on. Like other types of American social institutions, the American welfare institution has embraced the core social and cultural principles of American society, and embodied them to serve the demands and needs of American people through the implementation of both comprehensive and specific welfare legislations.

At the turn of the twentieth century, the first U.S. comprehensive welfare legislation was passed by the U.S. Congress. It was initially called the Economic Security Act of 1935, but its name was later changed to the Social Security Act of 1935. This landmark legislation ratified a wide array of social programs for various groups of Americans in need of support, such as the Old Age Assistance program for the poor elderly, the Aid to Dependent Children for low-income single-parent families with children (which later renamed as Aid to Families with Dependent Children (AFDC), the Old Age Insurance for the retirees (which was later called Social Security), the Unemployment Compensation Program for the unemployed, the Public Assistance Program for the poor, and many others.[8] This 1935 Social Security Act was national and legislative responses to cope with rising unemployment, shrinking family income, numerous political protests, and widespread social disorders (violations of law and order) that took place after the Great Depression. Moreover, this 1935 Social Security Act also reflected the core cultural values of American society at that time. On the one hand, collective obligation and a redistribution of income for people in need triggered the enactment of this legislation.[9] The other driving force behind the ratification of this 1935 Social Security Act was the underlying social atmosphere in which there was a strong wish to maintain the two-parent family structure and traditional family values, including the subordination of women to men within the family.

Since the mid-twentieth century in American society, the promotion of individual rights, equality, and social justice has continued to grow. To some degree, such general consensus of the American general public on those social ideas and values led to the passages of Disability Insurance for people who were injured or handicapped on the job under the name of the 1956 Social Security Amendments, the 1964 Food Stamps aimed at improving nutrition or alleviating hunger among the poor families, health care bills in the 1965 Social Security Amendments, such as Medicare for all Americans age sixty-five or over and Medicaid for people in poverty, and the 1968 Fair Housing Act that prohibits racial discrimination in access to any houses in sales or for rent. But, from the late twentieth century, this previously liberal approach to social welfare gradually shrank in the United States; the social climate became more conservative. Otherwise, this developing conservative outlook on social welfare policies culminated in the passage of the Personal Responsibility and Work Opportunity Reconciliation Act of 1996 (the PRWORA), which remains in effect today. By and large, this new welfare provision was deeply grounded on the views that poor people should work for the eligibility of welfare, that the eligibility requirements for any type of welfare should be more tightly regulated, and that the time for welfare benefits should be limited.[10] For example, Temporary Assistance to Needy Families (TANF), formerly known as Aid to Families with Dependent Children (AFDC), is a means-test program of federal-state partnership, which is in an important part of the 1996 PRWORA. In most cases, the recipients of TANF are required to work after two years and imposed to the five-year lifetime limit in assistance. TANF also barred assistance to illegal immigrants and even to legal immigrants for the first five years after arrival.[11] Overall, it cannot be ignored that some important shifts in some core social and cultural values of the times were a momentum for the historic changes in the rules of the American social welfare institution.

UNEMPLOYMENT INSURANCE

Unemployment Insurance (UI) is a social insurance program that originated from the 1935 Social Security Act. The main ideas behind this legislation were initially proposed by the Committee on Economic Security created by President Franklin D. Roosevelt. In the beginning of its enactment period, this unemployment insurance program was aimed at first at providing temporary financial support to those involuntarily laid-off workers, and second, stabilizing the economy during recessions by increasing their purchasing power.[12] Since then, the other two important, albeit undisclosed, goals of this UI program were to assist these individuals' reentry into the labor market as early as possible through employment services—e.g., job counseling, training, and placement, and to prevent further unemployment through legal ways to provide some tax credits to employers who comply with the federal law.[13] In general, the UI program is a social safety net program for workers. Moreover, the UI program is also referred to as a unique federal-state partnership program, in which states administer it on the basis of their own unemployment insurance laws under the assistance and guidelines of the federal government.[14]

More specifically, the federal government has imposed a uniform federal tax on employers for unemployment insurance. This tax collected by states is then transmitted to the Department of Treasury and deposited in the Unemployment Trust Fund. The Secretary of Treasury is responsible for investing all reserve funds and managing a separate account for each state. Typically, the federal government returned almost 90 percent of the tax on employers to the states that created their own unemployment programs in line with the standards of the federal government, while the remaining 10 percent of the reserve funds for states is used mostly to pay for both the federal government's costs of administration for the UI program and the bailouts for the states at times when they exhausted their own trust funds.[15] Although the federal government requires states to fulfill certain national-level administrative standards for the UI program, states have a great deal of latitude in the establishment and administration of their own separate policies and standards for it. Indeed, a designated department or agency of each state government—e.g., New York State Department of Labor or the State of California's Employment Development Department—administers the UI program throughout its own rules and guidelines with regard to contributions, coverage, benefit eligibility, benefit amount, benefit period, waiting time, and payment methods. Thus, states can enact and execute different policies, rules, and procedures for the administration of their UI program. For example, eligibility for the UI benefits differs across states, and its qualification is generally determined by the consideration of a range of factors, such as the duration of work, wage rates, and other state requirements that include the causes of unemployment and the availability for future work. Since 1986, the UI benefits have been taxable income for federal income taxes, but exempt from state income taxes. The annual count of UI claims was 8.8 million in 1992 to approximately 11.5 million in 2010.[16]

SOCIAL SECURITY

Social Security, previously named Old Age Insurance, was the chief social program of the 1935 Social Security Act. Many older people who have relied on their regular income from their economic activities before retirement often face immediate and long-standing economic insecurity after they stop working due to old age. For that reason, the principal goal of this 1935 Social Security legislation was to protect the older population by preventing their economic hardships likely to occur after their withdrawal from the labor market. In addition to the protection of retired older people, the lifelong economic security of their families, particularly their wives, was also guaranteed by Amendments to the Social Security Act of 1939. The Social Security program was further extended with new laws permitting benefits for disabled workers and their families who suffer economic hardships as a consequence of no or insufficient income after work-related injury or illness. Then the inclusion of the disability insurance program in Social Security was finally made possible by a couple of amendments to the Social Security Act of 1956, 1958, and 1960.[17] Overall, Social Security is understood as a comprehensive social insurance program that provides cash benefits for the aged, the disabled, and their family members.[18]

The procurement of funds for Social Security stems from payroll taxes of both employers and employees.[19] Both parties are legally required to pay 6.2 percent of the employee's salary to the Social Security fund. In other words, Social Security is compulsory and financed through wage-based contributions.[20] The Social Security payroll tax is deposited in the Social Security Trust Fund and managed by the Department of Treasury. As an independent agency of the federal government, Social Security Administration governs the diverse procedures and regulations of Social Security for its recipients and applicants, and manages its personal and organizational units. As of May 2013, the total number of Social Security beneficiaries was more than 54 million—39 million from retirement, almost 8 million from disability, and over 7 million from early retirement or young survivors.[21]

HEALTH PROGRAMS FOR LOW-INCOME AMERICANS

Basically, the U.S. health care system is divided into two parts; private- or employment-based health insurance programs, and public health care ones that are sponsored by the federal government, the states, or their partnerships. When individuals with low income and their dependents have no private health insurance or only limited medical coverage plans, they often rely upon government-sponsored health insurance programs. Of them, Medicaid is the best known government-sponsored health care program. It provides medical assistance to low-income people, including the elderly, the disabled, and the low-income parents, pregnant women, and children.[22] In history, Medicaid was enacted with the Social Security Act Amendments of 1965. It is being jointly funded by the federal and state governments. With the procurement of some funding for Medicaid, the federal government requires states to follow its federal guidelines, such as which population groups are eligible for it, the category of its medical coverage (e.g., hospital care, doctor visits, long term care, prescription drugs), other eligibility requirements (income, family size, legal status), and so on. However, each state government has a great deal of discretion to exercise authority on Medicaid in terms of its determination of specific eligibility criteria, coverage or benefits, the selection of its providers, and care management units and programs.[23]

Then, the stringent threshold of family income for Medicaid eligibility left many children of low-income families uninsured. It was the 1997 Balanced Budget Act that made it possible for more low-income children to have access to public health insurance by introducing the Children's Health Insurance Program (CHIP).[24] The CHIP is the kind of public health program that provides health services for low-income children who are ineligible for Medicaid but have no health insurance. Like Medicaid, the CHIP is administrated by each state government under the guidelines of the federal government. It is also jointly being funded by federal and state governments. In this respect, the states have the option of using CHIP funds to expand their state Medicaid programs, to cover low-income, uninsured children only, or to create a combination of both.[25]

Moreover, many states introduce their own separate, self-funded health care programs which provide health services to low-income adults aged 19 to 64 who have no or limited health insurance because their families' incomes are too high to qualify for Medicaid/CHIP and they are too young to qualify for Medicare. When they are eligible to enroll in such a state-funded health care plan, they should pay for a premium for the receipt of their health services on the basis of their family income level. As some cases of these state-funded health plans, there are Family Health Plus in New York, Family Care in New Jersey, and Healthy Families Programs in California. At the federal-government level, the designated agency in charge of Medicaid and the CHIP is the Center for Medicaid and CHIP Services (CMCS), an agency of the U.S. Department of Health and Human Services. In the states, health units—i.e., Department of Health Care Services in California, Department of Health in New

York—administer their states' Medicaid and CHIP programs along with their own state-funded health plans. According to the report, almost 66 million people were enrolled in Medicaid at some time during 2010, and more than 5.3 million children were enrolled in the CHIP as of June 2011.[26]

NUTRITION ASSISTANCE PROGRAMS FOR LOW-INCOME FAMILIES

Economic hardship makes it difficult for low-income families to put food on the table. These low-income adults and their dependent children need social services to protect them from hunger or nutrition deficiencies damaging the retention of their healthy life. Therefore, alleviating hunger and improving nutrition for them was the major goal behind the U.S. legislations of public food programs. Up till now, the largest public food program in the United States is the Supplemental Nutrition Assistance Program (SNAP), previously called Food Stamps. The SNAP is a federal assistance program for low-income individuals and families through which they can receive monthly benefits that allow them to purchase food at authorized food stores.[27] The SNAP is administered by the Department of Agriculture's Food and Nutrition Service and the state governments, but the states and their local agencies—e.g., in the State of New York, local departments of social services—can exercise a great deal of discretion in the administration of the SNAP.

As the sources of the SNAP funding, 100 percent of its benefits are paid by the federal government, whereas the federal and state governments share the administrative costs of the SNAP. In history, this food program was originally enacted by the 1964 Food Stamp Act aimed at strengthening the agricultural economy and improving nutrition for low-income families. Since then, major changes to this early food program, such as its updated eligibility requirements, retailer participation, taxation, benefit levels, benefit transaction, administration, and budgeting, took effect through the 1977 Food Stamp Act and other associated legislations, including the Hunger Prevention Act of 1988, the Mickey Leland Memorial Domestic Hunger Relief Act of 1990, the Personal Responsibility and Work Opportunities Reconciliation Act of 1996 (PRWORA), the Balanced Budget Act of 1997 (BBA), the Agricultural Research, Education and Extension Act of 1998 (AREERA), the Food Security and Rural Investment Act of 2002, and the Food, Conservation, and Energy Act of 2008.[28] As of July 2013, the number of SNAP participants nationwide reached more than 46 million.[29]

Another well-known public food program is the Special Supplemental Nutrition Program for Women, Infants, and Children (WIC) that provides nutritious foods, nutrition education (i.e., breastfeeding promotion and support), and other health and social services to low-income women, infants, and children up to age five.[30] Thus, the main goal of the WIC is to improve the health of pregnant women, and mothers with infants by means of food assistance, nutrition education, and health care. Annually, the federal government funds the total cost of the WIC, but the WIC is administered by the Food and Nutrition Service of the U.S. Department of Agriculture in partnership with the state agencies (state departments of health or human services). WIC participants receive checks, vouchers, or an electronic benefit card from state WIC agencies to purchase specific food items at authorized food stores. The WIC was created in 1972 as a two-year pilot program as part of an amendment to the Child Nutrition Act of 1966.[31] In 1975, it was established as a permanent national health and nutrition program. Some new rulings of the WIC, such as the updated eligibility requirements, the WIC food package, retailer participation, nutrition education, and the nutrition risk criteria, were further introduced through the Child Nutrition Amendments of 1978, the Child Nutrition and WIC Reauthorization Act of 1989, the WIC Farmers' Market Nutrition Act of 1992, the Healthy Meals for Healthy Americans Act of 1994, the William F. Goodling Child Nutrition Reauthorization Act of 1998, and the Healthy, Hunger-Free Kids Act of 2011.[32] As a result, in 2011, on average there were 8.9 monthly participants in WIC; of them, there were 4.7 million children, 2.1 million infants, and the remaining 2.1 million women.[33]

Likewise, the health risk of school children from low-income families due to malnutrition or hunger was also of great concern among policymakers. To deal with this social issue, two other public food assistance programs—National School Lunch Program (NSLP) and School Breakfast Program (SBP)—were created to provide nutritious meals at no or reduced cost to eligible school children.[34] Both programs are funded 100 percent by the federal government, but they are jointly administered by the Food and Nutrition Service of the U.S. Department of Agriculture and the state education agencies. The early legislation of the NSLP is known as the Richard B. Russell National School Lunch Act of 1946, while the SBP was first enacted with the Child Nutrition Act of 1966: the Healthy Hunger-Free Kids Act of 2010 amended the initial legislations of both programs by introducing some new provisions on policies, rules, guidelines, and funding.[35] In 2011, more than 31.8 million school children received free or reduced lunch each day through the NSLP.[36] In the same year, more than 12.1 million school children received breakfast every day through the SBP.[37]

HOUSING ASSISTANCE PROGRAMS

The federal government and the states support eligible, mostly low-income individuals or families directly or indirectly throughout many types of housing assistance programs. Since a detailed discussion of all of the housing programs they sponsor is of little interest here, here I will focus on two major public rental assistance programs for low-income individuals or families. First of all, the most well-known rental assistance program is the Public Housing Program that provides decent, safe, and sanitary rental housing to eligible low-income families, the elderly, and persons with disabilities.[38] The cost of managing the Public Housing Program, informally called public housing projects, is funded by the federal government, but this program is operated and administered by local housing agencies under the guidance of the U.S. Department of Housing and Urban Development (HUD). This Public Housing Program, authorized by the 1937 Housing Act at the beginning, was, in a way, directed to supply rental housing units for low-income families in recognition of their suffering from the acute housing shortage. As of 2009, there were nearly 1.2 million households living in public housing units.[39]

The second program, the Housing Choice Voucher Program, also known as Section 8, is another major rental housing program for low-income families and individuals—e.g., the elderly, persons with disabilities, homeless people, or displaced people.[40] Eligible participants of this program are responsible for finding their own rental housing units within public or mostly private housing markets, including single-family homes, townhouses, and apartments. When the landlords in the private housing market agree to rent their housing units under this program, public housing agencies (PHAs) determine whether those rental units meet minimum standards of health and safety. The cost of this program is funded by the federal government, but this housing program is administered by local PHAs. As a method of payments for rent, the PHA directly pays a housing subsidy to the landlords on the behalf of the participants every month, and the participants pay the difference between the actual monthly rent and the amount of housing subsidy provided by the program. This housing choice voucher program was made possible by the Housing and Community Development Act of 1974.[41] In the year 2009, more than 2.2 million households participated in this program.[42]

SOCIAL WELFARE AND SOCIAL CAPITAL IN THE KOREAN-AMERICAN COMMUNITY

Social networks are closely linked to the concept of social capital. Some of social networks create two forms of social capital—e.g., social resources and social support—among their participating members. For immigrants seeking information or assistance, their family networks in the host society often become a primary source of social resources that constitute information, capital, goods, credit, and services. In their family networks, social support comes into being when family members offer each other various forms of social resources and emotional support. This is also true for networks of Korean immigrant families in the United States. In a narrow sense, some members of these family networks become important informants to the other family members seeking information or advice. Thus, there is no doubt that they are willing to help their family members seeking information by complying with their requests.

Like other racial and ethnic groups in the United States, some Korean-American families live below the subsistence level and are in desperate need of health care, food, and shelter so that their last resort can be some public assistance programs offered by the federal government or the states of their residence. However, it is also a big challenge for them to understand the specific rules of the American welfare programs suitable for their needs and eligibility conditions. In that case, sometimes, their other family members who might have more familiarity with the rules of different types of welfare programs can become important informants who help them identify what programs they are eligible for, figure out for them what documents they need to prepare, and guide them on what to do after submitting the applications for approval. These family members can also play a big role in the way of offering information seekers emotional support. In turn, they are the kind of social supporters who offer their needy family members companionship, words of comfort, or encouragement. Moreover, other types of small-scale, informal networks composed of close Korean friends, coworkers, and neighbors are as important as their family networks in times of their search for information about the rules of the American welfare institution.

In many cases, participation in ethnic religious organizations offers their congregants an opportunity to join its social networks within which their network members interact more with one another, individually or collectively. In fact, this type of social network, which can be only accessed through participation in religious organizations, is of great importance among Korean immigrants in the United States. Surprisingly, Korean-Americans have a remarkably high participation rate in religious activities; nearly 75 percent of them are church-goers most of whom (over two-thirds) are Christians.[43] Wherever Korean immigrants in the United States live, they tend to gravitate to Korean churches in their local region of residence. Their predilection to attend Korean-American churches in such a high rate might have some connection with a personal sense of comfort they receive from regular interactions with co-ethnic religious leaders and congregants, not to mention their actual religious practices. What's more, most Korean-American churches offer their congregants in need some level of social services.[44] Indeed, their religious activities in

Korean-American churches make it possible for some congregants to assess useful information that helps improve their understanding about the rules of the American welfare institution. For example, most larger Korean-American churches regularly circulate information on various types of American welfare programs to their congregants even further by offering periodic seminars or lectures for these programs under which they invite various experts on the American welfare institution, particularly about its diverse programs such as public housing programs, means tested programs (Supplemental Nutrition Assistance Program, Supplementary Security Income, Temporary Assistance to Needy Families), Social Security, Unemployment Insurance (UI), and public health care programs (Medicaid, Medicare). Moreover, religious leaders in most Korean-American churches put a great emphasis on their informal role as emotional supporters through their attempts to provide personal counseling to their church members who are suffering or in needy situations.

Still, a greater number of the U.S. Korean populations live in the large gateway cities and their suburban areas in which there are many non-profit organizations run by Korean-speaking directors and staff members. These so-called ethnic Korean organizations also provide information, personal counseling, and workshops regarding the rules of the American welfare programs, and sometimes, they assist direct applications to certain social welfare programs for people in need at no or low cost. However, these non-profit, Korean-American targeted organizations in the realm of the American welfare institution generally differ in their mission statements, the target groups (children, families, the elderly, the disabled, the poor), the managerial structure, and the size of staffs. Nonetheless, making full use of the public welfare programs to support their targeted, disadvantaged groups in the U.S. Korean population is their commonly shared goal. In New York City, for example, some non-profit organizations, such as the Korean Family Counseling and Research Center, the Korean-American Senior Center of Flushing, and the Korean-American Community Center of NY, provide information about a wide range of American welfare programs for their targeted groups, along with their direct assistance for the preparation of the paperwork and applications of Social Security, public housing, Medicaid, Medicare, Supplementary Security Income, Supplemental Nutrition Assistance Program, and so on. Moreover, Korean populations living in large gateway metropolitan areas also have more opportunity to obtain information about American welfare programs through various local Korean language media, such as locally aired Korean televisions or radio stations, locally issued daily Korean newspapers, or monthly or weekly Korean magazines or periodicals. For example, a regular weekday program of the NY Radio Korea (a Korean-language radio station) often introduces a wide range of American welfare programs, providing answer times on the related inquiries raised by its callers via a direct connection with social workers and experts in the fields. The introduction of the American welfare institution and many rules of its diverse programs is also central to several weekday programs of MKTV (a NY-NJ Korean television station) that covers the areas of NY, NJ, CT, DE, and PA.

Many first-generation Korean immigrants in the larger U.S. gateway cities and their surrounding areas tend to subscribe to one of the two major Korean language newspapers—*The Korea Times* and *The Korea Daily*—delivered to their homes. Needless to say, their customary readings of these printed newspapers can further enhance their knowledge about the updated policies and procedures of certain American welfare programs, because these Korean-run newspapers regularly publish recent news and experts' columns about many American welfare programs. Nowadays, these U.S. Korean newspapers also post most of their articles on their online domains. One of its results is that even Korean-Americans living outside of the big gateway metropolitan areas can now have an opportunity to learn about American welfare programs through their direct access to these online-version Korean newspapers. Additionally, other recent improvements in media and information technologies can satisfy some Korean-Americans who want to obtain more detailed or particular information on certain American welfare programs suitable for their personal needs or interests. For instance, the online website of *The Korean Daily* issued in the United States runs a section that posts the messages of user questions about American welfare programs and experts' response messages under the heading "ASKAMERICA."

Likewise, some well-known Korean-American online websites, like MissyUSA (missyusa.com), HeyKorean (heykorean.com), Mizville (mizville.org), and Korean Community of US (there are 10 locally operating websites), also provide a section of questions and answers on all sorts of topics, including those of the American welfare institution and the rules of its various programs. In the case of this book's "MissyUSA" online community, some of its members who are facing financial or other difficulties seek information on the rules of the American welfare institution or those of its certain programs by posting their messages seeking information or advice on its "Life Q&A" message board. In response, some of its other members tend to post their response messages for those seeking information and/or their expressions of emotional support for these inquirers (information seekers). In other words, there are two broad groups of social supporters: instrumental guiders (information describers, analysts, confirmers, and advisors) and emotional supporters (companions, encouragers, and critics).

THE FIVE AMERICAN WELFARE PROGRAMS ON THE "MISSYUSA" COMMUNITY

Unemployment Insurance (UI)

The specific eligibility rules for the receipt of Unemployment Insurance (UI) are determined by the states on their own, but most states share the three basic criteria as the eligibility requirements of UI benefits. To qualify for UI benefits, first of all, UI claimants should have worked enough hours and earned a minimum amount of wages during the base period of their employment.[45] In the case of New York State, for example, UI claimants must have had paid employment in at least two quarters of their base period and received at least $1,600 in wages in one of the four quarters in their base period.[46] Second, the termination of their employment should have been through no fault of their own. Thus, their unemployment should be justified—i.e., layoffs from their companies. Hence, their UI claims will be generally disqualified if they quit their jobs voluntarily or were fired for misconduct. Third, they must be able to work and be available for work while applying for UI benefits and while receiving UI benefits. On January 3, 2012, one member of the "MissyUSA" community posted a message requesting information about the eligibility requirements for UI benefits on its "Life Q&A" message board. The six response messages followed this post:

> Q: I worked for my new company during the last four months. Before that, I quit my job after my six-year employment at another company. Now, I was laid off from my new company. Am I eligible for UI benefits? Also, I am not sure about which employer of these two companies would receive my UI application information from the state labor department.
> A1: You should have worked at least 6 months in your new company. You are also unqualified to apply for your UI from your previous employment at the other company because you left that job on your own decision.
> A2: I advise you to check this message board of "Life Q&A" on a regular basis if you want to learn more information about the eligibility requirements for UI benefits.
> A3: No, you are ineligible. The minimum employment period for UI benefits is at least 6 months in your new company.
> A4: I think you are eligible because you worked during some periods of the last 16 months. Try to apply for it. In case you are rejected, you have nothing to lose.
> A5: You are ineligible for UI benefits because you quit your job in your former company and worked less than 6 months at your new company.
> A6: I agree with A5.

Four respondents (A1, A3, A4, and A5) belong to the subgroup of information analysts for the inquirer because they explained why she is eligible or ineligible for UI benefits. Despite no direct response to the inquirer, Respondent 6 (A6) is positioned to serve an information confirmer who agreed to the description posted by Respondent 5 (A5). While Respondent 2 (A2) can be here regarded as an information advisor to the inquirer, Respondent 4 (A4) can be further seen as both an information advisor and an encourager for the inquirer.

As another illustration, a message requesting information on the eligibility rules for UI benefits was posted on December 1, 2012. Three response messages for it were as follows:

> Q: The store where I had worked was shut down yesterday. I and the other two employees were laid off. I am planning to apply for Unemployment Insurance. My questions are: 1) How many months are necessary to qualify for UI benefits? In the calculation of my work period, should I include the duration of the employment I worked for ahead of this store? 2) When can I start to apply for UI?, and 3) Do I need the signature from my employers in applying for UI? I cried all day long yesterday. I have no idea of how to live on and my family is near bankrupt this moment. . . .
> A1: Different states have different UI rules about the minimum period of employment months. You need to check the UI policy of the state you worked. It is unnecessary to get the signature from your employers. Your state labor department will contact them.
> A2: 1. On average, you need the total of 18 months, together with the inclusion of your past employment period. Check this at your state labor department. 2. You can apply for your UI one week after the day of your layoff. Interview and the submission of required documents will be followed thereafter. 3. Your state labor department will contact your employers. If they deny their decision of your layoff, you cannot receive your UI benefits. In case, you need to prepare all necessary documents refuting their arguments. Finally, search for more information about the labor department or unemployment in the State of California at Google.
> A3: Go to the State of California labor department website and apply for UI benefits on the day of your layoff. Your benefits will be calculated from the date of your application, not from your layoff day. In the State of California, you will not receive your UI benefits check for the first two weeks, and then, you will receive a maximum of $450 in each week. Therefore, don't forget to apply for your benefits on the labor department website on Monday morning every week. That is not difficult at all. Just put some basic information like your name, address, social security number, the duration of work and wages at both of your recent and past companies. . . . Don't be downhearted. I was laid off four times. . . . This is not the end of your life. You might find a better company later on . . .

In general, Respondent 1 (A1) takes on the role of an information describer to the inquirer. Two respondents (A2 and A3) belong to the subgroup of information analysts for the inquirer. All three respondents also belong to the subgroup of information advisors to the inquirer. Besides, Respondent 3 (A3) also becomes an emotional supporter, as she expressed encouragement and offered companionship for the inquirer in her message.

A UI application to the state office—e.g., The State of California Employment Development Department (EDD)—can be completed online, or through a telephone call, mail, or fax. The state office runs an online and automated telephone system to check UI weekly benefits and payment status. On October 8, 2012, a message asking a question about weekly benefits claim was posted on its "Life Q&A" message board. There were three short response messages and one more message from the inquirer:

> Q: Greetings! I want you to respond to my question I am very concerned about right now. I skipped the online application of my weekly benefits claim last one week. . . . Is there any way to receive it?
> A1: Apply for it right away and include the missing days in your weekly application.
> A2: You can receive it by mailing a letter requesting that weekly payment to the state office.
> A3: I don't know where you live. In my case, I can handle this matter through the state online service protocol that automatically provides information on unpaid periods.
> Q: I appreciate your replies. I was unable to sleep for fear that I wouldn't receive it.

All three respondents take on the role of information describers to the inquirer. Besides, two of them (A1 and A3) provided some instructions to the inquirer. Therefore, these two respondents are placed to be in the position of information advisors for the inquirer. It is interesting to observe that the second message from the inquirer contained both expressions of her appreciation to the respondents and her current emotional pain at the same time.

The completion of UI application, in addition to the preparation of its related forms and documents, is not an easy task for some UI claimants. On March 2, 2012, one member posted the message related to this topic. This message was commented by its four members. The inquirer herself added two more messages as her reaction to the response messages on her initial post:

> Q: In late January of this year, I was laid off and applied for my UI benefits at the EDD [CA] that sent me a letter indicating the amount of money I would receive weekly. After filling out the form sent to me with that letter, then, I mailed it back to the EDD. Then, the EDD resent me the same kind of letter and the form that includes job search information. That was two weeks ago. So far, I didn't hear any news from the EDD. Without dependence on unemployment benefits, my family is finding it hard to make ends meet. My efforts to search for a

new job didn't work so far, either. I am so frustrated now. Would you give me some advice about the projected time for receiving my unemployment benefits?
A1: You will receive it. It is almost impossible to have direct contact with one of EDD representatives by your telephone call. That's my experience. The fastest way is to use its online website in which you need to make your personal identification number, and then, you can see your record and request any inquiry there. Another convenient way to solve your problem is to use its automatic voice service system through which you should enter your social security number and personal identification number. . . . Once done, you will receive a Bank of America Debit Card from the EDD . . .
A2: In the form you received with the letter, you should write your job search information on its back page only when there is a check mark on its front page. In my case, I wrote my job search information in spite of no check mark there. . . . Like you, I received the second letter and the same form from the EDD. If there is no check mark in the form, don't write your job search record. After this correction, I received the EDD Debit Card eventually and weekly payment, alike.
Q: Thank you for your replies. I am now so relieved. . . . Do I have to open a new checking account at Bank of America? Like A2, I was likely to make the same mistake twice. . . . If I correct that error, do you think that I can receive my unemployment benefits?
A1: You don't have to open a checking account from Bank of America. Just use the EDD Debit Card like cash or a credit card. I didn't write my job search information when I noticed no check mark on the form. . . . I want to provide another advice to you. In the questions of your job refusal and school attendance, don't forget to answer "NO." If you put "Yes," you cannot receive unemployment benefits.
A3: Try to do your best. Check your case through the Internet. And continue your call to the EDD when you are not connected . . .
Q: I appreciate A1 for providing valuable information to me one more time. I also express my thanks to A3. I will continue my call . . .
A4: Check the top of the form where you can find your claim period and weekly benefits amount. When I saw my husband's form by chance, there was zero in the column of weekly benefits amount because of the first week as a waiting period. In the second form he received, there was information about a two-week claim period and a certain amount in the column of weekly benefits amount. Then he received a debit card from the EDD and weekly payment.

The multiple roles of information analysts, advisors, and encouragers for the inquirer can be detected through three respondents' messages (A1, A2, and A4). To some degree, these three respondents also belong to the subgroup of emotional companions for the inquirer because they shared their experiences with her. Besides, Respondent 3 (A3) is the person that belongs to the subgroup of information advisors for the inquirer.

Even if some recipients of UI benefits work on a part-time basis, they may qualify for the receipt of UI benefits. However, one thing that needs attention here is that their weekly benefit amount will be adjusted after deducting the amount of their weekly wages. Whenever their weekly wages exceed the UI weekly benefit amount—e.g., $405 in New York State, they are ineligible to receive UI benefits for that week. Besides, the extension of UI benefits can become available as far as the state experiences high unemployment, or when the federal government has approved a special extended UI benefit provision. On June 2, 2012, there was one post requesting information related to this topic. Two response messages were as follows:

> Q: I am now receiving UI benefits from the EDD for three months. In the meantime, I worked part-time and received a check. If I write the amount of this check on the EDD form, am I no longer eligible to receive UI benefits? My second question is whether or not it is possible for me to extend UI benefits after no balance on my EDD account.
> A1: If you worked at a contract job, you would receive your benefit subtracted from the amount of your check. In general, the extension of UI benefits is automatic, but that is not guaranteed. You need to call the EDD to get more information in your case.
> A2: The amount of your wage will be deducted from your weekly benefit amount. If your wage was more than your weekly benefit amount, your UI claim can be stopped. The six-month extension is usually possible, but your case is uncertain.

Both respondents take on the role of information analysts for the inquirer. The message of respondent 1 (A1) also places her in the position of an information advisor for the inquirer.

In addition, some members of the "MissyUSA" community sought other kinds of UI-related information, which include the payment period, the processing time of UI claims, the interview, the contact of employers, and the like. Once these types of questions were posted, some other members of the "MissyUSA" community responded to their posts as the respondents (social supporters), namely, either instrumental guiders and/or emotional supporters.

Social Security

To qualify for Social Security (retirement) benefits, people need to earn Social Security credits that are based upon the amount of their earnings at work.[47] In 2013, one credit needs at least $1,160 of earnings, and the maximum number of the credits they can earn each year is four.[48] When their credits reach forty over a lifetime, they can retrieve their retirement benefits. American citizens and legal permanent residents (green card holders) are eligible to receive retirement benefits. Eligible American citizens can also receive Social Security payments even when they are living outside of the United States. But, some eligible legal permanent residents may no longer receive Social Security payments if they stay outside the United States for six months or more. However, one exception to this is that they can continue to receive Social Security payment when their country of residence has a Social Security agreement with the United States. These countries are, for example, South Korea, Canada, and Spain. People can start to receive retirement benefits from the age of sixty-two. However, the monthly amount of their retirement benefits depends upon their retirement age and history of work. Generally, their benefit payment ahead of the reach of full retirement age (sixty-five) will be reduced, but their benefit payment after full retirement age will increase up to age seventy. On a regular basis, those messages requesting information on these issues of Social Security have been posted on the "Life Q&A" message board. Two related cases are in detail illustrated below. First, one member posted the message about its eligibility rules on December 1, 2012. Five of eight response messages for this initial post are introduced here in order:

> Q: Over the past 10 years, I paid for my social security tax from my work at an American company. I am not working this time, and if I remain unemployed before my retirement age, am I still eligible to receive my retirement benefits?
> A1: Yes, you are qualified to receive retirement benefits . . .
> A2: Are you talking about Supplementary Security Income? If not, you will receive some minimum amount of benefits because you have already met the requirement of ten-years work . . .
> A3: If you had worked for 10 consecutive years and earned $5,000 each year, you would have already made 40 credits necessary to receive your retirement benefits.
> A4: Yes, you can. . . . But your benefits will not be a great amount because your payment will be averaged from your 30 years of work.
> A5: Supplementary Security Income is the federal income support program for the needy people [the poor elderly, the blind, or the disabled]. This program is completely different from Social Security. When people work for 10 years or more, they may be eligible for retirement benefits. But, don't think of your social security payment as the secure source of your income for your retirement life. You will not receive as much as you expected. Please check the website of social security administration in which you can calculate how much you can be paid on average.

Both respondents (A1 and A4) were the subgroup of information confirmers for the inquirer. Four respondents (A2, A3, A4, and A5) belong to the subgroup of information analysts for the inquirer. Moreover, the role of an information advisor to the inquirer was revealed in the message of Respondent 5 (A5).

As another example, one message requesting information about the benefit amount and a list of the countries where the U.S. Social Security payment is sent by wire transfer was posted on January 4, 2012. Three members posted their messages in response to this post:

> Q: I am a permanent U.S. resident and reported my social security tax for more than 10 years. This year, I am expected to obtain American citizenship through naturalization. How much can I receive for my retirement benefits when I reach the age of 65? Also, is it possible to receive my benefits in Seoul [the capital city of South Korea] and the United States if I come back later on?
> A1: American citizens can receive their retirement benefits in Seoul.
> A2: The amount of retirement benefits differs on a case-by-case basis. If you want to know your monthly benefit amount, just make a phone call to the U.S. Social Security Administration.
> A3: There is no uniform amount in payment because different persons paid different amounts of social security tax based upon their earnings. The moment your date of retirement approaches, you will receive a letter from social security administration. There, you can find out more detailed information about your benefit amount.

Respondent 1 (A1) can be generally considered an information describer to the inquirer. To some degree, Respondent 2 (A2) takes on both roles of an information describer and an information advisor to the inquirer. Besides, both roles of an information analyst and an information advisor for the inquirer are conducted by Respondent 3 (A3).

When people die, Social Security benefits may be paid to their survivors (spouses and children) as long as they contributed to the Social Security tax as employed workers for more than ten years. To qualify for Social Security survivor benefits, those survivors need to be at least at age sixty for retirement benefits, or at least at age fifty for disability benefits.[49] Additionally, Social Security survivor benefits can be also paid to unmarried children under the age of eighteen, or children under the age of nineteen or a full-time student, or to children who were disabled before age twenty-two and remain disabled. The benefit amount that survivors will receive is calculated differently across individual situations. For example, Social Security benefits will be equivalent to the benefit amount of the deceased workers for widows or widowers of full retirement age or older. Widows or widowers aged sixty through sixty-four will receive 71.5 to 99 percent of the full benefit amount. Children under age eighteen will receive 75 percent of the full benefit amount. On October 7, 2012, one member posted a message requesting information about an average amount of Social Security benefits for widows. Five response messages followed it:

> Q: When a retired person dies, how much and how long can his widow receive her social security benefits?

> A1: I think that on average, she can receive half of his benefit amount . . .
> A2: There exists no restricted duration for receiving survivor benefits.
> A3: In Korea, she will receive 70 percent of his benefit amount. I don't know about this case in the United States.
> A4: In the situation of the death of a retired military member, she will receive 100 percent of his benefit amount. I am sure that this is the same for most people in this category. And she will continue to receive the same benefit amount up until her death. But, her benefits will be stopped after her remarriage. That's why most of the widows receiving survivor benefits tend not to remarry, but instead they prefer to have boyfriends.
> A5: My father worked in a public sector job and my mother has received 70 percent of his basic benefit amount.

Except for Respondent 4 (A4), the other four respondents can be categorized into the subgroup of information describers to the inquirer. However, their messages contained some inconsistent and inaccurate information that might have made the inquirer confused in her evaluation of social security survivor benefits. Respondent 4 (A4) plays the role of an information analyst for the inquirer.

To qualify for Social Security disability benefits, those who became disabled before full retirement age (sixty-five) should have at least six to twenty credits from their three to ten years of work before the diagnosis of their disability.[50] Their eligibility for disability benefits also takes into account the age at the time they became disabled. Taken together, for example, a disabled worker at the age of forty-four needs at least 5.5 years of work in order to be eligible to receive disability benefits. The amount of one's monthly disability benefit is based upon his or her average lifetime earnings. In 2013, average disability payments range from $700 to $1,400 per month. On June 7, 2012, one member posted a message of a general inquiry about disability benefits. Four members responded to this post:

> Q: I have a question about social security disability benefits. I know an acquaintance with severe physical disability so that he is now using a wheelchair. . . . He stopped working and has a tough time. He is a green card holder and lives on an insufficient income. Can he receive some benefits from public welfare programs? If possible, would you recommend me those agencies administering such programs?
> A1: He should consult with a social worker.
> A2: At least the five years of work are the eligibility requirements for social security disability benefits. I was disabled in the accident, but couldn't receive disability benefits due to less than five years of work. If you were born with a disability, meet a social worker and find out some welfare programs suitable for your case.

A3: If you are qualified for disability benefits, you will receive $800 per month. Also, don't forget to apply to a cheap apartment for the disabled . . .
A4: Call . . . to ask your questions. If you didn't pay for social security tax, you will not receive disability benefits. But I think that you will get Supplementary Security Income.

Respondent 3 (A3) appears to be the information describer for the inquirer, whereas two respondents (A2 and A4) take on the role of information analysts for her. Besides, all four respondents belong to the subgroup of information advisors to the inquirer.

Health Programs for Low-Income Americans

Medicaid is a federal-state medical assistance program for selected groups of people with low income. States set their own income standards for Medicaid eligibility under their criterion of the annual federal poverty level (FPL), which is regarded as one of the important federal Medicaid guidelines. Then, states are not the same in percentages of federal poverty level that meet Medicaid eligibility in income—i.e., in the case of parents of dependent children with no employment in 2013, 10 percent of FLP in Alabama, 100 percent of FPL in California, 150 percent of FPL in New York, and 200 percent in District of Columbia.[51] Another eligibility rule for Medicaid is proof of U.S. citizenship, or if applicants are immigrants, verification of legal permanent residence status, along with more than five-year residence in the United States.[52] In other words, legal permanent residents (green card holders) who have less than five-year residence in the United States are ineligible for Medicaid. However, as of 2004, twenty-three states, like CA, NY, WA, TX, IL, and NJ, provide state-funded health plans to legal immigrants (adults and children) under state Medicaid/CHIP programs, regardless of their date of entry into the United States.[53] Nonetheless, most undocumented and temporary immigrants are barred from any coverage of Medicaid without regard to their duration of stay in the United States.[54] On October 1, 2012, one message requesting information related to Medicaid eligibility in income was posted on the "Life Q&A" message board. After this post, there were four response messages:

Q: Over the past several months, I am really having a tough time. The total monthly income of my family is $540. I am worried about my children. Is my family eligible for Medicaid?
A1: I think you are qualified in your income level. Your status is also important. Legal permanent residents [green card holders] must have lived in the United States for over five years to be eligible for Medicaid.
A2: For immigrant children, their permanent resident status is enough to qualify for Medicaid [children's Medicaid].

A3: The total monthly income of your family with children falls substantially below in support of the basic needs of your family members. . . . Hurry up to apply for TANF, Food Stamp, Medicaid. . . . In your case, you should verify your American citizenship or legal permanent resident status with more than five-year residence in the United States. But, your children under 18 will be largely eligible regardless of their duration of stay in the United States.
A4: The determination of your status is likely to differ across states. I believe that in Maryland where I live now, legal immigrants, regardless of their length of residence in the United States, are eligible for Medicaid.

Two respondents (A1 and A3) belong to not only the subgroup of information confirmers, but also the subgroup of information analysts, for the inquirer. The other two respondents (A2 and A4) seem to be placed in the subgroup of information describers to the inquirer. In addition, both roles of an information advisor and an encourager are revealed in the messages posted by Respondent 3 (A3).

As another illustration, there was a message requesting information about income eligibility in Medicaid on December 6, 2012. Four short response messages with a second message from the inquirer followed this initial post:

Q: My circumstances are very difficult after leaving my job. So, I am going to apply for Medicaid in my state, California—Medi-Cal. I couldn't find out any information about income standards on Medi-Cal website. . . . All four members of my family hold American citizenship. My first child is suffering badly from asthma. My husband is working in a company without any health insurance plan and our total annual income is $32,000. Is our family eligible for Medi-Cal?
A1: States have their own income standards for Medicaid.
A2: If you are going to apply for Children's Medicaid, please see http://www.healthyfamilies.ca.gov/HFProgram/Income_Guidelines.aspx.
A3: Call Korean Health Education and Research Center—www.lakheir.org, which will help you how to apply.
A4: I found out the following information:

Table 3.1.

Family Size	Monthly Gross Income	Property Limit
1	$931	$2,000
2	$1,261	$3,000
3	$1,591	$3,150
4	$1,921	$3,300

No source, part of the quotation from the MissyUSA website.
Note: Each extra person income + $312 & each extra person property + $150

> Q: Thank you for sharing your information with me.

The role of an information describer for the inquirer is conducted by Respondent 1 (A1), while Respondent 4 (A4) becomes the information analyst for the inquirer. Additionally, the remaining two responders (A2 and A3) belong to the subgroup of information advisors to the inquirer.

Like income standards in Medicaid, states determine the criteria of coverage for their own Medicaid programs, which include "the type, amount, duration, and scope of services within broad federal guidelines."[55] For example, states are required to cover certain "mandatory benefits"—e.g., in- and out-patient hospital services, physician services, nursing facility services, laboratory and X-ray services, and so on—through the Medicaid program. However, states have discretion in determining their coverage of "optional benefits"—e.g., clinic services, physical therapy, dentures, personal care, hospice, and so on—through the Medicaid program. On May 3, 2012, one member posted a message related to Medicaid coverage for one of her family members. After this post, there were four response messages, two of which were messages from the same member, and one was a supplementary message from the inquirer:

> Q: Twelve years ago, my mother underwent a kidney transplant operation. . . . She as the beneficiary of Medi-Cal had regular checkups and blood tests from a kidney specialist every year. Now she can no longer meet this doctor, instead she should choose a general physician. . . . Her eligible time for Medicare is three years later. My questions are: 1) Are there some hospitals receiving Medi-Cal near Los Angeles? 2) Someone recommended me to meet a social worker. How would I come into contact with a social worker? 3) My mother needs to have a kidney doctor. Is she cared by a general physician? and 4) Is there any way for her to receive Medicare?
>
> A1: Before the start of July this year, Medi-Cal recipients should be required to register for a HMO [a health maintenance organization contracted with the Department of Health Care Services]. A couple of Korean hospitals receive Medi-Cal, but it depends on your HMO. Medicare is a federal health insurance program that is covered for people aged 65 or more or the disabled, based upon their past employment. If your mother had no work experience, she should wait until she becomes 65.
>
> A2: The best way is to check university hospitals or general hospitals in your area. You can consult with a social worker there. My father used emergency services from a university hospital and a social worker there helped him receive Medi-Cal, and continues to arrange his health examinations with certain physicians. Or go to your county human services office to contact a social worker. There, you can ask for translation service in Korean.

A3: UCLA Hospital is not in the network of HMO. And USC Hospital is in L.A. Care [a Los Angeles County health care system and a type of HMO]. . . . You should have written a waiver form that is required to receive lasting medical services under general Medi-Cal program. Also, try to contact kidney specialists in LA Koreatown.
Q: I submitted a waiver form, but it was denied. So is it your suggestion that I need to meet social workers in university hospitals to identify the coverage and services of Medi-Cal?
A3: You should continue to appeal that denial. Register for L.A. Care and go to USC Hospital. . . . It is strange that some kidney specialists in Koreatown would not receive Medi-cal. You should check this, as well.

Two respondents (A1 and A3) take on the role of information analysts for the inquirer. All three respondents belong to the subgroup of information advisors to the inquirer. Moreover, the role of an encourager to the inquirer by Respondent 3 (A3) is revealed in her message.

The Children's Health Insurance Program (CHIP) is another public health care program for uninsured children from low income families, including those whose family incomes are too high to qualify for Medicaid.[56] Like Medicaid, the CHIP is administered by the states under one of three programs, namely, the Separate State Child Health Plans (WA, TX, and thirteen other states), the Medicaid Expansions (D.C., MD, OH, and five other states), or the Combination Programs (CA, NY, and twenty-six other states). Under the CHIP, most states cover children up to or above 200 percent of the federal poverty level. Based upon the family income level and the types of the medical services offered, states impose copayment, premiums, and deductibles for children covered in the CHIP. In most states, lawfully residing children are eligible for the CHIP. On February 9, 2012, there was a message requesting information about the coverage of the CHIP. Two members responded to this initial post:

Q: I applied for Medi-Cal for my child and received plastic Benefits Identification Card [California Benefits Identification Card, or BIG]. When my child is sick, can I use emergency services through Kaiser [a health care provider contracted with the Department of Health Care Services]? In my Medi-Cal application, I didn't designate a primary doctor and a hospital. Would you please inform me of the dentist's, an ophthalmologist clinic, and a children's hospital that receive this card in or near the city of Santa Clara? What is the amount of my copayment from each visit of these hospitals?
A1: I think that the Santa Clara valley medical center in San Jose would receive a Medi-Cal card. Call those hospitals in your areas to check whether they receive Medi-Cal.
A2: There is no charge for the medical services through the Medi-Cal program that also covers emergency medical treatments. It seems that Medi-Cal has no connection with Kaiser. Also, check the hospitals around your area by accessing their websites.

Both respondents belong to the subgroup of information advisors to the inquirer. Individually, Respondent 1 (A1) can be identified as the information describer to the inquirer, whereas Respondent 2 (A2) becomes an information analyst for her. Then, Respondent 2 (A2) stated inaccurate, unreliable information in her message. Hence, it is unclear how the inquirer interpreted this respondent's message.

As stated earlier, the state-sponsored health programs, like Family Health Plus in New York or Healthy Families Programs in California, provide medical services for low-income families (or households) whose incomes are too high to qualify for Medicaid/CHIP. Thus, the eligibility for these types of state health programs is based upon the size of family and monthly family income. For example, the maximum amount of monthly income allowed to qualify for the New York Family Health Plus program is from $1,362 (one-person household) to $2,794 (four-person household), to $3,749 (six-person household).[57] Moreover, American citizenship or legal permanent resident status is further required in eligibility for this state health program. A co-payment for families enrolled in this Family Health Plus program is determined by the type and scope of their medical services. On October 4, 2012, one member posted a message requesting information about a public health program for some low-income families. This was followed by four short messages in reply:

> Q: It is almost impossible to apply for Medicaid that has very tight eligibility criteria. Would you inform me of any health insurance program that offers less than $200 payment per month? It is also likely that Healthy Families [State of California sponsored low-cost insurance for children and pregnant women] will no longer exist from next year. . . . I should do the ultrasound check regularly.
>
> A1: The uncertainty of Healthy Families Program is untrue. Apply for this right away.
>
> A2: Indeed, Healthy Families provides a good, low-cost service. Apply for it and then, you can use it one month after.
>
> A3: I will help you. Please call me at . . .
>
> A4: In California, go to the following link. . . . You can check your payment information. Besides, you can get more knowledge about Healthy Families when you check the following link . . .

Except for Respondent 3 (A3) whose role for the inquirer is unclear, three other respondents belong to the subgroup of information advisors to the inquirer, even though their comments are very different in content. The first two respondents (A1 and A2) also belong to the subgroup of encouragers for her. Besides, Respondent 2 (A2) can be the information describer for the inquirer.

Nutrition Assistance Programs for Low-income Families

The Supplemental Nutrition Assistance Program (SNAP), previously called as Food Stamps, is a federal food assistance program for low-income individuals and families.[58] To qualify for SNAP, its applicants (households) should meet both the gross and net income tests. Thus, they must have a gross monthly income below 130 percent of the federal poverty line and a net monthly income below 100 percent of the federal poverty line. Another eligibility rule for SNAP is a household asset limit, in which households may have up to $2,000 in countable assets, $3,250 if one person in the household is age sixty-five or older, or is disabled. SNAP is offered to both American citizens and legal immigrants who have lived in the United States for five years or more, or who are children under eighteen. Other groups of immigrants, such as legal immigrants with less than five-year residence, undocumented, or temporary immigrants are ineligible for the SNAP program. Though unlawful, their receipts of SNAP, WIC benefits, or school meal programs have no impact on their reentry into the United States, deportation, or the denial of their applications for permanent residence.[59] The benefit levels of SNAP vary across the size of household—e.g., $200 in one-person household, $367 in two-person household, $793 in five-person household. On January 5, 2012, one member posted a message requesting information about eligibility for SNAP. Six members responded to this post:

> Q: My family is having a difficult time because of my joblessness, child care, and low earnings in my husband's work. My child is an American citizen, but we are not green card holders yet. In our case, is it possible for us to qualify for the SNAP?
> A1: You are ineligible. But, you can apply for it under the name of your child because your child is qualified.
> A2: Our couple's applications for green cards are pending. . . . But, we have social security numbers and have lived in the United States for more than ten years. My children are American citizens. We are now receiving the SNAP through my children. Although states have different rules on the SNAP and social workers provide certain guidelines for it, I hope that this information is useful to you.
> A3: My family had a really hard time six months ago when my husband lost his job and my house was sold by a short sale. Right after that, we applied for the SNAP and are now using it. Try to apply for it under the name of your child by bringing in copies of your bank accounts, recent pay stubs, and income tax report. The allotment [benefit amount] for my family is $700 per month. My family of four are American citizens. In the beginning, it was so shameful to use it, but it really does help. . . . Don't be disheartened by your plight. Keep your courage up! The better day will come eventually.

A4: My immigration lawyer advised me not to receive the SNAP before the attainment of permanent resident status. You need to check this matter.
A5: In my immigration status, I am in the same situation as you. . . . Try to apply for it.
A6: I received the SNAP during some months after my child was born. I was not a green card holder at that time. I didn't renew the SNAP thereafter. The record of receiving the SNAP had no influence on the attainment of my green card.

The role of an information describer to the inquirer is taken on by Respondent 1 (A1). But, all six respondents belong to the subgroup of information advisors to the inquirer, while two of them (A2 and A3) can be also placed in the subgroup of information analysts for her. Expressions of companionship to the inquirer are revealed in the messages of four respondents (A2, A3, A5, and A6), three of whom (A2, A3, and A6) also take on the role of encouragers for the inquirer.

At authorized stores, SNAP households can buy certain food items, such as breads and cereals, fruits and vegetables, meats, infant formula, baby food in boxes and jars, and so on.[60] However, they cannot buy beer, wine, liquor, cigarettes, household supplies, pet foods, vitamins and medicines, hot foods, and so on. On February 6, 2012, there was a message requesting information about the food items approved through SNAP. There were four response messages from this post:

Q: I applied for the SNAP with the name of my baby. Can I buy milk powder by it? How about sandwiches and chicken wings at delis?
A1: Yes, you can.
A2: Those foods cooked or already made cannot be purchased through the SNAP.
A3: Yes, you can. Even some fast-food restaurants receive the SNAP. In addition to such foods pointed out by A2, you cannot buy any prepared foods at grocery stores.
A4: Some restaurants and grocery stores notify whether or not they accept an EBT [electronic benefit transfer, or a SNAP benefit card].You should check this when you go to any restaurant or grocery store. When you become eligible for the SNAP, you can also qualify for WIC [the Special Supplemental Nutrition Program for Women, Infants, and Children]. From WIC, you can get infant formula and baby foods.

The role of information confirmers to the inquirer is conducted by two respondents (A1 and A3). In general, three respondents (A2, A3, and A4) belong to the subgroup of information advisors to the inquirer, and two of them (A3 and A4) also belong to the subgroup of information analysts for her.

Low-income pregnant or breastfeeding women, infants, and children up to age five are eligible for the Special Supplemental Nutrition Program for Women, Infants, and Children, often called WIC, which provides nutritious foods, nutritious education, and health and other social services to them.[61] As for its income eligibility, 185 percent of federal poverty line is used as its threshold. WIC participants receive checks, vouchers, an electronic benefit card (EBT) to purchase foods, such as infant cereal, iron-fortified adult cereal, vitamin C-rich fruit or vegetable juice, eggs, milk, cheese, peanut butter, dried and canned beans/peas, canned fish, and so on. The immigration status of applicants is not an eligibility requirement for the receipt of WIC. On December 4, 2012, one member posted a message requesting information about the eligibility rules for WIC. Three members posted their response messages, and there was also another message posted by the inquirer:

> Q: I want to know the eligibility criteria for WIC program. Are they different across states?
> A1: Check the website.
> A2: Yes, they are. Search for it on Google.
> A3: Let me inform you of eligible persons and periods: pregnant women and up to six weeks after the birth of their child, up to age one for new-born child from non-breastfeeding or postpartum women with any nutritional risk, up to age five for children at nutritional risk. . . . Even if you hold health insurance, it doesn't affect your eligibility for WIC. Even if you are neither an American citizen nor legal permanent resident, your immigration status does not affect your eligibility, either. You should apply for it to your state of residence. What state do you live in?
> Q: Thank you. I live in New York.
> A3: Call. . . . Contact information by mail is . . .

All three respondents belong to the subgroup of information advisors to the inquirer. In addition, Respondent 2 (A2) takes on the role of an information confirmer, and Respondent 3 (A3) performs three different roles, namely, those of an information analyst, an information advisor, and an encourager, for the inquirer.

National School Lunch Program (NSLP) is a federally assisted meal program that provides eligible school children nutritious meals for lunch at free or reduced prices.[62] Children from low-income families—i.e., 130 percent of the federal poverty line—are eligible for free meals for lunch, and moreover, reduced-priced meals for lunch are available for the children within the other income categories of their families—i.e., between 130 percent and 185 percent of the federal poverty line. The immigration status has no impact on eligibility for the NSLP. On September 7, 2012, there was one post requesting information about eligibility for the NSLP. Six response messages followed it:

> Q: If the NSLP application without proof of income is handed in to school, can the NSLP be approved?

A1: You should verify your family income. Schools like increasing NSLP participants because they would receive more cash reimbursement from the USDA [the United States Department of Agriculture].
A2: Write your family income in the income column of the application form and submit it to the school office. It is not difficult at all and you don't need any additional documents. If your case is approved, you will receive the letter at your home. Schools have no objection to more NSLP applicants. My kid also takes free meals for lunch.
A3: My kid disliked it because he hated receiving its vouchers in the classroom.
A4: That's strange. Even homeroom teachers have no idea of who receives its vouchers in class.
A5: It's impossible to know who uses it due to its automatic payment system, except for cafeteria managers or cashiers.
A6: School districts have different rules for the processing of the NSLP applications. Some school districts require income verification . . .

Of these six respondents, two of them (A2 and A6) take on the role of information analysts for the inquirer, and Respondent 2 (A2) and Respondent 1 (A1) belong to the subgroup of information advisors to her. Encouragement was also expressed in the message of Respondent 2 (A2). Interestingly enough, the other three respondents (A3, A4, and A5) missed the point of the question raised by the inquirer: besides, two respondents (A4 and A5) commented on the message posted by Respondent 3 (A3).

Housing Assistance Programs

Some families or individuals, like the elderly or persons with a disability, are eligible to apply for the public housing program that provides rental units for them. However, low-income standards (or limits), established by HUD (the U.S. Department of Housing and Urban Development) and determined by local housing agencies (HAs), are another requirement they need to be eligible for this program.[63] In general, the eligibility requirements for their annual gross income are adjusted for by their family size, and it should be at or below 80 percent of the average median income of their county of residence, or their metropolitan area. For example, in a New York metropolitan area composed of New York City and its surrounding three counties, the low-income limits as of 2013 are $48,100 in a one-person family, $61,850 in a three-person family, $68,700 in a four-person family, and $74,200 in a five-person family.[64] The other public housing programs, like the housing choice voucher program (Section 8), also require verification of American citizenship or lawful permanent residency in the United States. Thus, undocumented immigrants and temporary immigrants are unqualified for it. When accepted in the program, its participants must pay up to 30 percent of their monthly adjusted income for rent. On March 3, 2012, one member requested information about the eligibility conditions for the public housing program by posting a message on the "Life Q&A" message board. There were two short messages in response to this post:

> Q: I want to know the eligibility criteria for public housing.
> A1: You can find out that information in the instruction of its application form.
> A2: The public housing program is one for low-income families. Their income level determines its eligibility.

Respondent 1 (A1) takes on the role of an information advisor to the inquirer, whereas Respondent 2 (A2) is, to some degree, considered to be the information describer to the inquirer.

The public housing program also offers rental units in a senior building only for the persons, and all their household members, at least at the age of sixty-two or over. In addition, the same eligibility and rental payment requirements of the general public housing program, as aforementioned, are applied to this type of public housing program targeted toward the elderly.[65] On December 6, 2012, one member posted a message requesting rental information in the senior public housing program. There were ten response messages, five of which were posted by two members:

> Q: I want to help an elderly couple I know very well. The other day, I heard a senior public housing program pay rent cheaply. I don't know how to apply for this program. I wish you can share your information with me.
> A1: You need to go to senior public housing apartments directly and question your inquiries to office staffs there . . .
> A2: Contact apartment offices. But, waiting lists for senior housing are very long. I don't know where you live, and in most areas of California, waiting times take several years. Then, some rental units in an apartment near Huntington beach are recently available for the low-income elderly. Waiting time for this apartment will be less than one year. The monthly rent payment for this apartment is one third of tenants' gross income. If you need more information about this apartment, I will inform you personally.
> A3: I need that information more in detail.
> A4: I also need that information.
> A5: Can you send me that information to me as well?
> A2: I sent you such information through your emails.
> A3: Thank you.
> A6: Someone I know is now looking for information about senior public housing units. I also want to help her. Can you also send me your information about that apartment to me?
> A7: My mother lives in a senior public housing apartment in the area of Santa Ana north of Irvine [CA]. She entered there after a year of waiting and paid about $500 per month for first two years. Since then, her monthly rent was set into about one third of her income. . . . She is very

glad to settle there because her location is so convenient to go to Korean grocery stores, Korean church, and Korean senior citizens association.
A2: Make a call at. . . . Ask someone there as to whether the applications are now accepted and pick up the application forms, if they are. That senior apartment is really spacious and at an affordable price.

The role of information analysts to the inquirer is performed by two respondents (A2 and A7). Like the case of Respondent 1 (A1), Respondent 2 (A2) also takes on the role of an information advisor not only to the inquirer, but also to the three respondents (A3, A4, and A5). In addition, Respondent 6 (A6), like the inquirer, becomes another information inquirer by requesting information to Respondent 2 (A2). Indeed, Respondent 2 (A2) is a central figure in this thread on rental information in the senior public housing program.

Unlike the public housing program, low-income families or individuals (the elderly, the disabled, homeless people, or displaced people) can rent housing of their own choice—i.e., single-family home, townhouse, and apartment—largely through the private housing markets under the housing choice voucher program, popularly known as Section 8, which is also administered by local housing agencies.[66] To qualify for this voucher program, its applicants' annual gross family income should not exceed 50 percent of the average median income of their residential county or metropolitan area. Additionally, verification of American citizenship or lawful permanent residence is required for its application. As for the payment of monthly rent, voucher holders (tenants) should contribute to at least 30 percent of their monthly gross income, and then, the remaining cost is covered by the voucher program. On June 6, 2012, one member requested information about the application for the Section 8 voucher program. There was only one response message:

Q: I want to apply for the Section 8 for my mother. She is 65 years old and her total monthly income, including Social Security and SSI [The Supplemental Security Income], is about $800. Where do I have to apply for it? And is my mother qualified?
A1: Ask for information at Korean Community Centers. When you have the lists of housing units accepting the Section 8, visit each apartment to ascertain whether they are accepting the applications this time.

The role of an information advisor to the inquirer is taken on by Respondent 1 (A1).

As another example, one member posted a message related to the Section 8 program, followed by a response message on March 7, 2012:

Q: I applied for the Section 8 within the territory of Orange county [CA] through the Internet. I thought that I had included the name of my youngest son in my online application. Then, his name was not in the email confirmation of my application. How can I correct this error?

> A1: Go to the website again and you can find contact information. Then, make a call and request the addition of his name in your application.

Respondent 1 (A1) is positioned to take on the role of an information advisor for the inquirer.

SUMMARY

There are many Korean-Americans who are helpless or at risk in economic and social aspects. For them, their interests in the rules of the American welfare institution will reflect their desperate need of social services. This chapter has addressed this point by focusing on the broad rules of its five major social programs: Unemployment Insurance (UI), Social Security, public health assistance programs (i.e., Medicaid, children's health insurance program), nutrition assistance programs (i.e., the Supplemental Nutrition Assistance Program), and public housing assistance programs. However, it will be not easy for people in need or in a difficult circumstance to obtain information about the rules of these social welfare programs. From that point on, this chapter has stressed the importance of an ethnic-centered online social network, the "MissyUSA" community that is also known as the largest online social network of married Korean-American women in the region of North America. At the same time, the notion that their actions for seeking certain information about the rules of social welfare program(s) are really subjected to their personal needs, interests, or concerns has also been one of this book's premises. First, this chapter has shown that this "MissyUSA" community clearly works as an important source of social resources (information)—a form of social capital—to the information seekers about these five social welfare programs. Thus, some members of the "MissyUSA" community looked for a wide range of information about the rules of each of these five American social welfare programs on its "Life Q&A" message board in which they posted the general or specific messages seeking information about policies, qualification requirements, procedures in application, government agencies in charge, its processing time, and the like.

Second, this chapter has also revealed that this "MissyUSA" community is the community and the network of social supporters for its information seekers (inquirers). In other words, some of its other members (respondents) have transmitted their knowledge, advices, or emotions, or have shared their own experiences about the rules of the American welfare institution in response to the messages posted by information seekers. Indeed, their postings of response messages are primarily predicated on their general sense of community that leads them to assist their ethnic members at stake. In other words, all the respondents largely belong to either or both groups of instrumental guiders (information describers, analysts, confirmers, and advisors) and emotional supporters (companions, encouragers, and critics) for information seekers. As demonstrated above by the broad examination of their response messages, overall, many respondents belonged to the subgroups of information advisors, analysts, and/or encouragers for information seekers. To put it more simply, this chapter of the American welfare institution has demonstrated that their roles as instrumental guiders for the information seekers have been much dominated, in contrast to their roles as their emotional supporters.

NOTES

1. Pyong Gap Min, "Growth and Settlement Patterns of Korean Americans."
2. Terrance J. Reeves and Claudette E. Bennett, *We the People: Asians in the United States*, Census 2000 Special Reports (U.S. Census Bureau, 2004).
3. About 60 percent of them were currently married, and the remaining 30 percent of them were never married (single).
4. 3.5 percent of them were male householder with no wife present.
5. Terrance J. Reeves and Claudette E. Bennett, *We the People: Asians in the United States*.
6. Chang-Hwan Kim, "*The Generational Differences in Socioeconomic Attainments of Korean Americans*," Paper presented at The Research Center for Korean Community at Queens College (April 7, 2013).
7. Ibid.
8. Mimi Abramovitz, *Regulating the Lives of Women: Social Welfare Policy from Colonial Times to the Present* (Boston, MA: South End Press, 1989); and Joel Blau and Mimi Abramovitz, *The Dynamics of Social Welfare Policy* (New York: Oxford University Press, 2004).
9. Mimi Abramovitz, *Regulating the Lives of Women*.
10. Ruth Sidel, *Keeping Women and Children Last: America's War on the Poor* (New York: Penguin Books Ltd., 1998).
11. The 1996 PRWORA also included those amendments to Food Stamps, Supplementary Security Income (SSI), and Medicaid programs. For immigrants, the same tight eligibility requirements as TANF were applied to Food Stamps, Medicaid, and SSI benefits (an assistance program for the low-income aged and adults with disabilities).
12. Mimi Abramovitz, *Regulating the Lives of Women*; and Joel Blau and Mimi Abramovitz, *The Dynamics of Social Welfare Policy*.
13. Mimi Abramovitz, *Regulating the Lives of Women*; and Michael B. Katz, *The Price of Citizenship: Redefining the American Welfare State* (New York: Henry Holt and Company, 2001).
14. Gwendolyn Mink and Rickie Solinger, *Welfare: A Documentary History of U.S. Policy and Politics* (New York: New York University Press, 2003).
15. Michael B. Katz, *The Price of Citizenship*.
16. Marios Michaelides and Peter R. Mueser, "Recent Trends in the Characteristics of Unemployment Insurance Recipients," *Monthly Labor Review*, July, 2012.
17. Mimi Abramovitz, *Regulating the Lives of Women*; Joel Blau and Mimi Abramovitz, *The Dynamics of Social Welfare Policy*; and Gwendolyn Mink and Rickie Solinger, *Welfare*.
18. Unlike Social Security, Supplementary Security Income (SSI), also known as a welfare program or as a federal means-tested income program, makes a weekly cash payment to low-income individuals who are age sixty-five or older, or disabled. Un-

like Social Security that is paid for by social security taxes, SSI is paid for by U.S. Treasury general funds: see the link, http://www.ssa.gov/.

19. Joel Blau and Mimi Abramovitz, *The Dynamics of Social Welfare Policy*.

20. Michael B. Katz, *The Price of Citizenship*.

21. See http://www.ssa.gov/docs.

22. See http://www.medicaid.gov/. Then, Medicare is a national health insurance program for people age sixty-five and over, and for people of under-sixty-five with long-term disabilities (http://www.cms.gov/Medicare). There are two parts in Medicare; Part A and Part B. Medicare Part A is also called Hospital Insurance that covers inpatient care in hospital, hospice care, and some home health care. It is compulsory because it is financed primarily with the 1.45 percent payroll tax while working. But, Medicare Part B is an optional health program because individuals receiving it should pay some monthly premiums for its coverage. It is also called Medical Insurance that covers doctor's services, outpatient care, and some other medical services excluded in Part A. Besides, since January 2006, Medicare has added a new program, Medicare Prescription Drug Coverage that is aimed at helping lower prescription drug costs. It is also another optional health program because its recipients should pay some monthly premiums for this coverage.

23. For more information, see http://www.medicaid.gov/.

24. Joel Blau and Mimi Abramovitz, *The Dynamics of Social Welfare Policy*.

25. Available at http://www.medicaid.gov/CHIP. The Affordable Care Act, known as a comprehensive health insurance program for low-income Americans, was passed by Congress and then signed into law by the President in March 2010. This new health care law is also the kind of amendment to both of existing Medicaid and the Children's Health Insurance Program (CHIP). For more detailed information on its key provisions, see https://www.medicaid.gov/affordablecareact/affordable-care-act.html.

26. Ibid.

27. Available at http://www.fns.usda.gov/snap.

28. Ibid.

29. Ibid.

30. Available at http://www.fns.usda.gov/wic.

31. Ibid.

32. Ibid.

33. Ibid.

34. Available at http://www.fns.usda.gov.

35. Available at http://www.fns.usda.gov/school-meals/legislation.

36. Ibid.

37. See http://www.fns.usda.gov.

38. A special rental assistance program only for low-income elderly is named the Section 202 program. HUD administers this program by financing direct loans to private and nonprofit developers with the aims of constructing and maintaining those housing units affordable for eligible elderly. Therefore, funds through this program help lower the tenants' burden on monthly rent payment. However, the tenants' contracts through this program are approved for three years only and its renewals are contingent upon the availability of this program's fund. This Section 202 program was authorized by section 202 of the Housing Act of 1959. For instance, the number of properties and units developed by the Section 202 program was 42,737 between 1959 and 1974, 37,363 between 1985 and 1988, and 35,281 between 2000 and 2006. For detailed information, see http://portal.hud.gov/hudportal/HUD?src=/program_offices/housing/mfh/mfinfo/sec202ptl.

39. See http://portal.hud.gov/hudportal/HUD?src=/program_offices/public_indian_housing/programs/hcv.

40. Available at http://www.huduser.gov.

41. Joel Blau and Mimi Abramovitz, *The Dynamics of Social Welfare Policy*.

42. See http://www.huduser.gov.

43. Pyong Gap Min, *"Korean Americans,"* in *Asian Americans: Contemporary Trends and Issues*, ed. Pyong Gap Min (Thousand Oaks, CA: Pine Forge Press, 2006), 230–259.

44. For detailed information, see Pyong Gap Min's "The Structure and Social Functions of Korean Immigrant Churches in the United States," *International Migration Review* 26 (1992): 1370–1394.

45. The base period is the period of employment for the determination of UI claim. This base period is classified into two types: the standard base period and the alternative base period. The standard base period is the first four of the last five completed calendar quarters prior to the current quarter. For example, if someone was laid off in December 2012, his/her standard base period is July 2011 through June 2012. The alternative base period is the last four completed calendar quarters prior to the current quarter. In the same case, his/her alternative period is October 2011 through September 2012.

46. Available at http://www.labor.ny.gov.

47. The eligibility for Social Security (disability) benefits should work for a certain period of time (the "duration of work test") based upon your age (www.ssa.gov). For example, if a person became disabled at the age of forty-six, six-years of work is generally needed to qualify for disability benefits.

48. Available at http://www.ssa.gov.

49. Ibid.

50. Since people get social security disability benefits for two years, they are automatically enrolled in Medicare that is known as the federal health insurance program for people who are sixty-five or older, and certain younger people with disabilities (www.ssa.gov).

51. Available at http://www.medicaid.gov.

52. In the State of New York, almost all children qualify for Children's Medicaid regardless of their immigration status, but based upon gross family income: see http://www.health.ny.gov/health_care/child_health_plus/who_is_eligible.htm.

53. Shawn Fremstad and Laura Cox, *Covering New Americans: A Review of Federal and State Policies Related to Immigrants' Eligibility and Access to Publicly Funded Health Insurance* (Center on Budget and Policy Priorities, November 2004).

54. Regardless of immigration status, Emergency Medicaid benefits for medical treatments at hospital Emergency Rooms are available to every group of immigrants, including undocumented immigrants.

55. Available at http://www.medicaid.gov.

56. Available at https://www.healthcare.gov/medicaid-chip/childrens-health-insurance -program.

57. Available at http://health.ny.gov/family_health_plus.

58. Available at http://www.fns.usda.gov/snap.

59. Ibid.

60. Ibid.

61. Available at http://www.fns.usda.gov/wic.

62. Available at http://www.fns.usda.gov/slp.

63. Available at http://portal.hud.gov/rental_assistance.

64. Available at http://www.nyc.gov/nycha.

65. One of the most well-known public housing programs for the elderly is the Section 202 program. For more details about it, see https://portal.hud.gov/hudportal/documents/huddoc?id=DOC_12821.pdf.

66. Available at http://portal.hud.gov/rental_assistance.

FOUR

The American Educational Institution on the "MissyUSA" Community

Most parents of school-age children are well aware that one of their most important tasks is to support a good education for their children; it is a common ground upon which most agree. In South Korea, education has been unquestionably an unfading buzzword over time among most Korean parents of school-age children. This pervasive Korean parents' belief in the importance of a good education for their children remains real and very strong even among most Korean parents living in the United States. Furthermore, the vast majority of Korean parents in the United States also have a strong assurance that the socio-economic status and well-being of their children in their new country heavily rely upon their children's good academic achievement or higher educational level. Indeed, the root of their firm belief on education might come from their generally shared perceptions that their children's attainment of a good education, especially higher education at prestigious universities, is directly linked to their children's bright career by way of enhancing access to professional jobs, more secure jobs, or jobs with high earning potential. However, many Korean parents in the United States realize at some point in their lives that there exists a gap between their outlooks on their children's education and the uncontrollable circumstances they face in reality.

Undoubtedly, Korean parents in the United States are composed of a very diverse group of people who are very different in their socioeconomic status, family structure, immigration status, duration of residence, family size, location of residence, and the like. Previous research on this topic shows that these family circumstances correlate with children's educational achievements.[1] More importantly, it should be noted that Korean immigrant parents' knowledge about the American educational institution is also very critical to their children's high educational attainment.

In other words, their parenting style and their plans and actions for their children's education will be less likely to produce positive results at a time when they struggle to figure out the rules of the American educational institution—specifically, within or across states, districts, schools, or grade levels, as well as how to make full use of them for the improvement of their children's education. Here, parental plans and actions for children's education refer to all kinds of their personal efforts necessary to make their children's education better—e.g., homework help, school activities (PTA, volunteering), communication with teachers and children, and the collection of education information.

Then, the gap between their great craving for their children's educational success and their plans and actions for it can originate really from some differences in the personal characteristics of Korean immigrant parents, which, for example, include their educational accomplishment, proficiency in English, participation in the labor market, experiences of discrimination, and their understanding of American society generally, and more narrowly, their understanding level of the American educational systems. My own stance on this is that their shortage or absence of adequate social networks or social capital is the missing link between their desire for their children's high educational attainment and their plans and actions for it. To put it simply, Korean immigrant parents' social networks become social capital, namely, the sources of social resources (information, tips, or advice about American educational systems and related issues) that can help initiate their plans and actions to intervene in the different-stage, educational processes of their children. In the Korean-American community, children's education, like child rearing, is mainly the woman's responsibility. In this respect, some of the Korean-immigrant or -American mothers' social networks might be the important terrains for discourse on their children's education or school activities, and furthermore, vital channels for the dissemination and circulation of education-related information before the mothers' effective involvement in their children's education.

One of the important social networks much more easily available for many Korean-American mothers of school-age children is the Korean-American women's online community, the "MissyUSA" community, which is also known as one of the largest Korean immigrant mothers' social networks in the United States and Canada. Basically, it is a great source of social resources, a form of social capital, to its information seekers about the rules of the American educational institution. Actually, many "MissyUSA" members have posted on its "Life Q&A" message board their inquiry messages about a wide range of the rules of the American educational institution and its specific organizational units that range from pre-schools to colleges or universities. For example, some popular themes or topics asked by its members include school registration, curriculum placement or selection, course materials, school programs, school policies, the roles of teachers or counselors, report cards, exams or tests, extracurricular activities, transferring schools, college selection, tuition, financial aid, scholarships, educational loans, and so on.

Full membership of the "MissyUSA" community requires both Korean nationality and current or past marital status. It goes without saying that there must be large numbers of its members with children who now attend elementary, middle, or high school, have graduated high school, or have even graduated college. Based upon their experiences, knowhow, or confidence from their children's education earlier, they constitute a massive group of counselors, advisors, or supporters to its other members who contrarily struggle to identify what to do for their children's better education or school life in the face of their unfamiliarity with the rules of the American educational institution. Thus, this Korean-American women's online community is not only a network and source of social resources in approaching it from the perspective of its information seekers (or inquirers), but also, it can be identified as a community and a social support network for them, as another feature of social capital, in the perspective of its respondents (or information providers). In this chapter of the American educational institution, this whole mass of social supporters is further classified into two groups. One of them consists of instrumental guiders (information describers, analysts, confirmers, and advisors), while the other belongs to emotional supporters (encouragers, companions, and critics). By analyzing their messages in response to the education-related inquiries, such specific patterns of social support for information seekers are in great detail examined below.

This chapter begins with an overview of the American educational institution in terms of its key educational goals, laws, policies, programs, different governing bodies, and school systems in modern American history. Here, the discussion about the rules of the American educational institution is generally put into focus in the realm of public schools from Kindergarten to twelfth grade and both public and private colleges and universities. Second, the Korean-American community is looked into within the conceptions of social capital and education, namely, social resources and social support, in the scope of education. Lastly, some selected messages requesting and providing information on the rules of the American educational institution among "MissyUSA" members (both of inquirers and respondents) are illustrated in the framework of social capital (social resources and social support). This is done by introducing a wide range of education-related themes and topics related to each of the American school systems that ranges from American primary school to junior high school to college and university.

THE AMERICAN EDUCATIONAL INSTITUTION: HISTORY, LAWS, AND ORGANIZATIONS

The American educational institution is, in this chapter, understood not only as all governing bodies (federal, state, and municipal or local educational departments, districts, and schools) designed to promote their defining goals of education by implementing their extant educational laws, policies, and programs or initiatives, but also as the collectivity of all school systems (public elementary schools, public secondary schools, and public and private colleges and universities) that are run to achieve their own concerted goals of education for the current and prospective learners with or without support from national, state, or local educational authorities. What is important here is that one unique feature of the American educational institution is its decentralized structure of governance, administration, teaching or research, and funding, which has led to the creation of dissimilar educational goals across its governing bodies. For example, the overriding educational goal that the U.S. Department of Education has prioritized is "to promote student achievement and preparation for global competitiveness by fostering educational excellence and ensuring equal access."[2] The New York State Education Department has set its own educational goal that is oriented to "raise the knowledge, skill, and opportunity of all the people in New York."[3] The New York City Department of Education's main educational goal is to "create equitable learning environment for all students" attending New York City's public schools.[4]

Like the cases of the three different governing bodies within the American education institution, educational goals are also not the same across districts and schools. For example, the central educational goal of a school district in the Borough of Manhattan in New York City is directed to the achievement of "excellence both academically and socially in order to be productive and industrious members in our global society."[5] Then, another school district in the same Borough has set its goal to "help all students become independent thinkers and give them the skills necessary for a productive fulfilling life."[6] A public elementary school in this latter school district in the Borough of Manhattan in New York City has put its top priorities on multicultural education, commitment to the community, and the encouragement of self-directed learning, whereas the educational goal of another public elementary school in the same school district is to provide "individual students the opportunity to extend and deepen his/her understanding in every classroom."[7] In turn, these illustrations unfold a distinctive feature of the American educational institution in which, in general, the educational goals stressed by its same or different organizational units are often contradictory, in focus and in content.

Nonetheless, more broadly, most of organizational units in the American educational institution basically embrace the ideas of equity and open access with the ideas of competition and advantage, as their main educational goals.[8] Each of these two conflicting educational goals of the American educational institution has been earlier justified in different historical backgrounds and reasons. The former has taken shape by the historical legitimacy and subsequent school practices relating to the idea of educational equity and open access to education. The development of citizenship skills critical for the promotion of a sense of community, the spirit of democracy and human and individual rights has historically been the core mission of American public educational systems that permit all members equal access to educational opportunity. In modern American educational history in particular, this political creed of mass education for all members has received a strong legal support, especially through the 1964 Civil Rights Act that prohibits discrimination in education.[9] This landmark legislation has provided people the right to have access to any educational agencies and entities (schools, colleges) receiving federal financial assistance by barring discrimination in those educational units on the basis of race, color, national origin, sex, disability, and age.[10] The conception and practice of equal educational opportunity in American educational systems has been further reinforced by the 1965 Elementary and Secondary Education Act (ESEA).[11] This 1965 ESEA, as a comprehensive educational law, has provided federal funding through concrete measures to meet the educational needs for children of low-income families or from high-poverty neighborhoods, children with English as a second language, children with disabilities, or neglected children. In fact, the ESEA has also focused on the gradual improvement of these children's academic achievement, with the goal of ultimately closing the academic achievement gap between them and children coming from relatively better economic and social positions.

As supplements to the 1965 ESEA, the 1968 Amendment of the ESEA has authorized the support of the development of bilingual education programs for non-English speaking children, and the 1975 Education for All Handicapped Children Act, now called Individuals with Disabilities Education Act, has also provided funding for schools to create special educational programs for students with disabilities.[12] In general, these two pieces of national legislation on equity and the rights of citizens have substantially affected the development of the policies and programs of public elementary and secondary schools, such as the implementations of compulsory schooling, age-based student placement in classes, uniform curriculum at each grade level, and cooperative learning.[13] Most recently, for example, the provisions on equal educational opportunity for all public-school attending students were included in the 2001 reauthorization of the 1965 ESEA, known as the No Child Left Behind Act (NCLBA). At the heart of this legislation are guidelines for improving students' reading and mathematics skills, and their or their parents' rights to choose better schools for their academic goals. As in the case of American elementary and secondary education, these ideas of equity and open access in education have materialized in American higher education. Indeed, this tenet of equal opportunity in postsecondary education has gained greater momentum especially with the Higher Education Act of 1965.[14] Educational assistance for low-income students pursuing college education is one important part of this educational law. Here, much attention was paid to financial support for college education and student living expenses. Especially, the major financial programs available for them were those of need-based grants (i.e., the Pell grant), low-interest loans (i.e., Perkins loan, the federal parent plus loan), and college work-study funding (i.e., part-time employment mostly in college campus).[15]

However, this American educational goal of equity and open access in education has often awkwardly coexisted with the ideas of competition and advantage as the other axis of the American educational goals. Thus, the truth is that in the modern American history of education, the ideas of competition and advantage have been also gradually implanted in the American educational institution.[16] On the whole, the public acceptance and policy effectiveness of these ideas have intensified with growing perceptions of American economic crisis due to international economic competition against other advanced capitalist countries, and shrinking employment opportunities of American adult work force due to less improvement in their overall job skills, training, scientific or mathematical knowledge, or technological competency. Some early educational laws were enacted to tackle these concerns about national economy and the quality of workforce. The related legislations include: the 1963 Vocational Educational Act that authorized more funding for vocational education schools, the 1984 Education for Economic Security Act that launched new science and mathematics programs at all levels of education, the 1994 School-to-Work Opportunities Act that provided federal funds for the schools established to prepare the students to find out their first jobs and continuing education, and the 2007 America COMPETES Act (or *America Creating Opportunities to Meaningfully Promote Excellence in Technology, Education, and Science Act*) that created new STEM (science, technology, engineering, and mathematics) programs in federal agencies to strengthen STEM education in schools, and implemented improvements for researchers, teachers, and students (National Center for Education Statistics 2011).[17]

Nowadays, a majority of Americans still take into account education, especially high-quality education, as one of the principal mechanisms for their socio-economic mobility, or for the continuous retention of their current socio-economic status, in the American class structure. Behind their more practical approach to the mission of education is their tacit agreement about the values of competition and advantage that rationalize, as the pivotal aim of education, higher academic achievement or better educational credential for personal career. For that matter, some educational programs at the levels of states, districts, or schools were oriented to meet their needs. The authorization of school choice programs was indeed legislative outcomes that reflect their concerns at the levels of states and community districts. One of the parents' options in school choice programs is to send their public-school attending children to charter schools that have greater autonomy in school governance (the creation of their school goals, the structure of the school's organization) and the hiring of teachers, curriculum, and instruction, but still have accountability for students' academic performance.[18] Basically, the attractiveness of charter schools is a better learning environment that can help students to improve their learning and academic achievement.

Magnet schools are another option. If children who have high academic ability or have special talents in particular areas are eager to pursue specific career paths before their postsecondary education, magnet schools can be a good option for their parents to consider. Magnet schools are public schools that are distinguishable from traditional public schools in terms of their selection of students (they may select from inside or outside districts, and rely on entrance examinations, interviews, or a lottery) and their curriculum concentration in specialized fields—i.e., performing and visual arts, mathematics, science, technology, fashion and design, food, foreign languages, the humanities, or social sciences.[19] Additionally, some schools run gifted and talented programs (G&T). Graduation from secondary-school G&T leads to a very promising prospect for admissions to a prestigious university, which is also linked to a positive factor of future career in the labor market or academia. This is why many parents want to send their children to gifted and talented schools. However, entrance into gifted and talented schools is very competitive, and therefore, these schools are only for children with exceptional academic capability or high intelligence level. For example, applicants to gifted and talented schools in New York City should score, in the entrance tests (verbal and nonverbal assessment), at the ninetieth percentile or above for district G&T programs, and score at the ninety-seventh percentile or above for citywide G&T programs, for them to be qualified.[20] As another option, some high-achieving students in public high schools can take advanced courses (honors or advanced placement classes) in preparation for applying to high-ranking or prestigious universities.[21] To put it shortly, there is a clear indication that American public school systems offer an array of various programs to enhance the academic achievement for all the students or their targeted students.

The American educational institution is very complex in its organizational structure and governance. But, its key legislative and governing units include the educational department of the federal government, the legislative and executive body of state education, the legislative and executive body of municipal education, districts, schools, and colleges and universities. Each of these educational entities conducts their own tasks and routines on the regular basis, but sometimes, their roles overlap with each other in some cases. At the national level, the key tasks and activities of the U.S. Department of Education are the management of federal finance for education (i.e., financial aid, student loan, funding), the collection of data and research on America's schools, the assessment of major problems facing American education, and the enforcement against discrimination in American education.[22] Then, in the case of the United States, the primary responsibility for public education is granted to individual states within which the key legislative and executive branches of state education are composed of the state governor, the state legislature, the state board of education, and the state education department or agency.[23] In general, the state governor, the state legislature, and the state board of education set their state goals for education, state policies and procedures for the establishment of schools and colleges, and state policies and rules for educational standards (i.e., curriculum, instruction, requirements for school enrollment and graduation), assessment (i.e., educational programs, school evaluation through student performance in testing), and for teacher certification.[24] They also set state educational budgets and the procurement and distribution of funds for elementary, secondary, and higher education. Besides, the operation of the approved state educational policies and rules is usually in the hands of state governors and state education departments or agencies that also take charge of the enforcement of national educational laws and policies within the state educational system.[25]

In the state, its municipal or local educational units, like city mayors and city education departments or agencies, should comply with state educational policies and rules so that their main role is to implement state measures within their jurisdiction. Without breaching these state educational policies and regulations, policymakers at this local level—e.g., city mayors, city councils, or members of city boards of education—also create their own educational measures, and authorize city education departments or agencies to oversee the implementation of these measures established in their local school system. In New York City, for example, these measures include a strong system of accountability (the closing of academically low performing schools), a series of learning standards (individual subject and each grade level), rigid assessment (teacher contract or tenure according to the academic performance of students), and the allocation of educational funds based upon its top priority (the academic achievement of students, graduation rate, school facilities).[26]

In a municipality, school districts are usually divided across the boundary of neighborhood zones—i.e., 32 school districts in New York City. After all, each school district is held accountable for the implementation of both state and city educational measures to public elementary and secondary schools in their jurisdiction. At the same time, each school district has also their own discretion in handling some important education-related issues. For example, the chief school administrator of the district (superintendent) has the authority to appoint principals in district schools and approval of teacher tenure decisions and school budgets, plays a liaison role between the community (and parental associations) and the district board of education, and has the right to develop new curricula and instructional methods in state learning standards.[27] Moreover, district boards of education have their own power in the creation of the educational policy reflecting the interests of community constituents, the approval of district employee hiring, the evaluation of superintendent, the contract negotiation with teachers or a teacher union, and the oversight of curriculum.[28]

One of the pillars of American school systems is public elementary and secondary schools. Most American public elementary and secondary schools, except for charter schools, are under the supervision of school district boards of education and superintendents. The grade span of public elementary schools in American schools is either K-5 or K-6. For American public secondary schooling, it ranges in grades through 6 to 12 (or 7-12), and it is often divided into middle schools (6-8 or 7-9) and high schools (9-12 or 10-12). As usual, placement of the students into different grades is primarily based upon student ages. Indeed, most students in the same grade levels of public schools are generally taught under similar curricula (the subjects taken) and have similar learning standards (the content and level of each subject). Likewise, most public schools also offer various academic programs within schools—e.g., gifted and talented programs, course-based ability grouping such as honors courses or advanced placement courses (AP), special education, or bilingual education—to meet the needs of their diverse student body.

By and large, American public elementary- and secondary-school structures are organized into administrators (principals, assistant principals), teachers, pupils, and staffs (guidance counselors, nurses, psychologists). Taken together, public school principals are usually held accountable for school management (facility, personnel, safety, services), the execution of state and local educational rules and policies in school (enrollment procedures, curriculum, student disciplines, retention, and the prevention of bullying, discrimination, or harassment,) and for the assessment of some educational measures (overall students' academic performance in testing, graduation rate). Their other important roles are the advancement of school missions and goals, the evaluation of teachers, the decision to create and implement new grade curricula aligned with state and local standards, and liaisons between schools and the school districts as well as between schools and parents.

In American public schools, teachers are the most important figures for pupils' learning. Groups of public school teachers can be generally sorted out by their appointment or contract (tenured, tenure- or non-tenure track, substitute), teaching fields or subjects, classroom management (homeroom teachers), hierarchy (the head of department, the coordinator of curriculum or instruction), and so on. Obviously, their main role as educators is to help their students experience a more and better learning on the ground of their relentless efforts, which involve the use of their best methods of teaching, the setting of a good learning environment in the classroom, the lasting observation of the intellectual and moral development of their individual students, regular homework assignments, and active communications with the parents of their students and school principals or guidance counselors with regard to their students' academic or non-academic development.

American higher educational institutions are another essential entity of American school systems. Their main organizational units are broadly divided into two-year colleges (community colleges), four-year colleges (liberal arts or women's colleges), and four-year universities (with curricula in liberal arts and sciences at both undergraduate and graduate levels). In most American states, the establishment of a college or university is possible by offering full degree programs (associate or bachelor's degrees), but it must be authorized by the state board of education (i.e., the Board of Regents in New York State). Relative to public elementary and secondary schools, then American public colleges and universities enjoy a high degree of institutional autonomy and academic freedom, free from the accountability of state and local educational assessment. However, public colleges and universities, as compared with private colleges and universities, must comply with some federal and state laws and policies (i.e., affirmative action, admissions to state and local residents, requirements for registration or degrees) because the funding for their operational budgets heavily relies upon the U.S. Department of Education and their state governments.[29] In most cases, American four-year colleges and universities have formed similar organizational structures, such as academic programs (departments, centers, institutes), administrations for academic and student affairs (presidents, provosts, deans), research or teaching support units (libraries, facilities, technology), and divisions of student, faculty, and staff services (admissions, registration, tuition, scholarships, loans, financial aid, degree completion, human resources, payroll).

SOCIAL CAPITAL AND EDUCATION IN THE KOREAN-AMERICAN COMMUNITY

In this book, social capital consists of both social resources and social support that are inherent in, or emanated from, social networks. Unfortunately, some international migrants who have to leave their country of origin cannot avoid the disruption of the social networks formed in their home country. However, their efforts to adjust better to their host society tend to motivate them to create their new social networks or to join them to some extant social networks in their new land. In discussions of the American educational institution from the perspective of Korean immigrant parents, it must be true that their participation in certain social networks of their host society is very conducive to their sons' or daughters' better education and schooling. One of such important networks might be their extended family networks that usually exist in Korean-American gateway (or enclave) communities as the result of chain migration of many family members from Korea. For example, the newly settled Korean immigrant parents in the United States can take advantage of these family-based networks when seeking information about American school systems—i.e., school registration, school courses, participation in school programs (band, G&T), children's school activities, application procedures for college admissions, educational loan, or scholarship—from the other members of their family networks who have some information or knowhow about American educational systems as parents of school-attending or -attended children. In addition, some parents under stress for their difficulties in understanding their children's school systems or school operations can receive some consolation or encouragement from the members of their family networks. For that matter, these family networks function as an important social support network for them. However, such networks as extended family networks are not always available to all Korean immigrants at arrival, and its effectiveness can be also very low when they lack social interactions among their other family members in the United States.

In typical Korean immigrant families in the United States, mothers are usually the primary planners and managers of their children's education and career development.[30] In fact, a great improvement in their knowledge about their children's education and schooling can be an outcome of their active participation in social networks of various sorts. For example, one loose but important social network for them is the one that is established through their interpersonal relationships with teachers, guidance counselors, or school officials who have inside knowledge about their children's academic performance and other activities in the school.[31] To them, the importance of this social network can intensify with their direct involvement in school events as school volunteers or as members of a school-wide parent-teacher organization, as well as with their regular participation or attendance at the school's open house nights, back-to-school nights, school career days, or classroom observation days. But, this kind of social network is less often utilized by those Korean immigrant mothers with limited English skills. Instead, many Korean immigrant mothers tend to participate in a Korean parent-teacher organization (KPTO) at the school- or grade- level, especially when they live in a larger Korean-American gateway city or community. They generally think of it as a critical medium to convey the uniqueness of Korean culture and identity to English-speaking school staffs and teachers, and likewise, to address their and their children's needs in school, collectively. More importantly, some Korean-American mothers participating in a KPTO gather together, regularly or informally, to exchange information and consult with each other on any issues related to their children's education, schooling, or career trajectory. Moreover, some of them are joining their neighborhood networks through which they tend to maintain close relationships with some Korean and non-Korean neighbors who have school age children, or who sometimes become their informants about the history, characteristics, or most recent updates of local schools.

Wherever Korean immigrants live in the United States, a vast majority of them attend Korean-American churches inside or outside their local communities. One feature of most Korean-American churches is that in church activities, church members are often set apart by age, gender, and residential area. That way, churchgoing Korean immigrant mothers can build up their own within-church networks through their repeated contact with each other, for example, by attending the meetings for female church members or same age women's gatherings, participating in the regular district meetings, or by sending their children to Sunday or summer church school. On the education side, some of these churchgoing Korean immigrant mothers express to other members in the same within-church networks their difficulty in finding the best ways to improve their children's performance in the academic subjects their children struggle with, or understanding certain areas of local school systems or policies. Some others can also request from their church-network members information or advice about what to prepare when their children move up to the next grade level, the colleges best suited to their children's abilities or their financial situations, or about the handling of other matters relating to their children's education. Here, they regard their tight, sometimes overlapping networks within church as a great source of information for their children's education. On the flip side, information providers (or respondents) tend to perceive such within-church networks as an important route for them to support these education-related information seekers. In turn, the ways these information providers support information seekers are usually revealed through transmissions of the requested information, expressions of their personal opinions or experiences, or their emotional support to those information seekers. Indeed, the networks of many Korean immigrant mothers are quite extensive due to their connectivity with other family members, teachers, school parents, neighbors, church members, or other acquaintances.

These days, most Korean immigrant mothers are very well aware of a tremendous emphasis put on students' academic achievement in American elementary and secondary schools, and the importance of SAT (Scholastic Aptitude Test) or ACT (American College Testing) scores in college admissions. To be sure, their connection with various types of social networks will also become a great resource in seeking information for their children's educational attainment outside of formal schooling. In the larger Korean-American gateway cities like Los Angeles, New York, Chicago, or Atlanta, there are numerous Korean-run private tutoring or SAT preparation institutions, known as cram schools.[32] Despite the expensive tuition of these cram schools, a major concern for many Korean immigrant mothers with children in high school in these Korean-American concentrated areas is to find out the best cram schools, the ones that have a reputation for making a great improvements in school subject tests, or for enhancing SAT or ACT scores in a short time.[33] Often, information on different outcome levels of student performance—e.g., the numbers of students who passed advanced placement (AP) exams, scored higher on SAT tests, or were admitted to elite or selective colleges—of each cram school in the city spreads, speedily and widely, among members of these various networks of Korean immigrant mothers. Additionally, some members of these networks also transmit information or exchange their opinions about other out-of-school studies like private tutoring, online courses, or a self-study through test-prep books (i.e., Princeton Review or Kaplan) or through problem-solving level-based worksheets in math or reading—i.e., Kumon.

In addition to Korean immigrant mothers' personal networks, their residence in larger Korean-American gateway cities provides them an opportunity to learn about American local educational policies, systems, and programs through ethnic Korean language media that include daily printed and online Korean newspapers, locally aired Korean televisions and radio stations, weekly issued Korean magazines, or periodicals. These days, however, it is not very difficult for Korean immigrant mothers with limited English skills who reside outside of Korean-American gateway communities to obtain a wide range of information on the rules of the American educational institution. Thanks to the innovation of information technology, they can really have a chance to improve their knowledge about them by reading the online education sections of Korean language newspapers, or assessing some popular Korean American online websites, such as "MissyUSA" (missyusa.com).

THE AMERICAN EDUCATIONAL INSTITUTION ON THE "MISSYUSA" COMMUNITY

The "Life Q&A" message board of the "MissyUSA" community is an important venue to exchange any kinds of messages about the rules of the American educational institution among its members. Given two forms of social capital, requesting information as a specific aspect of social resources is one type of messages posted on it, whereas responses to such messages requesting information, known as a pattern of social support here, are the other type of messages. Below, the occurrence of these two types of social capital is demonstrated by dividing the postings of education-related messages into the four distinctive layers of the American educational institution: Elementary School (K-1 through grade 5), Middle School (grades 6 through 8), High School (grades 9 through 12), and College Education.

American Elementary School Education

In this broad category of American elementary school education, information on various subjects was requested by some members of the "MissyUSA" community. In classifying them more generally, indeed, there were many different topics, which include the following list: school absence, school leadership, entrance to Kindergarten, gifted and talented program (G&T), skipping a grade, music or band classes, parental volunteering or participation in parent-teacher organization, school registration, class materials, course selection, extracurricular activities, school graduation, and so on. Of them, five specific examples are in detail introduced below. At first, a member posted a message requesting information about the school absence of her third-grade child on March 6, 2012. This post received three response messages:

> Q: I have to visit Korea with my child in third grade. I am not sure whether a two-week school absence is allowed. Also, what worries me after coming back to school is how to catch up with the undone schoolwork.
> A1: To a third-grade student, that's no problem.
> A2: School absence is fine in cases of family affairs and a visit to a foreign country under the permission of the school authorities. You also need to consult with your child's teacher about homework, the required reading during class absence, and so on.
> A3: In my case, my child was absent from school for three weeks on account of our visit to Korea. My child's teacher assigned [him or her] all the necessary schoolwork during our stay in Korea and checked them after our return . . .

In general, American public schools' district boards of education have established their own policies and procedures for the handling of the school absence of their district-attending students, which are much subject to the education law of their state. In the case of the state of New Jersey, for example, students' consecutive unexcused absences of four or more require their parents to consult with the school official or homeroom teacher. This is not the case in this inquiry message. All three respondents (A1, A2, and A3) belong to the subgroup of information confirmers to the inquirer, and two of them (A1 and A3) also take on the role of information describers for her. Both roles of an information analyst and an information advisor to the inquirer were conducted by Respondent 2 (A2). Furthermore, like Respondent 1 (A1), Respondent 3 (A3) is positioned as an encourager for the inquirer because this respondent expressed her confidence that the child's schoolwork would be handled well by the school teacher.

On November 8, 2012, there was a message requesting information (or advice) about what to do for her child who was elected student council president in an elementary school. There were six response messages and one additional post from the inquirer:

> Q: My daughter attending an elementary school became student council president. I have no idea of what I should do for her and her school. Can you give me some advice?
> A1: Congratulations! How about buying a present for her?
> A2: Praise her accomplishment, and advise you to participate in such school activities as volunteering or school PTA [parent-teacher association].
> Q: Do I have to join the school PTA? I really worry about my interaction with English-speaking parents.
> A3: There is a lot of work when you do volunteering in the school. So you don't have much time to interact with them.
> A4: Congratulations! Your daughter must be very smart. You need to encourage your daughter always and help her with your careful scrutiny of all the letters your daughter brings home. It is also a good idea to attend school PTA meetings frequently . . .
> A5: My daughter was elected vice president of her elementary school's student council. Before her participation in school council, I encouraged her every time because she worked very hard to prepare her election.
> A6: I envy you. I really hope that such achievement will happen to my child.

Generally, three respondents (A2, A4, and A5) belong to the subgroup of information advisors to the inquirer, and of them, Respondent 4 (A4) also takes on the role of an information analyst for her. The role of information describers to the inquirer is revealed in the messages of four respondents (A1, A3, A5, and A6). Then, the response messages posted by two respondents (A1 and A6) were completely off topic.

On September 6, 2012, one member posted a message requesting information about gifted and talented programs (G&T) in public elementary schools. There were two messages in response to this post:

> Q: My daughter was admitted to her school gifted and talented program. I know that gifted and talented programs are not the same across public elementary schools. But I have no knowledge of its goals, curriculum, the level of learning, and the intensity of study in the program. . . . Please post precious information for me.
> A1: My daughter is now in her gifted class. Don't expect too much. My experience is that this program introduces a new learning method to its students, but it is not exactly for academically talented students. I also

> think that offering a gifted and talented program and special education in public schools is a way to display outsiders that their schools try to integrate students of diverse backgrounds. For no follow-up step is taken from schools after the completion of a gifted class.
> A2: It is true that different public schools have varying policy and curriculum for their gifted and talented programs. In elementary schools, students in the program tend to learn advanced curriculum at math, the course materials of one grade up in social studies, and to conduct research projects that help them develop their creativity. . . . You need to meet your child's gifted program coordinator to learn more about it.

Clearly, this inquirer seems to seek information on the features of the G&T programs across school districts, not citywide G&T programs. Both respondents (A1 and A2) are very knowledgeable about the general characteristic of gifted and talented programs. Thus, they belong to the subgroup of information analysts for the inquirer. Besides, both respondents are also positioned to take on the role of information advisors to the inquirer.

The opinion of whether skipping Kindergarten is a good idea was raised in the message posted on the "Life Q&A" message board on September 5, 2012. Five members responded to this post:

> Q: My child learns fast and is very mature, compared to other kids of the same age. My child often complained to me that homework is too easy and school is boring. My friends suggested me to meet the teacher. I didn't do it because of my work schedule. Almost a month after school started, I received a letter from the teacher who recommended me to skip Kindergarten for my child. . . . My child has a very good character and social skill, but is short in height relative to the same-age other kids. My child also wants to attend first grade. My uncertainty is whether skipping a grade is the right decision.
> A1: When my child attended kindergarten, I received the same recommendation from the teacher. But, I continued to send kindergarten for my child who was very shy and unsocial at that time. This year, my child went to college and in retrospect, I think that my judgment at that juncture was correct. Now my child became a very social, diligent, and confident person.
> A2: Deferring a grade is recommended by some education experts for children's learning and school adaptation. But if your child feels school as a boring place, skipping a grade is not a bad idea.
> A3: In case your child can catch up with the course work, skipping a grade is fine and your child will enjoy school more.
> A4: My child skipped first grade and now is in eleventh grade. I am happy with and proud of my child. Till [his/her] middle school, I was worried about [his/her] height, but now [he/she] is 189 cm tall . . .
> A5: In the morning classes, my child studies in kindergarten, but in the afternoon classes in first grade . . .

As a whole, the district board of education under the guidance of the state board of education has their own standards of grade skipping for academically excellent students. In this message thread, three out of five respondents (A1, A2 and A3) belong to the subgroup of information advisors to the inquirer. To some degree, Respondent 2 (A2) can be also regarded as the information analyst for the inquirer. Then, the messages of two respondents (A4 and A5) place them in the subgroup of information describers to the inquirer. Besides, encouragement to the inquirer is contained in the messages of two respondents (A2 and A4).

As another illustration, there was a message requesting information about the dress code for elementary school graduation. Five messages were posted as responses to this post:

> Q: I have never attended a graduation ceremony held in American schools before. My first child will soon graduate from elementary school. I don't know what my child and I should wear at the graduation ceremony . . .
> A1: Try to wear formal suits.
> A2: I have attended many graduation ceremonies. In fact, there were not many people in formal suits. Most schools announce a dress code for kids in advance. If not, wear a dress for a girl and for a boy, a shirt with a color and khaki pants.
> A3: It is a little bit awkward to wear formal suits. A shirt with collar and long pants are much more natural.
> A4: Recently, my daughter graduated from school. I saw many girls wearing a summer dress and many boys wearing a shirt with collar and pants, not jeans. Some of them came to wear casual clothes. I also observed that many adults had worn comfortable clothes over formal suits.
> A5: The school your child attends will notify you [his/her] dress code ahead of the graduation ceremony. But I saw many Asian adults wearing formal suits in the schools a large proportion of which students were from Asian backgrounds.

Prior to graduation ceremony, schools usually provide proper dress codes for those students graduating from their schools. All five respondents belong to the subgroup of information advisors to the inquirer. Besides, generally, three of them (A2, A4, and A5) also belong to the subgroup of information analysts for the inquirer.

American Middle School Education

In this category of American middle school education, some popular topics posted on the "Life Q&A" message board of the "MissyUSA" community were course selection, gifted and talented program (G&T), band or orchestra participation, back to school night, summer camp, transferring schools, PSAT (the Preliminary Scholastic Aptitude Test) or SAT, detention, and so on. Of these distinctive topics, messages on four topics are in great detail introduced below. At first, a member posted a message requesting information about course selection on February 2, 2012. There were five short response messages, along with an additional post from the inquirer:

> Q: My daughter in 7th-grade does not want to take any foreign language course. If a foreign language course is not taken, does it cause a disadvantage in admissions to a selective college?
> A1: Prestigious colleges or universities require their applicants to take a foreign language course at least for three years.
> A2: Your daughter is now only in 7th grade. She can take one of many foreign language courses from 9th grade . . . At that time, your daughter will change her mind, I guess.
> A3: Most kids take a foreign language course from high school. For example, there are four different levels in the Spanish course and taking its first two levels is required. It really depends on what colleges your daughter will apply to. But many elite colleges or universities require the completion of a foreign language course . . . Some Ivy League schools also treat Korean as a foreign language course.
> A4: Your daughter cannot be admitted to a college without completing a foreign language course in high school.
> A5: Don't push your daughter too hard. She can take it in high school.
> Q: Thank you for posting your advice . . . Taking a break seems to be not a bad idea.

In American middle school education, students' course selection is usually taken in charge by a supervisor of instruction or a guidance counselor in school. All five respondents belong to the subgroup of information advisors to the inquirer. Additionally, Respondent 3 (A3) is also positioned to take on the role of an information analyst for the inquirer.

On January 1, 2012, there was a message requesting information (or advice) about the selection of a music instrument for the seventh-grade son of the inquirer. There were four response messages that had followed this post:

> Q: My son has played violin over two years, but he doesn't want to play strings any more. Instead, he is interested in playing wind instruments like bassoon or clarinet. As more kids likely play clarinet in school orchestra, then relatively, there are few to play bassoon. But, this instrument is too expensive and finding a musician is not easy, either. He wants to join both school orchestra and band. . . . I am not sure of what instrument is the right choice for him.
> A1: My son had no interest in playing an instrument before, but the bassoon left a deep impression on him in a concert he attended. Then, he could easily join school band after expressing his interest in the bassoon. A school bassoon can be used and schools offer bassoon lessons. But the bassoon is too expensive if you decide to buy it.

A2: Playing unique instruments, rather than playing popular instruments, is of great advantage. Music teachers will give more care and attention to them.
A3: Playing a bassoon is good to your son. You don't have to buy it, you can use the school bassoon. But, its leather costs a lot.
A4: The price of bassoon is $7,000 on average. Finding an instructor to teach bassoon is a more serious problem.

Many Korean-American parents want their children to participate in schools' music programs, and through them, they also expect their children to do well in music, or to play a music instrument very well. Often, they also want to know the school policies on the selection of students for participation in the school's music programs. In evaluating those four response messages, all four respondents belong to the subgroup of information advisors to the inquirer. Moreover, the first three respondents also take on the role of encouragers to the inquirer.

On October 4, 2012, a member with a daughter in seventh grade posted a message requesting information about summer camp. Five response messages followed it:

Q: I have a daughter in 7th grade. My family came to the United States quite recently, so I don't know much about American educational systems. One day, I had a chance to converse on the importance of school districts with my acquaintance who also suggested me to send my daughter to a summer writing or leadership camp program at UCLA. I also learned that each program costs six or seven thousand dollars. Is this really true? Without a good record of academic performance, is it also difficult to get admissions to such summer camp programs?
A1: The cost of a two-week summer camp program for high school students is 1,500 dollars or so. I am talking about one of them offered in Massachusetts, with the inclusion of a dormitory fee. My child failed to get into this program in spite of her good academic standing and the submission of a teacher's letter of recommendation. I guessed that her essay seemed to be not so great. All applicants for summer camp programs are not admitted.
A2: You don't have to worry about it too much. Your child can go to a selective college without any record of attendance in summer camp programs. Many universities offer summer camp programs for middle and high school students. And there is no close linkage between participation in a summer camp program in a certain college or university and admission to it after high school graduation. The range of the cost of summer camp programs is six to seven thousand dollars . . .
A3: I have two children, one in a middle school and the other in a high school. For middle school students, summer camp programs are not much effective. . . . And the cost of these programs is four to five thousand dollars at least. But there are some good, specialized summer camp programs for high school students. My conclusion is that you don't have to spend a lot of money by sending your child to a summer camp program. Colleges run summer camps for profit. That's it.

A4: You can send a college summer camp program when your child becomes a 10th or 11th grader. It is better to send your child to a cram school that provides an intensive summer writing course. College writing summer programs are run for profit. But, sending one to a college summer program is a good strategy if your child thinks of an early application to that college.
A5: Sending your child to a college summer camp program is not required in the college application package. I spent more than three thousand dollars for a three-week program.

Some Korean-American parents, like this inquirer, believe that children's attendance in college summer camp during middle or high school has a positive factor on their admission to prestigious American colleges or universities. The messages of all five respondents unveil their roles as information advisors to the inquirer. Respondent 2 (A2) also takes on the role of an information confirmer to the inquirer. With this respondent, three other respondents (A2, A4, and A4) also belong to the subgroup of information analysts for the inquirer.

On December 1, 2012, a member posted the message requesting information (or advice) about the teacher's judgment regarding the teacher's decision to place her teenager in seventh grade in detention. There were three response messages for this post:

Q: My child was excelling in his studies. Before the start of another class, my child's homeroom teacher noticed that my child was helping two other classmates with homework. As a result, my child received detention and zero points on that assignment. . . . I thought that helping other students is not part of cheating. So I wrote the teacher a letter requesting the reconsideration of [his/her] earlier decision. However, my appeal was not accepted on the ground of school policy. . . . Still I don't get it. Does it also have a negative impact on my child's access to junior honor society next year?
A1: You need to check the school policy on homework help in class from the student handbook, school website, or school district website. If these sources are unclear in the description, you can request from the school principal a formal copy of school detention policy in your child's case. . . . If your child helped with some part of the assignment for the other two students without letting them copy the entire homework, the detention decision should be reconsidered. I don't know its impact on your child's future disadvantages.
A2: The context is very important. If that homeroom teacher announced the completion of that homework on their own like take-home exams, the detention would be justified.
A3: It doesn't matter in a team project. It can be treated as a cheating case if that was an individual assignment. My child's school has exactly the same policy.

American public schools under the guidance of the state board of education and the district board of education have the written statement of their schools' integrity policy, academic honor code, or code of student conduct, for cheating, lying, and stealing. The message posted by Respondent 1 (A1) shows her role as an information advisor to the inquirer. Generally, all three respondents belong to the subgroup of information analysts for the inquirer because they attempted to explain the conditions determining differences in cheating and no cheating.

American High School Education

In the category of American high school education, there were many posts on diverse topics that include the purchase of textbooks, sports, music classes, volunteering, AP (Advance Placement) class, PSAT (the Preliminary SAT), SAT (the Scholastic Aptitude Test) or ACT (American College Testing), school policy violations, counseling for college, teachers' letters of recommendation, majors in college, recommendations on certain colleges or universities, college loan, aid, or scholarship, the FAFSA (the Free Application for Federal Student Aid) or CSS (the College Scholarship Service), college interview, college tuition, and the like. Of them, some messages on six topics are introduced below. First of all, one member posted a message requesting information about an advanced placement course (AP) on September 9, 2012. Four members responded to this post very shortly:

> Q: My daughter in 11th grade applied to take AP chemistry, but she could not get into that course. She should take it. Is there any idea to take it?
> A1: It seems to be late. My son got the announcement about his AP courses before the start of summer break.
> A2: If there is no seat available at this time, it will be difficult to get into that course. You need to ask the school to have an option to take an online AP course, instead.
> A3: Your child can take it either from a community college near your community or during summer. Schools accept such credits.
> A4: It is possible to take AP exam by self-study.

In general, eligibility for taking an AP course in school needs recommendation from current year's teacher and supervisor in the subject field. In this message thread, all four respondents belong to the subgroup of information advisors to the inquirer. Moreover, encouragement to the inquirer is contained in the messages of two respondents (A3 and A4).

On October 1, 2012, there was a message requesting information about how to report SAT and ACT scores to the colleges that the student will apply to, from a member who has a teenager in twelfth grade. This post received ten response messages, the first five of which are introduced here:

> Q: Like me, this time must be a very stressful time for all the mothers having their children in 12th grade. . . . My child received the score for ACT. I am not sure whether this ACT score should be sent to the colleges being applied. My child took the SAT three times earlier and the highest score was 2,290, but 710 only in critical reading. This relatively low score in critical reading initiated her taking of ACT. Her ACT scores were 33 in writing and science and 34 in critical reading . . .
> A1: Someone told me that critical reading in SAT is a little bit more difficult than that in ACT. The school counselor I met advised me that the science score in ACT is of no particular importance. Don't take tests any more. The test scores taken from the SAT and ACT are very similar so that you need to report both to the colleges being applied. This time, your focus should be on improvement on essays.
> A2: Your child can take as many tests as your child wants. The scores are at higher tier. GPA [grade point average] is also very important. In addition, it is necessary to prepare other important things required by the colleges that select their students on their own criteria.
> A3: The score of 2,290 in SAT is the same as 34 in ACT. The change in ten points up and down has no substantial meaning. One merit of ACT is that the students weak in critical reading can raise their score because the critical reading of ACT is less difficult than that of SAT . . .
> A4: When applying to selective colleges, the score of 710 in critical reading is not a bad score at all.
> A5: Your child's scores in SAT and ACT are similar to my child who received 2,290 in SAT and 34 in ACT. . . . An admission to one of the top American colleges or universities was very challenging in my case. Your child also needs to have a good GPA, strong letters of recommendations, well-written essays, and the record of other extra-curricular activities.

The SAT (the Scholastic Aptitude Test) and ACT (American College Testing) are two most well-known standardized tests widely used for college admissions in the United States. The score of either test is a critical part and condition for college admission. To some degree, three respondents (A1, A3, and A5) can be classified into the subgroup of information analysts for the inquirer because they attempted to explain implications about the scores from both tests. Overall, all five respondents belong to the subgroup of information advisors to the inquirer.

On May 7, 2012, a member posted an inquiry message on a letter of recommendation from teachers for the college admission of her high school child. There were four response messages from three members and four additional posts from the inquirer:

> Q: My child is now in 10th grade. When applying for colleges, is it correct to include a letter of recommendation from a teacher in the application package? From what subject teacher should that letter be obtained?

A1: Most private colleges and universities tend to request two letters of recommendation. Those two letters are requested to the teachers mostly taught in their 11th or 12th grade. Or one letter can be asked for to their guidance counselors who know the students very well. . . . Your child needs to show some impression to the teachers whom your child is thinking to ask for a letter of recommendation.
Q: Now I can understand what you mean. . . . Let me add one more question. If teachers are asked for by students, do they write a letter of recommendation for them?
A1: Most teachers will write a letter of recommendation for students of good academic performance and behaviors in their teaching classes. I attended an American high school where all three teachers wrote letters of recommendation for me upon my requests. But I remember the refusal of my art teacher to write a student a letter of recommendation. . . . After receiving the letters of recommendation, don't forget to send a thank you card and a small gift like a $20 Starbucks gift card. . .
Q: Thank you for posting detailed comments.
A2: Try to receive letters of recommendation from the teachers who have liked your child or who have taught the subjects your child will major in college. Often, three letters of recommendations are needed; two from teachers and one from a guidance counselor.
Q: Thank you for providing valuable information.
A3: To get letters of recommendation, my child has tried to be acquainted with the teachers of subjects similar to my child's major in college. Moreover, my child often left school to help those teachers or to work on projects with them and their other students.

All three respondents belong to the subgroup of information analysts for the inquirer. Likewise, they all take on the role of information advisors to the inquirer, alike. For example, as both an information analyst and an information advisor, Respondent 1 (A1) informed the inquirer of the total number of letters of recommendation needed, and also provided the inquirer her explanations and advice about specific things needed to be done so as to receive a letter of recommendation from teachers.

A message seeking information about some universities in the state of Texas was posted on February 5, 2012. Four members responded to this post:

Q: I would like to know some information about dormitory facilities, the atmosphere of the campus, and the racial and ethnic composition of students in the six best universities in the state of Texas; University of Texas at Austin, Texas A&M University, Texas Tech University, Baylor University, University of Texas at Dallas, and SMU [Southern Methodist University].
A1: SMU has a beautiful campus, many white students, and many students from wealthy families. And it is very safe, as well. The campus of the University of Texas at Austin is big and many Asian students attend this school.

> A2: If you consider an undergraduate-level university, I think that the University of Texas at Austin is best, especially the atmosphere of the campus and a relatively large number of international students.
> A3: The dormitory of the University of Texas at Austin is not in a good condition. . . . But it must be the best university in Texas. Texas A&M University is also a good university, but its surrounding environment is not much attractive. . . . Both universities have many international students.
> A4: Actually, the best university in Texas is Rice University.

The first three respondents (A1, A2, and A3) take on the role of information analysts for the inquirer. The role of an information advisor to the inquirer can be also revealed in the message of Respondent 2 (A2), while Respondent 4 (A4) can be treated as the only information describer to the inquirer in this message thread.

On March 6, 2012, one member posted a message requesting information on college financial aid for low-income students. Thereafter, there were six response messages, the first four of which are introduced below:

> Q: My family came to the U.S. almost a year ago. I am living in California, currently working, and my average hourly earnings are 20 dollars or so. . . . Somebody told me that college tuition here is very expensive, but financial aid is available for low-income students. Can you inform me of the eligibility of college financial aid based upon annual income? If my child gets admission to the University of California, for example, how much do I have to pay for college tuition from my pocket? And how much can my child receive financial aid? My husband cannot find a job yet and we came to the U.S. for my children's education. There will be no hope for my family if college financial aid is unavailable.
> A1: Don't worry about it. Your child will receive a substantial financial aid package from the colleges.
> A2: Your child will receive some financial aid in attending a public university in your state of residence. But, one condition is that the period of your in-state residence should be more than 365 days. If your family's annual income is below 60,000 dollars, try to apply to private universities and if admitted, a 100 percent financial aid will be provided to your child . . .
> A3: Given your family's permanent resident status, the degree of financial aid for low-income students will vary according to the number of their family members. Even if your child cannot receive it entirely, your child can use educational loans and pay for them after college graduation. In addition, your child can also apply for state grants or many types of scholarships provided by companies to make up the payment of college tuition.
> A4: College students from low-income families can use government-sponsored grants through FAFSA [the Free Application for Federal Student Aid], and they don't have to pay them back. In Korea, the college scholarship is based upon merit, whereas in the U.S. it is based upon need.

There are a wide variety of scholarship and financial aid programs available at federal, state, and college levels. As stressed above, at the federal level, those high school students admitted in college and current college students are considered to receive need-based grants, low-interest loans, or a financial support through the federal work-study program. Moreover, most American states offer various types of financial support—e.g., grants, scholarships, low-interest educational loans—to those students attending their state public colleges or universities. In the series of these posts, the roles of both information analysts and information advisors for the inquirer are clearly revealed in the messages of three respondents (A2, A3, and A4). Respondent 1 (A1) can be also identified as an information advisor to her. Besides, two respondents' messages (A1 and A2) posted the texts that contained encouragement to the inquirer.

On January 6, 2012, one member posted a message requesting information about the application of the FAFSA (the Free Application for Federal Student Aid). After this post on the "Life Q&A" message board, there were three response messages and another post from the inquirer:

> Q: I am in trouble in the section of income tax in FAFSA form. Can my child's school counselor help fill it in if I bring this form with my document of income tax return? Or do I have to do this through a CPA [certified public account] or any other organizations? And I am not sure whether CAL Grant [the grant funded by the State of California] is separately prepared, or part of the application of FAFSA . . .
>
> A1: After applying for FAFSA and filing your child's GPA [grade point average] by school before March 1st, CAL Grant is automatically applied. You should make sure whether your child's school reports your child's GPA. You and your child should prepare for the FAFSA application on your own. But you can ask for help to a CPA when you are in trouble.
>
> A2: You can do the application of FAFSA yourself. Read the instruction carefully and follow it. . . . In my case, I spent less than half an hour to complete it. When you ask for help to someone like a CPA, of course, you should pay for a service fee. That is your unnecessary spending of money . . .
>
> A3: One FAFSA application determines the eligibility and amounts of all grants provided by the federal government, the state, and the school. In the section of annual income, report information separately in the columns of father and mother, generally fill in information according to the numbers assigned to 1040E and 1040EZ [tax forms]. . . . Please try it. If you have trouble during your time of preparing FAFSA and post your problem on this message board, I will try to answer your inquiry.
>
> Q: Thank you for responding to my post. I will attempt to prepare the FAFSA application with my child . . .

The FAFSA (the Free Application for Federal Student Aid) is the financial assistance programs for those entering college or current college students who hold American citizenship or legal permanent resident status, and it is being offered and administered by the U.S. Department of Education. By an annual application of the FAFSA, students are determined to receive certain federal grants, loans, or work-study funds.[34] In the perspective of social support, two of these three respondents (A1 and A3) belong to the subgroup of information analysts for the inquirer. The role of information advisors to the inquirer is revealed in the messages of all three respondents. Additionally, two respondents (A2 and A3) appear to take on the role of encouragers to the inquirer.

American College Education

In the category of American college education, many topics were posted on the "Life Q&A" message board of the "MissyUSA" community. The list of major topics in this category includes college transfer, college grade, college tuition, college loan, aid, or scholarship, the FAFSA (the Free Application for Federal Student Aid), college club activity, online class, health insurance, ROTC [Reserve Officers' Training Corps], job searching, dormitory life, and so on. Of these different topics, some messages on four topics are in detail illustrated below. At first, one member posted a message requesting information about the eligibility of in-state college tuition on January 6, 2012. Five members responded to this post:

> Q: After attending a college for a year, is it qualified to receive in-state tuition? I am talking about The University of Michigan, Pittsburgh University, New York University, Boston University, and Ohio State University. Can in-state tuition be applied if working part-time there, or if just living there?
> A1: The policy of in-state tuition varies from state to state. You need to check it from each university. The eligibility of in-state tuition requires residence in the state, with its verification.
> A2: In private universities, there is no concept of in-state or out-of-state tuition. Let me add more. First, the eligibility of in-state tuition necessitates the parent's real move toward the states where their children go to colleges and then, their residence over one year. Second, in-state tuition is ineligible for those students who are younger than 24 years old. Third, those students of no surviving parent or at age 24 and over can change their residential address and are eligible for in-state tuition after their one-year residence.
> A3: In my state, in-state tuition for students younger than 24 years old is related to the amount of their parents' income tax return. Another important condition of the eligibility for in-state tuition is proof of your full-time employment. You need to contact each university for this matter.
> A4: That is inapplicable to the state of Michigan.

> A5: The policy of in-state tuition varies from state to state. One state I know uses citizenship status as the important requirement in determining in-state tuition.

Different eligibility rules for in-state college tuition are well stated especially from the posting of two respondents (A2 and A3). By and large, four respondents, except for Respondent 4 (A4) who is positioned as the information describer, belong to the subgroup of information analysts for the inquirer. Two of them (A1 and A3) also take on the role of information advisors for her.

On January 5, 2012, a member having a youngster in college posted a message requesting information about the application of the FAFSA. This post received eight response messages, the first five of which are introduced here:

> Q: My family has two income sources, one from me and my husband and the other from my son who worked part-time. His income was almost $3,000 and our combined income was less than $75,000. Can we get some financial aid through FAFSA? Is it also possible to receive the CAL Grant [a financial aid program administrated by the California Student Aid Commission]? His GPA was 3.4. If it is eligible for receiving a financial aid through the FAFSA, what about the CAL Grant?
> A1: As far as I know, student aid funds will be available if the total annual income of your family ranges below $60,000 or $70,000. Given its qualification, there are some free grants.
> A2: Everyone can file for the FAFSA regardless of their total annual income. Even private universities use the FAFSA to provide financial aid for their students. For example, Princeton University offers some financial aid to their FAFSA applicants whose annual family income is even more than $200,000.
> A3: If the application of the FAFSA is accepted, the CAL Grant is automatically filed. . . . In the UC [University of California], college tuition is paid off from the FAFSA if the total annual income of college student families is below $70,000. The Cal Grant is also eligible with 3.0 GPA as a minimum.
> A4: In this year of 2012, college tuition in the University of California is fully assisted from the FAFSA when the total annual income of college student families is below $80,000, not below $70,000. I found this information filing the FAFSA from my two students attending the UC.
> A5: The deadline for the FAFSA application is on March 2nd. If you didn't report income tax yet, put your expected income in the income column of the FAFSA. Later on, you can correct it.

Three out of these five respondents (A1, A3, and A4) can be regarded as the subgroup of information confirmers to the inquirer. Like Respondent 2 (A2), they also belong to the subgroup of information analysts for her, whereas the role of an information advisor to her is revealed in the message of Respondent 5 (A5).

On May 2, 2012, there was a post requesting information about registering for classes without health insurance. After this post, there were the eight messages in response to it, the first five of which are introduced here:

> Q: The health insurance of my child in the college was covered by a health plan provided by the company. But there will be unlikely for my child to have health insurance due to my move to another company. In my memory, the registration for the class last year seemed to be done with the verification of a health plan. Without it, is it impossible to register for the class? I am not sure whether health insurance is required or just optional.
> A1: You can buy a health plan from the college. The total cost per year is nearly $2,000. This amount is actually the cheapest . . .
> A2: Your child cannot register for the class without a health plan. In my case, I purchased a health insurance from my college . . .
> A3: In the case of my college, international students should have had a health plan, but it was an option to American citizens.
> A4: If Obamacare [or Affordable Care Act] is enacted, the children aged up to 24 will still become dependents in their parent's health plans.[35]
> A5: My child in the college is a dependent in the company's health plan. So we do not have to buy the college's health plan.

Two respondents (A1 and A2) can be classified as the subgroup of information advisors to the inquirer. Respondent 3(A3) is positioned as the information analyst for the inquirer, but the messages of the two other respondents (A4 and A5), as the subgroup of information describers, had no direct information sought by the inquirer.

A message seeking information about a payment method to a college dormitory was posted by a member on September 7, 2012. Four response messages were posted after it:

> Q: My daughter is now a sophomore at UC-Riverside. In her freshman year, she stayed in its dormitory. Today, she moved into its apartment because of her aversion to the food menu in the dormitory, and I paid for $700 at the time of receiving her apartment key. Do I have to pay for this amount of money every month? We applied for the FAFSA and I thought that her apartment fees would be covered by it. I am a single mom and earned almost $12,000 last year . . . I don't know what's going on.
> A1: Based upon your tax return of last year, your daughter's college tuition, in addition to some aids to other educational expenses, would have been fully funded through the FAFSA, but it does not cover the dormitory cost. I am also a single mom and had an experience similar to yours before. If your daughter is attending a public university in your state, why not commute from home to school? To save the dormitory fee, my child commuted from home to school. It is not a good attitude to request a full support from government in the name of a poor single mom with children.

A2: In the annual package of your daughter's educational grants or loans, all educational expenses like tuition, room or board, and meal plan are usually included. Check this from your daughter who might not have shared this information with you.
A3: I believe that your daughter must receive a financial aid that includes the cost of her apartment. . . . You should talk to your daughter on this matter.
A4: Ask your daughter to check her bank account in which her loan or grant for the amount of dormitory cost might be deposited.

Two respondents (A1 and A2) are positioned to take on the role of information analysts for the inquirer, and all four respondents (A2, A3, and A4) belong to the subgroup of information advisors to the inquirer. Besides, companionship to the inquirer is revealed in the message of Respondent 1 (A1).

SUMMARY

Most Korean mothers with a school-age child or children in the United States have a strong commitment to their children's education. Some of these Korean-American mothers make their constant efforts for promoting their children's academic performance and adjustment at school in various ways, such as through communicating with their children about school life, helping them with homework, participating in school activities (PTA, volunteering), or contacting teachers or school officials. Moreover, they also recognize that their information or knowledge about the formal or informal rules of the American educational institution and its national or local school systems is as equally important as their concerns about, or their direct involvement for, their children' education and better school life. Here, an important point is that a great deal of valuable information can be obtained usually through participation in social networks. Thus, membership in social networks often leads their members to have greater access to certain valuable information that is unlikely or sometimes very difficult for non-members of these social networks to gain. This is also true of the case of the American educational institution.

As stressed earlier, the Korean American women's online community—specifically, the "Life Q&A" message board of the "MissyUSA" community—is one of such social networks by which some of its online members can request a wide range of information about the rules of the American educational institution to its other members. From the perspective of information seekers (or inquirers), in particular, this Korean-American women's online community has become a network of social resources (or information), which is known as one form of social capital. In this chapter, some of its members' inquiries on information about the certain formal or informal rules of the American educational institution and its local school systems have been specifically illustrated by focusing on such topics as school absence, gifted and talented program (G&T), school dress code, grade skipping, detention, AP class, the SAT or the ACT, educational loan in college, in-state college tuition, college health insurance, and the like.

Social support is another form of social capital. As the online social network, the "MissyUSA" community also generates social support among its participating members. Indeed, this Korean-American women's online community becomes not only the network of social resources for its inquirers (information seekers), but also a network of social supporters from which its respondents transmit their information, knowledge, or advice, or express their encouragement for their other members (inquirers) who sought information or advice. In general, this chapter of the American education institution has shown that many respondents to the postings seeking information about the various rules of the American educational institution belong to the group of instrumental guiders, especially either subgroups of information analysts or information advisors, or both, to most inquirers. Additionally, some respondents' messages have also shown that they sometimes belong to information describers, information confirmers, or emotional supporters, especially encouragers, to those inquirers in trouble or in distress.

NOTES

1. Jamie Lew, "The 'Other' Story of Model Minorities: Korean American High School Dropouts in an Urban Context," *Anthropology & Education Quarterly* 35 (2004): 303–323; Yongmin Sun, "The Academic Success of East-Asian-American Students: An Investment Model," *Social Science Research* 27 (1998): 432–56; and Nazli Kibria, *Becoming Asian American: Second-Generation Chinese and Korean American Identities* (Baltimore, MD: The Johns Hopkins University, 2002).
2. For more information, see the link on the website of the U.S. Department of Education: http://www2.ed.gov/about/overview/mission/mission.html.
3. For more information, see the website of the New York State Education Department: http://usny.nysed.gov/about.
4. For more information, see the website of the New York City Department of Education: http://schools.nyc.gov/default.htm.
5. Available at http://insideschools.org/districts/manhattan/district-5.
6. Available at http://csd3.nycdoe.org/.
7. Ibid.
8. David F. Labaree, *Someone Has To Fail: The Zero-Sum Game of Public Schooling* (Cambridge, MA: Harvard University Press, 2010); and David F. Labaree, "Consuming the Public School," *Educational Theory* 6 (2011): 381–394.
9. Further information on the 1964 Civil Rights Act barring discrimination in education is available at http://www2.ed.gov/about/offices/list/ocr/docs/hq43e4.html.
10. Ibid.
11. Detailed contents of Elementary and Secondary Education Act of 1965 are available at http://www2.ed.gov/policy/elsec/leg/esea02/pg1.html.
12. National Center for Educational Statistics, *Digest of Educational Statistics* (Institute of Education Sciences, 2011).

13. David F. Labaree, "Consuming the Public School"; and David F. Labaree, "Public Goods, Private Goods: The American Struggle over Educational Goals," *American Educational Research Journal* 34 (1997): 39–81.

14. The original document of the Higher Education Act of 1968 can be assessed at ftp://ftp.resource.org/gao.gov/89-329/00004C57.pdf.

15. The Office of Federal Student Aid provides information on eligibility requirements, comprehensive types of the student financial assistance programs (scholarships, loans, and work-study funds), and for specific procedures to apply for it (Free Application for Federal Student Aid called FAFSA), see the link: http://studentaid.ed.gov/about.

16. David F. Labaree, *Someone Has To Fail*; and David F. Labaree, "Consuming the Public School."

17. National Center for Educational Statistics, *Digest of Educational Statistics*.

18. Pearl R. Kane, "The Difference between Charter Schools and Charterlike Schools" in *City Schools: Lessons from New York*, eds. Diane Ravitch and Joseph P. Viteritti (Baltimore, MD: The Johns Hopkins University Press, 2000), 65–87. As of 2012, most states (forty-two) passed a charter school law that permits the establishment of charter schools. For example, charter school became part of New York State's public education after the enactment of the New York State Chart Schools Act of 1998. For more information about charter schools in New York States, see http://www.p12.nysed.gov/psc/. In addition to charter schools, another well-known category of school choice program is homeschooling that allows parents to educate their children at home and vouchers. There are specific rules and procedures for homeschooling. For the case of New York City, see the link: http://schools.nyc.gov/documents/d75/district/attendance/home_schooling/HOMESCHOOLING_PROCEDURES_bb.pdf.

19. For more information, see the link on the website of the U.S. Department of Education: http://www2.ed.gov/programs/magnet.

20. For more information, see the link on the website of the New York City Department of Education: http://www.schools.nyc.gov/Academics/GiftedandTalented.

21. Honors and AP classes have been established at the high school level. Both Honors and AP classes are for high-achieving students from individual subjects. Thus, advanced-level courses are offered in both Honors and AP classes. The main difference between them is that those students taking AP classes learn college-level contents in the subjects and should take the AP test for college credits based upon exam scores. A good illustration of the eligibility requirements for Honors and AP classes in New York City public high schools is available at http://schools.nyc.gov/SchoolPortals/10/X141/EducationalSupport/Guidance/hs+guidance.htm.

22. U.S. Department of Education, *Overview of the U.S. Department of Education* (Washington, DC: Office of Communications and Outreach, 2010).

23. U.S. Department of Education, *Overview of the U.S. Department of Education*; and Institute for Educational Leadership, *Leadership for Student Learning: Recognizing the State's Role in Public Education* (Washington, DC, 2001).

24. Ibid.

25. Ibid.

26. For more information, see the link on the website of the New York City Department of Education: http://schools.nyc.gov/default.htm.

27. Ibid.

28. For further information, see the website of a school district in the State of New Jersey: http://www.wearenorwood.org.

29. For more information, see the link on the website of the New York State Education Department: http://www.highered.nysed.gov/ocue/lrp/rules.htm.

30. Hakyoon Lee, "I am a Kirogi Mother: Education Exodus and Life Transformation Among Korean Transnational Women," *Journal of Language, Identity, and Education* 9 (2010): 250–264; and Seungsook Moon, "Immigration and Mothering: Case Studies from Two Generations of Korean Immigrant Women," *Gender & Society* 17 (2003): 840–860.

31. Thurston Domina, "Leveling the Home Advantage: Assessing the Effectiveness of Parental Involvement in Elementary School," *Sociology of Education* 78 (2005): 233–249; and Annette Lareau, "School Class Differences in Family-School Relationships: The Importance of Cultural Capital," *Sociology of Education* 60 (1987): 73–85.

32. Min Zhou and Susan S. Kim, "Community Forces, Social Capital, and Educational Achievement: The Case of Supplementary Education in the Chinese and Korean Immigrant Communities," *Harvard Educational Review* 76 (2006): 1–29.

33. Soo-yong Byun and Hyunjoon Park, "The Academic Success of East Asian American Youth: The Role of Shadow Education," *Sociology of Education* 85 (2012): 40–60.

34. For more information, see the following link on the website of the U.S. Department of Education: https://studentaid.ed.gov/sa/about.

35. The Affordable Care Act, also known as Obamacare, is a comprehensive health care law proposed by President Obama and passed by the Congress. Its full passages are available at http://www.gpo.gov/fdsys/pkg/PLAW-111publ148/pdf/PLAW-111publ148.pdf.

FIVE

The American Housing Institution on the "MissyUSA" Community

Most domestic migrant families heading towards their new destinations will wish to have or look for their housing with good quality—i.e., physical structure, interiors, and/or amount of space. Family-friendly communities—i.e., the schools in the area, safety, good neighbors, open space, and local convenience facilities—are also important to them when searching for their new housing.[1] This is also true of most immigrant families. In the case of housing choice, immigrant families' migration process from their homeland to their new host country, or from one location to another in their host country, entails their efforts to find adequate housing for them to live in, including their decision of housing tenure, namely, homeownership or rental housing. Making a good decision about whether to buy or rent a house is not easy for them, especially when they lack proper knowledge about how the rules of the housing institution of their host country work. Likewise, their judgement to dwell in the same house or to move out of it also demands them to comprehend certain rules of the host country's housing institution, which include formal regulations and procedures on the rental agreement or its cancellation, payments of mortgage and property tax, a renewal of home insurance, refinancing, or the house for sale, and so forth. For them, particularly new immigrant families, their ethnic networks with family, friends, or acquaintances in the host society often stand on an important leverage that can help lower, or avoid, their uncertainty about their housing search, evaluation, and choice.[2]

Korean immigrant families in the United States are a diverse group of people in terms of their demographics, socio-economic statuses, legal immigration statuses, residential settlement patterns, and their housing preferences or needs, including their housing tenure choice: as of 2010, the homeownership rate of Korean-Americans was 48 percent, compared with 58 percent of all Asian Americans and 65 percent of the U.S. population overall.[3] To be sure, their worries or difficulties related to housing, given their generally limited proficiency in English and their relatively insufficient knowledge about the rules of the American housing institution, can be considerably alleviated by the acquisition of housing information through their personal networks or their ethnic networks—i.e., ethnic churches or non-profit organizations. Nowadays, some Korean immigrant women in the United States and Canada also make use of another type of social network, here the "MissyUSA" community, to obtain a wide range of information about the rules of the American housing institution. Indeed, this online social network has two important implications to them. First, it is a unique type of social network or community formed, and to be maintained, through an online platform. As is well known, to typical married women, their thoughts and preferences are critical for the selection of their family house because the home is so closely linked to their primary responsibilities, family and child care, as well as home management or housework, such as decorating, cleaning, and cooking.[4] Obviously, the "MissyUSA" community becomes a great online site for its participating members to exchange information about such housing-related topics, as well as a choice of their new family house or a change of the house.[5] What's more, this ethnic online community of married women is the network that also makes it possible for its members to transmit other types of housing-related information to one another—i.e., lease contract, home financing, closing, or management, the resale of owner-occupied housing units, housing search, and so on.

Second, the "MissyUSA" community is the kind of social network that creates social capital for its members. Dividing social capital into its two forms—social resources and social support, the group of information seekers (inquirers) has an unusual opportunity to seek social resources (information) by accessing the "MissyUSA" community, more specifically, its message board of "Life Q&A." Indeed, the "MissyUSA" community becomes an important medium or network, in the perspective of information seekers who want to know certain categories of information—i.e., sources, background, processes, outcomes, and/or advice—about the rules of the American housing institution. One of this book's premises that those information seekers of the "MissyUSA" community see the American social institution in the angle of their own personal interests or concerns is further applied in this chapter of the American housing institution. The reason is that most of its information seekers have a propensity to seek particular kinds of information—i.e., loan processing for a home mortgage, the amount of down payment, property tax, security deposit in rental housing—among the wide range of rules of the American housing institution on the ground of their personal interests, needs, or concerns. By and large, in this chapter, the postings of information inquiries about the rules of the American housing institution on the "MissyUSA" community are broadly divided into four thematic categories: the financing of homeownership, the home-buying process, homeowners' options and burdens, and rental housing. Thereafter, this chapter introduces some major topics in each of these four categories with specific illustrations in great detail.

Social support is the other form of social capital that also results from participation in the "MissyUSA" community. For its information providers (or respondents), this online community indeed functions as both a community of their own and a social support network for its information seekers. As was stated in earlier chapters, in this chapter, they are also classified into two broad groups in accordance with patterns of their messages in response to inquiry messages: instrumental guiders (information describers, analysts, confirmers, and advisors) and emotional supporters (companions, encouragers, and critics). As is the case of information seekers, information providers also see the rules of the American housing institution from their own perspective in responding to inquiry messages. This means that their response patterns are primarily based on their past or present participation in the American housing institution, their expertise about it, their earlier experiences with it, or hearsay about it.

In the beginning, this chapter reviews the nature of the American housing institution in modern American history in terms of its major goals, landmark laws, policies, programs, and key governing bodies: note that this succinct overview about it focuses on the private owner- and renter-occupied housing markets only. Second, this chapter discusses the relationship between both offline and online ethnic social networks of Korean-Americans and their accessibility to housing information and other related resources. Lastly, two forms of social capital (social resources and social support) are explored with some specific illustrations of online posts (inquiries and responses), from each of the aforementioned four thematic categories of the American housing institution.

THE AMERICAN HOUSING INSTITUTION: HISTORY, LAWS, AND ORGANIZATIONS

The major goals the American housing institution is on target to achieve differ substantially between its public and private sectors. For its public sector, the American housing institution primarily aims to improve housing affordability for low- and moderate income households by planning, financing, and supervising the production of more housing stock and effectively distributing existing or new housing stock in order to assist all those seeking housing, including public housing. When people are faced with the lack of affordable housing, it is quite difficult to expect them to have a normal lifestyle because the absence of suitable living space can undermine their sense of balance or rhythm in life, their health, the development of their potential, their regular economic and social activities, the dream of having their own families, and more. Although the financial situation of households creates differences in access to affordable housing, providing decent housing to all members in society must be the government's important task and responsibility. The American housing institution, at the level of the public organizational unit, ranges broadly from the U.S. Department of Housing and Urban Development (HUD) and its federal-level housing program offices or agencies (i.e., the Federal Housing Administration) to state-level housing program divisions (i.e., housing and mortgage finance agencies), to local-level housing program units (i.e., local or municipal housing authority).

On the other hand, one of the most important goals for most private, for-profit organizations of the American housing institution appears to be the pursuit of more economic interests through investment in the housing market or its related industries (home finance, real estate, construction). The collectivities of all the for-profit individuals (investors or developers) and organizations (or corporations) stretch from national to local ones in the realms of home finance (mortgage companies, banks, savings and loan associations, insurance companies) and residential housing markets (real estate and construction industries). Despite some potential conflicts of interest between the public and private sectors in the American housing institution, public-private partnerships in the home finance and housing markets become currently very strong at the jurisdiction of many state or local governments that try to supply as many houses as possible to meet the housing needs for their target groups of people.

The Financing of Homeownership

The initial step and the most important factor for homeownership is the acquisition of home finance from a mortgage lender. Before the Great Depression in 1929, most mortgage loans for single-family homes were made by private, local, or state banking institutions—i.e., savings and loan associations, life insurance companies, commercial banks, mortgage companies, and others.[6] From these mortgage lenders, most loans were granted to their borrowers on very stringent terms: higher down payment with the low loan-to-value ratio of the property (50 percent or less), the full payment requirement of the outstanding loan balance in very short terms (five to seven years), and mostly, adjustable interest rates.[7] Under the National Housing Act of 1934, the Federal Housing Administration (FHA) was established in the aftermath of the Great Depression which had caused massive foreclosures and mortgage defaults.[8] Since the enactment of this legislation, the FHA issued mortgage insurance for qualified lenders to prevent the risk of future foreclosures and mortgage defaults from borrowers as an institutionalized device to stabilize the volatile housing and mortgage markets.[9] Thus, the FHA guaranteed qualified lenders the disbursement of defaulted loans through its reserve fund that originated from a half-percent additional interest charge (mortgage interest premium) imposed on the borrowers of FHA-insured loans.

Moreover, the lenders of FHA-insured loans could raise more money for future mortgages by selling their FHA-insured loans to the government-sponsored mortgage company, known as the Federal National Mortgage Association (FNMA or Fannie Mae) launched in 1938.[10] Later on, the Veterans Administration, under the Servicemen's Readjustment Act of 1944, created its own home finance program (the VA program) similar to the FHA program to promote home purchases among military servicemen returning home.[11] In 1948, Fannie Mae also purchased VA-insured mortgage loans from these lenders. Indeed, the mortgage insurance policy of the FHA for the lenders of FHA-insured loans led to a substantial shift in mortgage terms and conditions: the high loan-to-value ratio (up to 93 percent of the property) with lower down payment, longer-term mortgage payment (25 to 30 years), and generally, very low interest rates as the result of the introduction of fixed interest rate mortgage loans.[12]

While the mortgage business continued to thrive at the time among the lenders providing the mortgage loans insured by the FHA and the VA, those lenders of non-FHA (or VA) insured loans (conventional loans)—here, mostly savings and loans and mutual savings banks called "thrifts"—were still struggling with their mortgage business that kept their loan terms very strict, as compared to those FHA-insured loan providers. Another impediment in their mortgage business was also associated with the federal regulation that prohibited them from reselling their approved loans to Fannie Mae. However, there was a breakthrough for these mortgage lenders to cope with their plight in mortgage business, as well as to compete with the lenders of FHA-insured loans in the home mortgage market, later on.[13] First, they could at last adopt less tight terms and conditions in their financing of home mortgages because they were able to have their mortgages insured by private companies—i.e., the Mortgage Guarantee Insurance Corporation of 1957 and GE Capital. Second, a legal route to sell their mortgages to raise more funds was made possible by the establishment of the Federal Home Loan Mortgage Corporation (Freddie Mac), under the Emergency Home Finance Act of 1970 that also permitted 90 percent loan-to-value ratio and a thirty-year payment term for uninsured mortgages.[14]

Third, they made aggressive attempts to raise more capital by increasing adjustable rate mortgages (ARMs) instead of fixed-rate mortgages that usually impose upon them a greater risk for borrowers' default, invest some of their deposits on other money markets (i.e., mutual funds), or to sell off below-market-rate mortgages, under the Garn-St. Germain Congressional Act of 1981.[15] Then, some provisions of this legislation were set back due to a new financial law, the Financial Institutional Reform, Recovery, and Enforcement Act of 1989 (FIRREA), which required at least 70 percent of all their loan funds in a housing or related investment as a reserve fund, along with the legal prohibition of their direct investments in real estate.[16] Taken together, the influence of these mortgage lenders (thrifts) in the mortgage market weakened further under this 1989 Act and a relatively substantial growth in the share of the nation's mortgages by Fannie Mae and Freddie Mac (i.e., more than 50 percent in 2003) and privately insured mortgage companies (i.e., almost 10 percent in 2003); thrifts shared less than one third of the nation's mortgages in 2003.[17]

To achieve the goals of making homeownership more available and affordable for low- or moderate income households, Congress and the federal government have exerted concerted efforts not only to construct a better housing finance system—as stated above, but also to develop a much more effective system to regulate housing discrimination, including discrimination in mortgage lending. In the latter case, the Fair Housing Act of 1968 was the initial comprehensive legislation to bar housing discrimination on the basis of race, color, country of origin, or religion, under the oversight of the U.S. Department of Housing and Urban Development (HUD).[18]

As for the home mortgage market, this legislation prohibited discrimination in the dissemination of loan information, the process of loan application, and loan decision. According to this law, even included in mortgage discrimination were those mortgages which were already approved but carried with more stringent requirements, such as the higher down payment, the higher interest rate with an adjustable-rate mortgage (ARM) over a fixed-rate mortgage, a certain loan type (FHA-insured loan), or short-term payment periods (fifteen or twenty years). Since then, all sorts of mortgage-related discrimination were more strongly regulated by the Equal Credit Opportunity Act of 1974 (ECOA) that authorized the Department of Justice and the other federal agencies—i.e., the Consumer Financial Protection Bureau, the Office of the Comptroller of the Currency, the Federal Reserve Board, and the Federal Deposit Insurance Corporation—to monitor the mortgage businesses of national, state, and local-level lenders, regulate their mortgage discrimination, or otherwise, to promote their fair practices in mortgage lending.[19] In the following year, the Home Mortgage Discloser Act (HMDA) of 1975 was passed by Congress and administered by the Bureau of Consumer Financial Protection to regulate local mortgage lenders' discrimination against qualified mortgage applicants from center-city, low-income, or minority neighborhoods.[20] As a supplement to the 1975 HMDA, the Community Reinvestment Act was passed in Congress in 1977 for the purpose of regulating various federal agencies that have the authorization to examine or evaluate local mortgage lenders with regard to the distribution of mortgages in number and amount for low-income minority neighborhoods.[21]

Moreover, state home financing programs were introduced in the 1968 Housing and Urban Development Act to meet the housing needs for low- or moderate-income households in the state, and to preclude their exposure to discriminatory practices in the private mortgage lending market at the state level. By 1992, all fifty states created their own housing finance agencies to finance mortgages for state and local developers and homebuyers, especially low-income first-time homebuyers, at below-market mortgage interest rates.[22] Most of these state housing finance agencies have worked in collaboration with the housing or home finance agencies of their local governments, such as the county or municipality. A large fund of state home financing programs has especially been used to promote the purchase of housing properties in urban target areas of the state, the areas designated by the federal government as economically distressed. For example, the State of New York Mortgage Agency (SONYMA) provides various mortgage programs to assist the financing of first-time homebuyers who are willing to purchase their new homes in the State of New York.[23] One of its mortgage programs, the *Achieving the Dream Program,* offers borrowers low fixed interest rates, financing up to 97 percent of the property, a 30-year payment term, and down payment assistance. But, eligibility for this program is restricted only to first-time home buyers with limited household incomes, relative to the median- or high-income households who have stable jobs, relatively good credit scores, and adequate financial assets for down payment, closing costs, and mortgage payments.

Overall, the relentless interference of U.S. federal, state, and local governments into the housing and home finance markets has been so far the key to the substantial rise in American homeownership rates since the Great Depression. Consequently, homeownership rates for American households rose from 47.8 percent in 1930, to 55 percent in 1950, 62.9 percent in 1970, and to 65 percent as of 2013.[24]

A Home-Buying Process

For prospective homebuyers, the determination of their home finance is an outcome of direct and indirect collaboration among a real estate firm (sales agent), a mortgage broker or firm (originator or processor), a mortgage bank (underwriter), the credit bureaus, an appraisal company (appraiser), and a real estate law firm (a buyer's lawyer).[25] On behalf of a customer (a loan applicant for a mortgage), a mortgage broker or firm (originator or processor) works with a real estate agent (usually, a buyer's agent) and a mortgage bank's underwriter who determines whether or not to grant a mortgage loan and the specific options and terms of a pending or approved mortgage by reviewing his or her application form and its supporting materials (work history, income, assets), the report of his or her credit history and score from the credit bureaus, and an appraiser's evaluation of the market value of a house for sale.

Before mortgage banks make their loan decisions for loan applications, the Truth in Lending Act of 1968 requires them to prepare the Truth in Lending Disclosure Statement that includes such loan information as the annual interest rate, the monthly amount of principal and interest payment, estimated property tax, and their financial charge for the loan.[26] In addition to this 1968 legislation, the Real Estate Settlement Procedures Act of 1974 (RESPA) further requires mortgage brokers and banks to provide their borrowers a notice of loan information, known as Good Faith Estimate (GFE) that should include loan terms, the loan interest rates, and specific settlement charges for each loan.[27] Even prior to the completion (or closing) of a home-buying or selling transaction, this 1974 legislation requires mortgage brokers and banks to prepare the HUD-1 Settlement Statement that discloses all itemized charges for their loan origination and all other services, including the commission for real estate agents. Indeed, both laws were enacted to protect loan borrowers against higher interest rates and more financial charges imposed from mortgage lenders. When that does happen unfortunately, loan borrowers are permitted under both laws to cancel the loan contract they had already signed.

Other private agents and companies and public-sector divisions are also involved in this typical process of home-buying and selling transactions; mortgage banks are required by the 2008 RESPA Rule to include these units' disparate service charges in the HUD-1 Settlement Statement.[28] First of all, a title company—i.e., National Land Title Agency—issues title insurance policies for both mortgage banks and prospective homebuyers to prove and secure the legal ownership to the property. Second, a land surveyor's report that the property boundaries of dwellings, yards, or fences are certified is required to be submitted to mortgage lenders. Third, prospective homebuyers must also purchase a homeowner's insurance policy on the property and submit its evidence to mortgage lenders; in some areas, the purchase of a flood insurance policy is additionally required. Fourth, most of the housing purchase process accompanies the home inspection of the property in the market through the home inspectors often hired by prospective homebuyers in order to identify its physical conditions, and many states further require sellers to perform a radon test of the property—a measure of the level of a radioactive gas in the property—to prevent the health risks of new home occupiers. Fifth, prospective homebuyers should contact county recording offices to record the deed of trust that shows the official ownership of the property and a mortgage lien within which mortgage banks can claim the ownership of the property in the event of homeowners' defaults on mortgage payments. Lastly, the transaction is completed after homebuyers sign all necessary documents—i.e., borrower's closing affidavit, the mortgage note, a certificate of occupancy, tax authorization notice, uniform residential loan application, a truth in lending statement, and so on, which are reviewed and certified by their settlement agent (buyer's attorney).

Homeowners' Options and Burdens

The refinancing of a mortgaged home, similar to the general process of home finance, needs direct and indirect collaboration among mortgage brokers or banks (originators, underwriters, and attorneys as settlement agents), the credit bureaus, an appraisal company, and a title company for title search and title insurance. For most homeowners, mortgage payments are usually the biggest item in their household expenditures. As a way to alleviate the financial strain caused by their higher monthly mortgage payments, some homeowners consider the option of their mortgage refinancing that often makes it possible for them to improve their mortgage terms and conditions—i.e., the cancellation of mortgage insurance premium applied to less than 20 percent down payment, the transition into fixed-rate mortgages from current adjustable rate mortgages (ARMs), lower interest rates, or longer payment periods—after negotiations with their own or other mortgage banks.

Another important reason why some homeowners refinance their mortgages is to cash out their home equity for money. Homeowners' regular and continuous payments of monthly mortgage bills gradually contribute to a rise in the market value of the properties over the balance owed on mortgages (debts) for which these homeowners accumulate equity from their homes. Some homeowners in this situation can have an opportunity to take out their equity through their new home equity loans. To protect them from high-cost refinances or home-equity loans from mortgage banks, the Homeownership and Equity Protection Act of 1994 (HOEPA) includes such provisions that mortgage banks are legally required to avoid certain high-interest loan terms or any prepayment charges for a loan process, and to disclose their mortgage origination fees.[29] Because of this tight regulation on mortgage refinancing, recently, many homeowners have faced difficulties in obtaining refinances or home-equity loans from mortgage lenders in spite of good records of their regular mortgage payments. In fact, this also has to do with the U.S. housing market crisis of 2006 from which the market value of their properties dropped substantially and it has yet to fully recover. Luckily, some homeowners in financial troubles have been eligible to obtain their mortgages since 2009 through the Home Affordable Refinance Program (HARP), which is known as one specific program of the Making Home

Affordable Program (MHA) administered by the Federal Housing Finance Agency (FHFA).[30]

Instead of mortgage refinancing, some homeowners experiencing financial hardship and in no default of mortgage payments will consider selling their homes, for whatever reason. Throughout the process of selling their homes, property sellers need to work closely with their real estate agents and settlement agents (attorneys) to contact their mortgage banks in cases that their mortgage loans are not in the state of full payment, and to handle their real estate transfer taxes and their pre-paid or unpaid property taxes with state or local government's taxation divisions.[31] Unfortunately, selling homes by mortgage banks can also occur at a time when homeowners default on mortgage payments for certain months in a row. There is no question that a loan modification with the mortgage lenders or the federal agency (the Federal Housing Finance Agency) will be typically their first serious attempt to lower their monthly mortgage payments.[32] When their efforts to modify their mortgage terms fail, then, they have two general types of involuntary options to sell their homes: short sale, also called "preforeclosure," and foreclosure.[33] As a common procedure of house short sales, mortgage lenders allow homeowners to sell their homes, but their selling prices are determined by their mortgage lenders who also have the right to negotiate with prospective homebuyers.

In contrast, some lenders use the foreclosure option within which they issue a notice of default, repossess the properties from defaulted homeowners, and resell the properties in the market. However, some mortgage lenders are less inclined to choose the foreclosure option. For example, the foreclosure laws of twenty-one states—e.g., New York, New Jersey, Illinois—require the judicial process through the court, which often causes the delay in the foreclosure of the properties or can make it very difficult to foreclose on the properties.[34] Anyhow, as long as the properties are owned by homeowners, they have to pay property taxes to their municipal or local finance or taxation departments on a regular basis (semi-annual or quarterly payments).

Rental Housing

Since the early 1970s, some U.S. states adopted all or part of the Uniform Residential Landlord and Tenant Act of 1972 (URLTA) that states the uniform terms and conditions of the rental agreement between a tenant and a landlord.[35] For those states who did not entirely adopt the URLTA, their tenant-landlord laws were, or can be, introduced not only by state legislatures (statutes) and state Supreme Courts (case laws), but also by local jurisdictions (ordinances) within a state—i.e., city, county, or town. In most states, their residential laws and provisions have been mostly regulated by state or local government agencies (i.e., Department of Consumer Affairs). Below, tenants' and landlords' rights and obligations in residential leases are briefly summarized by looking into the tenant-landlord laws and provisions of three states (California, New Jersey, and Tennessee) that embraced the URLTA completely.[36]

As usually manifested in the lease contract, prior to moving into a rental unit, the tenant has the right to inspect its physical conditions—i.e., kitchen, windows, bathroom, floor, electricity, heat, air conditioning—and then, can request that the landlord fix any malfunctioning equipment or damaged items. Basically, this rule of residential lease, called "the warranty of habitability," was enacted to protect tenants' health and safety during their occupancy in the rental unit. On the other hand, the landlord can request the tenant to pay a security deposit—i.e., usually one and a half months' amount of the monthly rent in the state of New Jersey—which can be used by the landlord in such happenings of the tenant's nonpayment of rent caused by the early termination of lease or for repairs of damaged property after the termination of lease. During the occupancy in the rental unit, according to the lease contract with the landlord, the tenant should comply with some of its certain rules. Here, the most important compulsory obligation for the tenant is to pay rent at the beginning of each month, usually on the first day of each month. It is also important for the tenant to maintain the rental unit in a clean, safe, sanitary, and good condition. But, making all necessary repairs or replacements to the malfunctioning facilities of the rental unit—i.e., the heating, the plumbing, or the electricity—is generally on the landlord's responsibility. Moreover, the landlord should abide by another legal tenant-landlord rule, "the covenant of quiet enjoyment" that prohibits him or her, without the tenant's permission, to enter into the dwelling units rented to the tenant. This regulation protects all the tenants under the provision of the unlawful access to their rental units by the landlord or others, as well as under the legal prohibition on the landlord's harassment against the tenants.

A yearly rental agreement terminates when the tenant gives no indication of a renewal of the lease after receiving a sixty-day advance notice from the landlord. A yearly lease contract also ends as the tenant addresses the vacation of the rental unit in the writing of a thirty-day advance notice toward the landlord. When there is no written notice from either party until the end of the lease term, the lease will be automatically renewed on a month-to-month basis. At the end of the lease, before moving out of the rented property, the tenant should make repairs to its damaged parts and leave it clean. If no defect in the rental unit has been found after an inspection, the landlord should return the full amount of the security deposit to the tenant. If that is not the case, the landlord can deduct a certain amount of the security deposit that corresponds to the costs of repairing or cleaning up the rental unit. In some cases, a convincing reason such as a job transfer to another region can cause the tenants to break the lease agreement before the end of its term. Despite such unavoidable circumstances, the tenants are responsible for the payment of the rent up to the remaining months of the lease term on the condition that the rental unit would remain vacant during that time. Otherwise, the tenants may continue to stay in the rental unit without payments of rent even after the expiration of the lease term. In this situation, the eviction of the tenants directly by the landlord, called a "self-help" eviction, is regarded as unlawful. Instead, the legal eviction process of the tenants must start from the landlord's complaints to local courts, proceed with the court hearing, and end with the sheriff's removal of the tenants from the rental unit with the judge's decision to evict the tenants.

HOUSING AND SOCIAL CAPITAL IN THE KOREAN-AMERICAN COMMUNITY

For Korean immigrants—particularly, new Korean immigrants, the existence of their social networks with earlier settled family members and friends in the United States can be very important for them to reduce their uncertainty that may come out on the housing search, the acquisition of a house, or a decision of their settlement in certain areas. It is because these earlier settled family members and friends in the United States tend to take on the role of their housing searchers in place of them before immigration or after arrival. It is also because they often become their reliable informants or communicators who share with them information on the size, quality, price, or location of the rental units found, or information for homeownership that includes housing finance and other required steps for it. In some cases, these U.S. family members and friends also become their co-signers of the lease contract when they have poor credit or employment history, or as financial helpers for rent security deposit or a down payment on a house.

Other types of social networks, such as those through co-ethnic businesses or organizations, also thrive, especially in the larger Korean-American gateway cities or suburban communities. As for housing-related matters in one of these areas, for example, the collectivity or spatial cluster of a greater number of Korean-American mortgage brokers or real estate sales agents is one of those social networks. Otherwise, the relatively large size of Korean-American populations in these selected large Korean American gateways—i.e., Los Angeles, New York, Chicago, San Francisco, Honolulu, or Atlanta—leads the prosperity of these Korean-owned or -targeted real estate business firms or services. For Korean-American customers looking for housing within these areas, therefore, they can rely on those co-ethnic real estate brokers or agents who have the ability to communicate with them in Korean, comprehend their specific needs and preferences for housing, and assess current local real estate listings more easily. When ethnic immigrants have their own housing submarkets in a U.S. urban area, their homeownership rates also rise.[37] In the same context, the possibility of becoming homeowners will also be expected to increase among Korean-Americans living in their urban gateway metropolitan areas where many potential homebuyers among them have little or no difficulty contacting their co-ethnic real estate brokers or agents. In addition to a good understanding of their Korean-American customers' housing choices or preferences and their better knowledge of the U.S. financial and real estate markets in both mortgage financing and the updated transactions of residential units, the direct or indirect connections of these co-ethnic real estate brokers or agents to some of the mortgage lenders (or companies) can also work as another positive factor for promoting Korean-American families' homeownership rates, especially within the territories of Korean-American gateways.

In a typical, larger Korean-American gateway city or community, there exist not only many Korean-American owned- or -targeted real estate firms of different scales, but also many other Korean-American small business owners, such as those of restaurants, nail salons, wholesale trades or markets, financial, medical, and law offices, among others.[38] Besides, the vast majority of their work force there is made up of Korean-Americans, many of whom are recent arrivals from Korea and whose social networks include some informants for various kinds of housing information, including the referral of co-ethnic real estate brokers or agents. Korean immigrants in pursuit of information on housing can also benefit from their residence in Korean-American communities where they have a greater chance to obtain housing-related information and knowhow from their interactions with co-ethnic neighbors. Furthermore, Korean-American religious organizations are another important network many of them can assess without much difficulty in their time of seeking certain housing-related information. In another sense, their regular church attendance, regardless of whether Korean-American churches are located in or outside of Korean-American gateways, also allows them to develop social networks with other Korean church members, some of whom might work at either Korean-owned or mainstream real estate firms, as real estate brokers, mortgage loan originators or processors, or mostly, sales agents. A noticeable feature of most Korean-American churches is the operation of their district meetings designed to hold Bible studies grouped by age and residence, usually on a monthly basis. In general, the members regularly attending their church district meetings tend to maintain strong personal relationships with each other, enough to share their housing experiences or provide information on housing to the others.

For those limited English-speaking Korean immigrants seeking information on housing, their residence in a larger Korean-American gateway also makes it possible for them to assess Korean-language local media that often helps improve their knowledge about a wide range of housing-related matters, such as the trend or current state of the national or local rental and homeownership markets (the number of the properties sold, vacant, or built, or a shift in property prices), the conditions or requirements for home financing (loan interest rates and types or the degree of down payments), and national- and local-level housing laws, programs, and so on. As stated in previous chapters, for example, there are two major Korean-language daily newspapers—*The Korea Daily* and *The Korea Times*—which are issued daily in both print and electronic forms in the NY-NJ-CT metropolitan areas. Moreover, the website of *The Korea Daily*, for example, also devotes a great deal of space to reports on a recent movement in national and local housing markets, a regular column in home financing and real estate markets for mortgage applications and the transaction process to buy, sell, or rent a house, and to mortgage and real estate experts' prompt responses about all sorts of housing-related questions through its section of "ASKAMERICA." Another important source of various housing information for Korean-Americans in these northeastern territories of the United States, for example, comes from the broadcasting service of NY Radio Korea (a Korean language radio) and MKTV (a Korean television station) both of which provide up-to-date economic news and regular business programs, including the news and programs on trends in the mortgage and real estate markets and experts' analysis of national and local housing markets. In the same areas, local housing information is further found from dozens of Korean-language real estate magazines or periodicals that print lists of houses on sale in the local markets and the contact numbers of local Korean-American real estate brokers and sales agents.

For many Korean-Americans living outside of gateway metropolitan areas, their social networks consisting of people of the same co-ethnic background are generally limited in number and size, and less extensive in scope. However, this does not mean that Korean language media is completely inaccessible to them. With the help of the Internet, for example, even many Korean immigrants living outside the NY-NJ-CT metropolitan areas can obtain American housing information from their online connections with electronic versions of *The Korean Daily* and *The Korea Times*, as well as live or recorded programs of NY Radio Korea and MKTV. Moreover, a wide variety of housing information posted online in Korean can be obtained through their connections with, or their memberships of, some well-known Korean American online communities, such as MissyUSA (www.missyusa.com), HeyKorean (www.heykorean.com), Mizville (www.mizville.org), and Korean Community of US (there are ten locally operating websites).

THE AMERICAN HOUSING INSTITUTION ON THE "MISSYUSA" COMMUNITY

The Financing of Homeownership

In this section of the financing of homeownership, some of the most frequently posted topics include the selection of mortgage lenders, the period of mortgage payments, the mortgage interest rates or types, monthly mortgage payments, mortgage interest rates being paid, the mortgage insurance (private mortgage insurance or PMI), the amount of a down payment on a house, the ratio of income to debt for mortgage approval or the appropriate ratio of income to monthly mortgage payments, the mortgage applicants' legal status, and the like. Below, specific cases of these different but related topics are individually introduced as fully as possible in order to evaluate them in the framework of the two forms of social capital (social resources and social support). First, in the topic of mortgage finance, an inquiry message on legal permanent resident status at the time of the purchase of a new house was posted by a member on May 1, 2012. Four members responded to this initial post:

> Q: My husband and I are going to apply for green cards this year. We are also considering the purchase of our own house because of higher rent costs. Are there some disadvantages when we buy a house without having our permanent legal resident status? I want to hear opinions from those "MissyUSA" members who bought their houses with no permanent legal resident status.
> A1: Your credit score and good income are important. Permanent legal status has nothing to with your mortgage finance. We purchased our current house before the approval of our permanent legal resident status, but we got a very good mortgage term with a low interest rate.
> A2: When you resell your house, you will pay more sales tax because you are foreigners . . .
> A3: Green card holders are also foreigners, but they tend to report their taxes. Then, there are some non-green card holders who own their homes in the United States without reporting their taxes. When they sold their houses, the IRS [Internal Revenue Service] holds the 10 percent of their house values sold, and then, they return the remaining money after deducting their sales tax.
> A4: My husband and I bought our current house without having our green cards. We were also very worried about that. The best idea now is to consult with experts in the area of home finance.

For many Korean-Americans, homeownership is central to the achievement of their American dream. To that end, they often seek information about the requisite qualifications for their mortgage finance, such as this initial poster's inquiry about legal permanent resident status. All four respondents belong to the subgroup of information advisors to the inquirer. Besides, two of them (A1 and A3) also take on the role of information analysts for her. To some degree, two respondents (A1 and A4) can also be classified as the subgroup of companions to the inquirer because they shared their experiences similar to this inquirer's.

A message asking a question about the extent of monthly mortgage payments was posted on March 3, 2012. Seven short responses followed this post:

> Q: What amount per month should be paid in a mortgage of $220,000 with a 15-year mortgage term?
> A1: It depends on the interest rate on your mortgage.
> A2: Almost $2,000?
> A3: I borrowed a mortgage of $170,000 with a 15-year mortgage term. I pay a total of $1,400 per month, including mortgage principal and interest, insurance, and tax [property tax].
> A4: Your monthly payment might be the range of $1,800. Your additional cost like property tax should also be considered.
> A5: Put your information on Zillow.com to figure out the amount of your monthly payment.
> A6: I pay for almost $1,500 per month with a 3.3 percent of the interest rate for 15 years. Property tax is not included in this monthly payment.
> A7: Your loan amount is exactly the same as mine . . . I pay for $1,059 in mortgage principal and interest per month based upon a 4 percent interest charge for a 30-year fixed rate mortgage.

Like many of both prospective and current other American homeowners burdened with higher mortgage payments, meeting monthly mortgage payments is a matter of great concern to many of both prospective and current Korean-American homeowners, including this inquirer. Three respondents (A3, A6, and A7) take on the role of information analysts for the inquirer. While the first two respondents (A1 and A2) can be classified as the subgroup of information describers to the inquirer, two other respondents (A4 and A5) appear to be in the subgroup of information advisors to her.

A member asked about the possibility of obtaining a mortgage loan without a down payment in a message posted on April 3, 2012. There were five response messages that followed it:

> Q: Is it possible to get a mortgage loan of $300,000 from a bank without any down payment? There is no substantial difference between rent and mortgage payments when I buy the home valued at that amount . . . I have a good credit score, but I have never purchased any house before. I really have no knowledge about the process of home finance, so please understand my ignorance.
> A1: This time, a down payment of at least 20 or 30 percent is required even to higher income applicants.
> A2: I believe you should put some down payment for your home mortgage loan. You need to consult with experts in home finance.

> A3: It is very difficult to borrow 100 percent of the home value from mortgage banks. But, you can apply for the FHA loan with the 3.5 percent down payment that equals almost $10,000.
> A4: You should prepare at least $10,000 for your down payment. Also, you should have an additional $200 per month as the cost of mortgage insurance [private mortgage insurance or PMI] that should be considered in case of no down payment.
> A5: Buying a house without any down payment is almost impossible this time, but it was possible five years ago like my case. I was so lucky . . .

In most prospective homebuyers in either American society or Korean society, their general conception is to put a certain amount of down payment on a house. Then, the inquirer in this message thread looked for information on mortgage programs of no down payment in buying her new home in the United States. The first four respondents (A1, A2, A3, and A4) are positioned to take on the role of information advisors to the inquirer. Two of them (A3 and A4) also belong to the subgroup of information analysts for her. Additionally, the role of an information describer to the inquirer was conducted by Respondent 5 (A5).

On June 7, 2012, a member posted a message requesting information on the amount of mortgage interest payments from the total monthly mortgage payment. There were ten response messages, the first five of which are as follows:

> Q: Recently I bought a new house with a 15-year mortgage term. Someone I know told me one day that my monthly mortgage payments for the first five years are just for mortgage interest payments without any repayment of my mortgage principal. Is it true?
> A1: In the beginning of your monthly mortgage payments, your mortgage interest payments are relatively high, but the repayment amount of your mortgage principal is relatively low. But, as time passes, you repay the amount of your mortgage principal more.
> A2: You are going to gradually pay your mortgage interest payments less and less with time.
> A3: For the first five years, the total repayment amount of mortgage principal is not much. But, since then, you will notice more payment of your mortgage principal.
> A4: Your friend's remark is untrue. You will repay some amount of your mortgage principal even for the first five years. You can find out more accurate information from some websites with a mortgage calculator on the Internet.
> A5: In my case, I am paying down some amount of my mortgage principal, though not much.

Some homeowners, like this inquirer, can feel a considerable sense of discomfort as their home equity is not much rising over time due to the relatively high rate and amount of mortgage interests in their mortgage payments. Two respondents (A2 and A5) belong to the subgroup of information describers to the inquirer. The role of information analysts for the inquirer is taken on by the three other respondents among whom Respondent 4 (A4) is also considered to be the information advisor for the inquirer.

On January 3, 2012, a member posted a message requesting information about the desired mortgage amount level on the basis of income. Five members responded to this post:

> Q: My husband and I are working and earn a total of $7,200 every month as our net income. We have two children of third and fifth grades in elementary school. Now we have almost finished paying off our college loans and the loans on two cars. On a monthly basis, we spend $600 at the expenses of my two kids' swimming, piano, and cello lessons. In our case, what is the desired monthly mortgage amount in proportion to our total monthly income?
> A1: Your mortgage amount should not be more than 25 to 30 percent of your income.
> A2: Monthly payments of $2,000 are reasonable.
> A3: It is hard to predict it in the absence of other information, such as your down payment amount and mortgage terms, and the location of your new house.
> A4: As your children grow older, there will be a steady rise in your expense for their education. . . . So try to buy a house of a reasonable price based upon your projected cost of living and income.
> A5: My family's income is similar to yours, but we have no children. We are planning to buy a house worth half a million dollars in the next two or three years. To achieve this goal, we are saving $2,000 every month and considering the 20 percent down payment . . .

To some extent, four respondents, except for Respondent 3 (A3), can be identified as the subgroup of information advisors to the inquirer. Then, the role of Respondent 3 (A3) appears to be the information describer to the inquirer.

On February 4, 2012, a member posted a message requesting information about her selection between two available mortgage payment options. There were ten response messages, the first five of which are quoted below:

> Q: I am planning to buy my first house soon. The price of a house I am looking to buy is around $450,000. The amount of its down payment affordable to me is $150,000 and the mortgage amount from a bank is $300,000. . . . Whenever I have extra money, I will try to pay down my mortgage loan. My goal is to pay off my mortgage debt in the next five years. Can you suggest which option is better between 15- and 30-year mortgages?
> A1: If you pay your loan off early, a 15-year mortgage is the better choice than a 30-year one.
> A2: I suggest you to select a 30-year mortgage. If any extra money is available, try to pay down your mortgage principal. Such an action can

help shorten the period of your mortgage payments. That is more secure for you.
A3: The future is always unpredictable, so I also recommend you a 30-year mortgage. The interest rate of a 15-year mortgage is not much different from that of a 30-year one.
A4: Your monthly payments calculated from your mortgage of $300,000 are approximately $2,300. If I were you, I would delay buying a house for a couple of years to prepare more money for the down payment. Thereafter, your burden of mortgage payments can be very much reduced.
A5: There is no question that the period of a 15-year mortgage is better than a 30-year one if you can afford to pay your monthly mortgages more.

All five respondents take on the role of information advisors to the inquirer because they provided their own thoughts, ideas, or advice to her. Likewise, all of them can be also identified generally as the subgroup of information analysts for the inquirer because they stated some general or specific reasons for the validity of their judgments or evaluations.

A Home-Buying Process

From this theme of the home-buying process, there were many posts among which some popular topics include the search for new homes for sale, new house purchases, home inspections, negotiations with home sellers for purchasing prices, the cancellation of the contract already signed, title insurance, the roles of real estate sales agents or lawyers, and all the costs or the closing costs for purchasing houses. Of them, some specific cases of different but related topics are introduced below. First, a member posted a message seeking information about an issue that comes at the time of making an offer for a new house, on April 6, 2012. There were ten response messages, the first five of which are quoted here:

Q: I found a house I really like. A check was requested by my agent [buyer's agent] to make an offer to the listing agent [seller's agent] of that house. Should we give a check to our agent when we make an offer to buy a house?
A1: Yes, you should. That check is called the earnest money deposit that indicates the seller your strong interest in the purchase of his or her house.
A2: It is a right way for you to write your check certain amounts and give it to your agent.
A3: I am living in New Jersey. Making an offer on the house accompanies the buyer's check which amount usually ranges from $1,000 to $5,000. The larger amount on the buyer's check gives a strong impression to the seller. Your agent will not deposit your check into the bank until your offer is accepted . . .

A4: That is the earnest money deposit. Write a check of $1,000 and give it to your agent.
A5: Your agent will forward a purchase offer letter and a copy of your check to the listing agent. Your agent will hold your check until all conditions are met. When your offer is declined, your check will be returned to you.

In the United States, legal steps to buy a new home are not the same in all states. Therefore, knowing its proper, legal procedures in the state of residence is important to prospective homebuyers. In this series of messages, all five respondents belong to the subgroup of information confirmers to the inquirer, and four of them, except for Respondent 2 (A2), also take on the role of information analysts for the inquirer. In addition, the messages of two respondents (A2 and A4) also place them in the subgroup of information advisors to the inquirer.

On March 10, 2012, a member posted a message requesting information on the hiring of a real estate attorney in the purchase of her new house. There were eight response messages, five of which are introduced below:

Q: I am preparing to buy my first house, and I am a person of sensitive character. . . . I don't want to be a victim of fraud in the process of buying my new house. I cannot trust my agent 100 percent. Therefore, I am thinking of hiring a real estate attorney.
A1: I bought my house by hiring a lawyer.
A2: I didn't think that the transaction of a house without hiring a real estate lawyer is possible. During the processing period of the house I now bought, my lawyer prepared and checked all the necessary and legal documents for me.
A3: You need to hire a lawyer who will take charge of the secure transfer of your funds associated with the purchase of the house and your escrow account and make sure of your legal ownership to the property through a title company.[39]
A4: In New York, hiring a real estate lawyer is legally required.
A5: As for me, my agent introduced me to a lawyer who handled many documents to be legally signed. I paid $350 for such service.

In general, all five respondents belong to the subgroup of information confirmers to the inquirer. Additionally, two respondents (A2 and A3) also take on the role of information analysts for the inquirer, whereas the remaining three other respondents can be also sorted out as the subgroup of information describers to her.

The inquiry about the necessity of a home inspection was asked in a message posted on February 10, 2012. Four members responded to this post:

Q: I signed a contract to buy a house that was unoccupied for almost over three months, and I found many dead bugs in the living room and bathrooms of that house. When I request a home inspection, does an

> inspector check bugs and mold in the house? Or is this problem different from a general home inspection?
> A1: You should do the inspection of that house. It costs several hundred dollars, but you may spend more money without it. If there were some problems found after the inspection, your seller will fix them. If not, you have the right to cancel your contract.
> A2: You need a home inspection. From it, you can find all the problems of your purchasing house, including bugs . . .
> A3: You should do the inspection of that house. Don't worry too much about dead bugs. Before you move in, that house needs fumigation.
> A4: I understand your concerns. I had the same feeling when I bought my house. . . . A home inspection is needed, but it is fine to move in if there is no serious flaw in the house.

Moving into a newly purchased house in a good condition must be the wish of all new homebuyers. Whether or not a new home is well cleaned before moving in there is a very sensitive matter for most housewives. In exploring the messages of four respondents in the context of social support, all four respondents belong to the subgroup of information advisors to the inquirer. Respondent 1 (A1) can be also identified as the information analyst for the inquirer. Moreover, companionship and encouragement to the inquirer was revealed in the message posted by Respondent 4 (A4).

On July 4, 2012, a member posted a message requesting information about whether title insurance is obligatory or optional for a home purchase. Three response messages followed it:

> Q: Is it mandatory to have title insurance? I bought my house three years ago without purchasing title insurance. Recently, one of my coworkers talked about the purchase of title insurance. I have no idea about that yet.
> A1: It is optional. I don't have title insurance. But it is a kind of insurance from a lien put on the house after the bankruptcy in business. It occurs very rarely to most of us. Purchasing title insurance is a conventional practice. . . . I also know someone who doesn't have home title insurance.
> A2: Mortgage banks request loan applicants to have title insurance.
> A3: Having your title insurance means that you can find any lien put on your purchasing house and any unpaid property tax from your former homeowner. You are legally protected from such occurrences once your title insurance fee is paid for . . .

Title insurance is the type of insurance to protect both a homeowner and one's mortgage company (lender) from unforeseen claims that may arise against his/her own property. Above, two of these three respondents (A1 and A3) belong to the subgroup of information analysts for the inquirer. In an array of these posts, Respondent 2 (A2) is just positioned as the information advisor to the inquirer.

A message requesting information on all the costs involving the purchase of a house was posted on April 3, 2012. Four response messages followed it:

> Q: I am thinking to buy a house of $200,000 in cash. How much do I have to prepare as the closing costs for such priced house?
> A1: There is no sales tax on the purchase of a new house. But, a certain amount of property tax should be prepared, and for example, that amount in LA [Los Angeles] is almost 1.25 percent of your purchasing house value that should be paid twice a year.
> A2: You should include the buyer's closing costs.
> A3: There are fees for the title company and your attorney handling the closing.
> A4: In all the closing costs, your attorney's service, a home inspection, and other fees are included. Closing costs vary across areas, but the average cost is almost $5,000.

All four respondents generally belong to the subgroup of information advisors to the inquirer. Besides, two of them (A1 and A4) also take on the role of information analysts for the inquirer, whereas two other respondents (A2 and A3) can be classified as the subgroup of information describers to her.

Homeowners' Options and Burdens

Some of the most popular topics posted by some of the "MissyUSA" members, in this broad theme of homeowners' options and burdens, include mortgage payoff, the shortage in the amount of mortgage payment, housing maintenance or management costs, home remodeling, refinancing, loan modification, property tax, house foreclosures, and house sales or short sales, among others. This section introduces some specific cases on five different but related topics. First, on April 1, 2012, a member posted a message requesting information on property tax. There were three response messages after this initial post:

> Q: I am living in New Jersey Bergen County. The current market value of my house is less than my loan amount, but my yearly property tax is as high as $12,000. Can I share your success story about a property tax appeal? Is the deadline of property tax appeal on April 15th this year?
> A1: A property tax appeal is no big deal. After filing it, your county will send you the result as to whether your property tax is down.
> A2: I am living in California and bought my house a year ago. Unfortunately, the market value of my house dropped greatly since then. I appealed my property tax amount and then, got a refund check from my county. If you need more information about this, just call to your county office. That's the way I did it.
> A3: I am living in a county in California. I did a property tax appeal early this year and received a reduced tax bill that should be paid for

before April 10th. Go to your county's assessor's website and in it, check the section of property tax appeal or reassessment. There are one or two documents very easy for you to prepare.

In New Jersey Bergen County, many Korean-Americans live together in such towns as Palisades Park, Leonia, Fort Lee, Tenafly, and Closter. The U.S. financial and housing crisis of late 2000s caused some Korean-Americans living in these areas to struggle to pay their high-interest mortgages. This inquirer might be a victim of such a nationwide economic recession. In general, all three respondents belong to the subgroup of information advisors to the inquirer. Two of them (A2 and A3) also display their companionship and encouragement to the inquirer in their messages that contain their early experiences similar to the concern raised by the inquirer. Besides, Respondent 1 (A1) can be identified as another encourager to the inquirer.

A message requesting information on home refinancing was posted on March 8, 2012. Five response messages followed it:

Q: The market value of my house dropped markedly so that I applied for the refinancing of my mortgage from a bank last year. But, it didn't work. The main reason for the disapproval in my early attempt of getting a refinancing mortgage was too high in the loan to value (LTV) ratio for my property. After paying more of my mortgage debt during this year, I am also planning to refinance my mortgage. Can I apply my mortgage refinancing to two or three different mortgage banks at the same time? If I do this now, the probable loss of my credit score is my worry. My husband said to me that it would be fine.

A1: You need to consider the heavy cost of your mortgage refinancing applications, such as your payments for several appraisals of your property. Therefore, apply your refinancing to a mortgage bank, and when that fails, apply it to another mortgage bank with more preparation.

A2: Don't apply your mortgage refinancing to several mortgage banks. Do it from only one of them.

A3: Try to apply your mortgage refinancing to only one mortgage lender. As another option, contact a mortgage broker who can apply it to several lenders on behalf of you. In that case, you cannot avoid losing some points of your credit score.

A4: When you apply your mortgage refinancing to several mortgage banks, each lender will check your credit score so that such procedure will hurt your credit score. Try to consult with an experienced mortgage broker.

A5: Recently, I did my mortgage refinancing. To do this, I contacted several mortgage banks to find out closing costs, the possibility to get a loan, and the time period to complete its applications. It took almost two months to get its approval. Try to contact each mortgage bank.

For refinance loan applicants, their good credits usually work positively in the approval process of their loans from mortgage companies. It is also likely that checking their credit scores from multiple mortgage companies during a short period of time leads to some drop in their credit scores. By and large, all five respondents belong to the subgroup of information advisors to the inquirer, and four of them (A1, A3, A4, and A5) can also be considered as the subgroup of information analysts for her. Besides, the message posted by Respondent 4 (A4) also places her in the position of the information confirmer for the inquirer.

On March 3, 2012, a member posted a message requesting advice concerning mortgage payoff. There were twenty response messages, the first five of which are introduced here:

> Q: The remaining balance of my mortgage principal is over $180,000, and its monthly payments in mortgage interest only are almost $800. A problem occurring in the case of the full payoff of my remaining mortgage is that my tax payment will be expected to rise to $6,000 from $2,000 per year. Despite such a large loss, I believe that it is a better idea to pay off my remaining mortgages. But, I am also very confused about what to do . . .
> A1: There is no clear answer to it. The selection depends upon homeowners' own personalities. Some of them will feel so relieved after the complete payoff of their mortgages.
> A2: Last year, I paid off my mortgage loan. I have a house worth $1,100,000 and save $6,000 in my bank account per month. My tax deduction was reduced, but I also feel at ease now. My two children will go to college in the next two or three years so that I am saving money for their tuition.
> A3: Paying off your mortgage much earlier is a good judgment.
> A4: If you don't have enough money to pay off your mortgage this time, try to refinance your mortgage which interest rate seems very high. When you negotiate mortgage banks with no or lower closing cost and below 3.0 percent of the interest rate, your monthly payments in mortgage interest will be reduced to around $500.
> A5: I have paid a lump sum for my mortgage that will be originally paid off in next spring.

All five respondents generally take on the role of information advisors to the inquirer, and two of them (A2 and A4) also belong to the subgroup of information analysts for her. And two respondents (A2 and A5) belong to each subgroup of information confirmers, and companions, and encouragers to the inquirer, respectively. In addition, Respondent 3 (A3) can be identified as another encourager to the inquirer.

On January 3, 2012, there was an inquiry message about the maintenance cost of a condominium. Four response messages followed this post:

> Q: Given the possession of a condominium, what is HOA? And is it the same as or different from the condominium fee?

> A1: Both terms are the same. HOA fee is an abbreviation of "Homeowners' Association" fee.
> A2: I believe that both are the same. I am paying $420 in HOA per month, but its fee includes all the costs of using electricity, water, gas, heater, and air conditioner.
> A3: In Korea, HOA is a kind of maintenance cost of the condominium. In the case of possessing it, some regular payments, such as the HOA fee, property tax, home insurance, and mortgages, occur.
> A4: It really depends on the condominium you possess and its community. Thus, the condominium fee is not exactly the same as the HOA fee. My two friends who bought their condominiums recently told me that they pay both fees separately . . .

Like the query asked by the inquiry, it is not easy to figure out all the sources of monthly payments related to the ownership of a unit in the condominium building. In some condominium or homeowners' communities, both fees are regularly collected together without any separation, but in some other communities, they are collected separately. In the latter case, a condominium fee is the total cost handling the upkeep of one's own condominium unit (i.e., roof, siding, gutter cleaning and its regular maintenance, (electricity, water, cable, sewage, heating, air conditioning), whereas a HOA fee is collected to manage the common areas and facilities of these communities (pools, tennis courts, parking lots, street lights, club house, gyms). In this series of messages, the role of information analysts for the inquirer is taken on by two respondents (A2 and A4). Respondent 4 (A4) also becomes the information advisor for the inquirer. Here, two other respondents (A1 and A3) belong to the subgroup of information describers to the inquirer. Then, there were conflicting comments between the messages of first three respondents (A1, A2, and A3) and the message posted by Respondent 4 (A4).

An inquiry about the home foreclosure was raised in a message posted on December 3, 2012. There were eight response messages, the first five of which are cited here and an additional message from the inquirer:

> Q: Now, I cannot pay my mortgages any more. I received from my bank a letter indicating the foreclosure of my house. I don't understand the phrase "trustee sale day." Is this the day I have to vacate my house?
> A1: That is the day for the foreclosure of your house. To avoid it, apply for bankruptcy, and then, you can delay foreclosing on your house for several months or more. You can do this by hiring a lawyer or visiting yourself at your county's sheriff's office.
> A2: A short sale through a real estate agent is a way to protect your credit and delay the imminent foreclosure of your house . . .
> A3: A short sale is the best option for you to avoid many hassles . . . I sold my house on a short sale because it was so painful to live in the house in the state of no mortgage payments. Now I feel so relieved. If your house is foreclosed, you may have to move out without a plan.

> Q: On average, how long does it take to sell houses on a short sale?
> A2: It will take several months.
> A4: The phrase "trustee sale day" is the day to sell your house at auction by the court [the Supreme Court]. If your house is sold to the third party, the ownership of your house is changed, and then, you should move out. If that is not the case, there is the next step waiting for you, and different states have different policies about it. Try to consult with experienced experts in the field. All four respondents take on the role of information advisors to the inquirer.

Two of them (A1 and A4) also belong to the subgroup of information analysts for to the inquirer. Additionally, companionship to her is contained in the message posted by Respondent 3 (A3).

Rental Housing

On the "Life Q&A" message board of the "MissyUSA" community, there were many posts related to rental housing. Some of the most popular topics on it include the search for a rental unit, a lease contract or re-contract, its cancellation, security deposit, prospective tenants' credit scores, a rent increase, late payment or late fee, the maintenance cost of a rented house, and move-in or move-out, among others. Of them, the specific cases of five different but related topics are introduced in this section. First of all, a member posted a message requesting information about a lease contract, on August 7, 2012. There were ten response messages, the first five of which are quoted here, as well as two additional messages from the inquirer, one of which is introduced below:

> Q: I am now searching for a space for rent not in Manhattan [a Borough of New York City], but in Queens [a Borough of New York City]. The monthly rent in an apartment there is approximately $2,000, but my monthly income for tax report is $1,600. I wonder if the apartment manager will agree to sign a rental contract.
> A1: Your monthly income should be 2.5 or 3 times at the level of your monthly rent. Or show evidence that you have enough savings to pay for your rent all year around.
> A2: It seems very difficult. Your monthly income needs to be at least $6,000 for a $2,000 rent. Ask someone to co-sign your rent contract.
> A3: It is unlikely.
> Q: I receive $3,000 every month from Korea for my sibling's college education. . . . How about this as a proof that I have a regular income?
> A4: You cannot use it.
> A5: We are student couples and are living currently outside of New York City. Our total income is less than the amount of our monthly rent. A staff at the apartment management requested us to prove whether we have the money equal to one-year rent. So we did it by receiving that amount of money from Korea.

In recent years in the United States, there has been a continuous rise in rental costs across many urban areas. As a result, high rents in these areas have made it very difficult for people with low or moderate incomes to rent homes. In this series of posts, the role of information advisors to the inquirer is conducted by three respondents (A1, A2, and A5). Here, the other two respondents (A3 and A4) belong to the subgroup of information describers to the inquirer. Besides, the message of Respondent 5 (A5) contains expressions of both companionship and encouragement to the inquirer.

On September 5, 2012, the information on security deposit was requested from a message posted by a member. It was followed by four response messages and an additional message from the inquirer:

> Q: I lived in a single house for three years, and after moving out of the house, I got my security deposit back. The original amount of my security deposit was $2,600, but I received only $837.5 after the deduction from those fees of house cleaning ($400), repairs ($765), carpet cleaning ($450), the repair of the dish washing machine ($80), and a toilet lid's cleaning ($67.5). There was no carpet cleaning during my three-year residence there. . . . Is this deduction reasonable?
> A1: That's too much. I rented a house owned by a white landlord, and cleaned its kitchen and refrigerator only, not its carpet. . . . Within two weeks after moving out of the house, I received 100 percent of my security deposit. I thought that the landlord would take out some of my security deposit to clean up the carpet and window curtains. . . . House cleaning fee depends on the number of the rooms in the house.
> Q: The house is relatively big and there were six bedrooms.
> A2: The owner charged too much for both house and carpet cleaning.
> A3: As far as I know, no deduction occurs from the repainting and cleaning of the house if tenants lived in the house more than two years. But, there might be some deduction when its carpet was tainted or damaged . . .
> A4: I don't understand $765 in repairs and $67.5 as the cost of a toilet lid's cleaning, plus $400 for house cleaning.

An unanticipated, low amount in the return of rental deposits from landlords arouses anger among those tenants who have already vacated their rented units, as shown in the case of this inquirer. Here, two respondents (A1 and A3) can be to some degree classified into the subgroup of information analysts for the inquirer. Furthermore, three of them (A1, A2, and A4) belong to the subgroup of companions to the inquirer.

On December 9, 2012, a member requested information on late fees for rent. There were four response messages and an additional message from the inquirer:

> Q: I am living in a rented apartment for two years. I used to pay my monthly rent on time, but my rent payments were late this time for several months. Then I received a notice letter that I should pay late

fees of $100 five days after the due date and $150 after ten days. No item of such fees was indicated in my lease contract. . . . My monthly rent is $1,300. Does it make sense?
A1: As a late fee for rent, there is usually some amount written in your lease contract. I pay $30 for it.
Q: There was no indication about it in my original lease contract. But my home owner directly told me about this new addition in my lease contract.
A2: There is no legal way to protect you.
A3: The amount of a late fee for rent should be indicated in a lease contract. But, the only solution this time for you is on-time lease payment.
A4: Such amounts of a late fee make sense. I also paid my late fees twice, so I recorded its due day on the calendar to pay it on time.

Overall, three of four respondents (A2, A3, and A4) belong to the subgroup of information advisors to the inquirer. Of them, Respondent 4 (A4) also takes on the role of an information confirmer to the inquirer. Besides, two respondents (A1 and A3) become information analysts for her.

The information about the maintenance of a rented house was requested by a member who posted a message on April 7, 2012. There were eight response messages, the first five of which are cited here:

Q: I am living in a single house in rent and not long after moving into this unit, there were many problems, such as termites in one of its rooms, no running water from its kitchen sink, and the dysfunction of its heating system. At that time, all of them were fixed together by my landlord. Now six months passed, and termite droppings were in the corner of the living room of the house . . . I called to the landlord with the request to treat them. . . . But, there was the landlord's response that I should fix it myself. . . . Is this the landlord's responsibility? I am thinking to move out after the termination of this lease contract . . .
A1: This time is your turn because your landlord did it already once.
A2: The termite problem in the house should always be taken care of by the landlord.
A3: The landlord should handle such a problem . . .
A4: It is one of the homeowner's responsibilities. We have several rental properties and we take care of annual termite service. But I would suggest you to check your lease agreement if there is any clause regarding termite issue.
A5: Treating termites is the landlord's responsibility, but handling ants in the house is the tenant's.

The responsibility for maintaining a rented housing in a habitable condition is sometimes a matter for negotiation between landlords and tenants. In this series of messages, all five respondents take on the role of information advisors to the inquirer. Moreover, the message posted by Respondent 5(A5) also puts her in the position of an information analyst for the inquirer.

On January 4, 2012, a member requested information about the foreclosure of the house from the perspective of a tenant. There were four response messages after this post:

> Q: I am living in California. My rented house has been foreclosed, and I received from the bank a notice letter to leave the house soon . . . I didn't find out a new rental house to move into yet. I need extra time to search for it. Unless I can move out of the house on the day the bank set in the letter, what will happen to me? I need your advice for me.
> A1: You need to contact the bank to explain your situation. If that deal doesn't work, request moving costs to the bank. Also, try to search for a rental house that is not difficult to find out this time.
> A2: You should vacate your rented house until on the designated day from the bank. But, the bank will pay you several thousand dollars for your moving costs.
> A3: You can continue to live there on condition that you pay your rents. However, the homeowners should move out of the house.
> A4: The sheriff will lock the foreclosed house on the day set by the court. You need to check that day.

In general, both roles of information analysts and information advisors to the inquirer, as requested by her, are performed by all four respondents.

SUMMARY

Some members of the "MissyUSA" community posted the messages requesting or providing information about the rules of the American housing institution which themes have been, in this chapter, divided into four categories: the financing of homeownership, the home-buying process, homeowners' options and burdens, and rental housing. Then, the two different types of messages (inquiries and responses) have been further identified by two distinctive forms of social capital—social resources (information) and social support. As evidence showing that the "MissyUSA" community becomes the important source of social resources (information), many of its members posted their messages requesting a wide range of information about the rules of the American housing institution. Interestingly enough, then, there have been two disparate patterns of their information inquiries about them.

The first has been the seeking of information about the stated or formal rules, regulations, or procedures of the American housing institution. In the theme of the financing of homeownership, for example, it included a wide variety of specified rules in home finance, such as mortgage types (fixed-rate, adjustable rate, or interest-only), monthly mortgage payments (mortgage principal and interest payments), down payment levels on new homes for sale, the periods of mortgage payments (fifteen or thirty years), and others. The second type of their inquiries has been largely the seeking of information about the rules of the American housing institution that reflect a series of informal, unwritten but generally agreed-upon procedures, guidelines, or practices. In the theme of rental housing, as an example, the terms of a lease contract included a refund of the tenants' security deposits within certain days (twenty-one days or thirty days) after they move out. Though there is no clear-cut rule on a standard refund amount of their security deposits, an informal rule here is that the amounts are often, fully or partially, refunded after the landlords' own inspection of the properties and all the deductions according to the damaged items in the property.

Social support to the inquirers (information seekers) by some other members of the "MissyUSA" community has been the other form of social capital that is indeed inherent in most posts in response to the inquiry messages. More specifically, these social supporters (respondents) have been classified into two broad groups: instrumental guiders (information describers, analysts, confirmers, and advisors) and emotional supporters (companions, encouragers, and critics). Of these instrumental guiders, some respondents have belonged to the subgroup of information describers to the inquirers by posting their response messages that refer to facts only, or direct or indirect answers or comments without making any further explanation, suggestion, or advice. The role of information confirmers to the inquirers has also been revealed in some messages posted by its respondents. Relative to these two subgroups of instrumental guiders, more respondents have taken on the role of information analysts for the inquirers. In their response messages, information analysts generally shared a common task to one another, namely, explanations of, or evaluations about, the conditions, reasons, the core issues, processes, and/or short- or long-term outcomes, with or without uttering their own experiences. Then, there have been some response messages that were unclear, or sometimes, outside the main focus of the inquiries, in explanation.

As already observed through many response posts related to the rules of the American housing institution, many respondents have taken on the role of information advisors for the inquirers. Thus, this subgroup of information advisors to the inquirers has been the most important subgroup in the group of instrumental guiders. It is because many inquirers (information seekers) wrote the messages seeking those information types that contain some ideas, advices, or suggestions from their respondents, with their aim of coping with the issues they face now or will face in the future. Correspondingly, their information advisors posted their messages that usually include their advice, ideas or options, or even their thoughts regarding what to do now or next on the basis of their past experiences, expertise, hearsay, or guesswork. Taken together, in this group of instrumental guiders, some respondents took on a single role, but some others took on multiple roles across its four subgroups. Compared with the respondents' strong roles as instrumental guiders to the inquirers, especially those as information analysts and/or advisors, however, they considered their roles of emotional supporters for the inquirers as less important. This is not to say that no expression of companionship or encouragement is found in their response messages. In fact, some of their response messages revealed their role of companionship for the inquirers in their texts that depict their own experiences or what steps they should take to cope with, and/or their role of encouragers to the inquirers who expressed no hope, disappointment, or disheartenment. Lastly, there were some respondents who belong to both groups of information guiders and emotional supporters to their inquirers. In short, this chapter of the American housing institution substantiated the "MissyUSA" community as the online space where some of its members, as information seekers or respondents, post their messages embracing social capital.

NOTES

1. William A. V. Clark, Marinus Deurloo, and Frans Dieleman, "Residential Mobility and Neighbourhood Outcomes," *Housing Studies* 21 (2006): 323–342.

2. George J. Borjas, "Homeownership in the Immigrant Population," *Journal of Urban Economics* 52 (2002): 448–476; Michael Hann, "The Homeownership Hierarchies of Canada and the United States: The Housing Patterns of White and Non-White Immigrants of the Past Thirty Years," *International Migration Review* 41 (2007): 433–465; Gary Painter and Zhou Yu, "Immigrants and Housing Markets in Mid-Size Metropolitan Areas," *International Migration Review* 44 (2010): 442–476; and Carlos Teixeira, "Cultural Resources and Ethnic Entrepreneurship: A Case Study of the Portuguese Real Estate Industry in Toronto," *The Canadian Geographer* 42 (1998): 267–281.

3. *The Rise of Asian Americans* (Pew Research Center, 2013). For more information, see http://www.pewreasrch.org.

4. Tamara K. Hareven, 1991. "The Home and the Family in Historical Perspective," *Social Research* 58 (1991): 253–285; and Madigan Ruth, Moira Munro, and Susan J. Smith, "Gender and the Meaning of the Home," *International Journal of Urban and Regional Research* 14 (1990): 625–647.

5. A "family house" means a single detached house, an apartment, a condominium, a townhouse, a duplex house, or a mobile house.

6. William N. Eskridge, "One Hundred Years of Ineptitude: The Need for Mortgage Rules Consonant with the Economic and Psychological Dynamics of the Home Sale and Loan Transaction," *Virginia Law Review* 70 (1984): 1083–1218.

7. Richard K. Green and Susan M. Wachter, "The American Mortgage in Historical and International Context," *The Journal of Economic Perspectives* 19 (2005): 93–114; and Alex F. Schwartz, *Housing Policy in the United States: An Introduction* (New York: Routledge, 2006).

8. This 1934 Act introduced the FHA section 203 (b) program that provides mortgage insurance to qualified lenders for protecting them from the default of the mortgages granted to their borrowers (homebuyers or homeowners). The summary of this program is available at http://portal.hud.gov/hudportal/HUD?src=/program_offices/housing/sfh/ins/203b--df .

9. Adam Gordon, "The Creation of Homeownership: How New Deal Changes in Banking Regulation Simultaneously Made Homeownership Accessible to Whites and

Out of Reach for Blacks," *The Yale Law Review* 115 (2005): 186–226; and Alex F. Schwartz, *Housing Policy in the United States*. In the private mortgage market, mortgage insurance is also known as private mortgage insurance (PMI).

10. At that time, the major mission of the Federal National Mortgage Association (FNMA or Fannie Mae) was to purchase FHA-insured loans from private lenders, and then, to hold or sell them. Its action of purchasing mortgages from private lenders indeed helped them to possess the cash needed to fund new loans. The history of government-sponsored enterprises is concisely summarized at http://fhfaoig.gov/LearnMore/History.

11. Ibid.

12. Alex F. Schwartz, *Housing Policy in the United States*.

13. William N. Eskridge, "One Hundred Years of Ineptitude"; Richard K. Green and Susan M. Wachter, "The American Mortgage in Historical and International Context"; and Alex F. Schwartz, *Housing Policy in the United States*.

14. For more information, see http://fhfaoig.gov/LearnMore/History .

15. Richard K. Green and Stephen Malpezzi, *A Primer on U.S. Housing Markets and Housing Policy* (Washington, DC: The Urban Institute Press, 2003).

16. Ibid.

17. Alex F. Schwartz, *Housing Policy in the United States*, 55–61.

18. For more detailed information, check the link of the U.S. Department of Justice website: http://www.justice.gov/crt/about/hce/title8.php.

19. For the passages of the ECOA, check the link of the U.S. Department of Justice website: http://www.gpo.gov/fdsys/pkg/USCODE-2011-title15/. Under the ECOA, any unfair discrimination in mortgage loans or credit transaction has been regulated by the Department of Justice, the HUD, or other federal agencies (see http://www.justice.gov/crt/about/hce/housing_ecoa.php). For further information, see John Yinger, *Closed Doors, Opportunity Lost: The Continuing Costs of Housing Discrimination* (New York: Russell Sage Foundation, 1995).

20. All the provisions of the HMDA are available at the website link of Federal Deposit Insurance Corporation (FDIC): http://www.fdic.gov/regulations/laws/rules/6500-3030.html.

21. For more information, see the website link of the Federal Financial Institutions Examination Council (FFIEC): http://www.ffiec.gov/cra/ .

22. Margaret M. Brassil, *The Creation of a Federal Partnership: The Role of the States in Affordable Housing* (Albany: State University of New York Press, 2010).

23. The mortgage programs available for first-time homebuyers in New York State are Homes for Veterans Program, Remodel New York, Achieving the Dream, Construction Incentive Program, and Low Interest Rate Program. For detailed information, see the link: http://www.nyshcr.org/Topics/Home/Buyers/SONYMA/SONYMAProductsforFirstTimeHomebuyers.htm.

24. The historical trends of national- and state-level homeownership rates between 1900 and 2000 are available at the link: http://www.census.gov/hhes/www/housing/census/historic/owner.html.

25. The three national credit reporting bureaus or agencies are Equifax, TransUnion, and Experian.

26. The key rules, regulations, and procedures of the Truth in Lending Act of 1968 are available at the link in the Compliance Manual section of the FDIC (Federal Deposit Insurance Corporation) website: http://www.fdic.gov/regulations/compliance/manual/pdf/V-1.1.pdf .

27. The HUD took charge of the implementation of the RESPA and then, since July 21, 2011, it has been administered and enforced by the Consumer Financial Protection Bureau (CFPB). For more information about specific passages of the RESPA and its amendments, see Consumer Compliance Handbook: http://www.federalreserve.gov/boarddocs/supmanual/supervision_cch.htm .

28. Ibid.

29. See the 2013 Home Ownership and Equity Protection Act (HOEPA) Rule: Small Entity Compliance Guide by Consumer Financial Protection Bureau. Sources: http://files.consumerfinance.gov/f/201305_compliance-guide_home-ownership-and-equity-protection-act-rule.pdf .

30. For specific HARP eligibility requirements and refinancing steps, see the link: http://www.makinghomeaffordable.gov/programs/lower-rates/Pages/harp.aspx .

31. A 3.8 percent real estate taxes is applied on the conditions of their gross income and the sale price of their properties.

32. For more detailed information on the Home Affordable Modification Program (HAMF) administered by the Federal Housing Finance Agency (FHFA), see the link: http://www.makinghomeaffordable.gov/programs/lower-payments/Pages/hamp.aspx.

33. Terrence M. Clauretie and Nasser Daneshvary, "The Optimal Choice for Lenders Facing Defaults: Short Sale, Foreclose, or REO," *The Journal of Real Estate Finance and Economics* 42 (2011): 504–521.

34. Karen M. Pencer, "Foreclosing on Opportunity: State Laws and Mortgage Credit," *The Review of Economics and Statistics* 88 (2006): 177–182.

35. The summary of the 1972 URLTA is available at the link in the website of the National Conference Commissioners on Uniform State Laws: http://uniformlaws.org/ActSummary.aspx?title=Residential+Landlord+and+Tenant+Act .

36. *California Tenants: A Guide to Residential Tenants' and Landlords' Rights and Responsibilities* (California Department of Consumer Affairs, 2011); *Tenants' Rights in New Jersey: Legal Manual for Tenants in New Jersey*: http://www.lsnjlaw.org/Publications/Pages/Manuals/TenantsRights.pdf (Legal Services of New Jersey. 2007); and *Tennessee Code Annotated*: http://tn.gov/consumer/documents/UniformResidentialLandlordandTenantAct7.12.12.pdf (the State of Tennessee, 2012).

37. For the literature dealing with the impact of ethnic immigrant enclaves or communities on their homeownership rates, see George J. Borjas, "Homeownership in the Immigrant Population"; Gary Painter, Lihong Yang, and ZhouYu, "Homeownership Determinants for Chinese Americans: Assimilation, Ethnic Concentration, and Nativity," *Real Estate Economics* 32 (2004): 509–539; Gary Painter and ZhouYu, "Leaving Gateway Metropolitan Areas in the United States: Immigrants and the Housing Market," *Urban Studies* 45 (2008): 1163–1191; and Carlos Teixeira, "Cultural Resources and Ethnic Entrepreneurship."

38. Pyong Gap Min, *Caught in the Middle: Korean Communities in New York and Los Angeles* (Berkeley and Los Angeles, CA: University of California Press, 1996); and Kyeyoung Park, *The Korean American Dream: Immigrants and Small Businesses in New York City* (Ithaca, NY: Cornell University Press, 1997).

39. At closing, an escrow account is set up by the mortgage lender who wants to ensure a new homebuyer the timely payment of his or her county property tax, homeowners insurance, or mortgage insurance if his or her down payment is less than 20 percent of the property value. For more information, see the link: http://www.banks.com/articles/understanding-escrow-accounts . The rules to create and maintain escrow accounts are specified in the Real Estate Settlement Procedures Act of 1974 (RESPA) and its amendments: see http://www.federalreserve.gov/boarddocs/supmanual/cch/respa.pdf.

SIX

The American Financial Institution on the "MissyUSA" Community

One of the important goals immigrants of different racial and ethnic backgrounds want to achieve in their new country is to reach their good financial standing. To that end, attaining their good sense of competence about the financial institution of the host society can be a very important prerequisite. Undeniably, their greater sense of competence in their own or family financial management in their new country must be based upon their good knowledge of its financial institution. More specifically, it is also connected closely to their deft ability in managing their routine financial arrangements and handling their other significant financial affairs or plans both of which can be regarded as the most basic aspects of their own or family financial lives in their host country. In most cases, their routine financial arrangements in their host society are made possible by opening and managing their bank accounts (checking, savings, or credit cards) with which they can regularly conduct cash deposits or withdrawals, money transactions, bill payments, or the purchases of consumer goods or services, proceeding well with their good knowledge about the detailed rules, products, and services of a set of its banking sectors. Moreover, another thing that should be considered here is that there are many immigrants dealing with some other financial matters regularly, facing some financial affairs, and/or making the financial plans for themselves or their families, all of which, for example, cover the acquisition or payment of personal loans for a car, business, home, or education, payment delinquency or debts on credit cards, capital or retirement investment, the purchase, change, or cancellation of insurance for life, health, or accidental or property damage, or regular reports and payments of personal income tax or other taxes like property tax. Indeed, these significant financial matters to be experienced in their new country can be much more wisely planned and managed if they have a great deal of knowledge and understanding with regard to the rules of its certain financial sectors that lie at the heart of their concerns.

However, there is evidence that overall, immigrants in the United States participate substantially less in its formal financial sectors than native-born Americans, and that their lesser participation in its mainstream financial sectors—banking, insurance, pension, and investment (stocks and bonds)—usually tends to reflect their relatively short duration of residence, unstable employment status, lower income level, fewer total years of education, and so on.[1] To put it differently, in fact, the awareness of how the mainstream financial institution of the host country works is never easy for many immigrants, particularly recent immigrants, who have difficulty in understanding its financial systems, the specific financial instruments or services offered from each of its financial sectors, and the language of finance itself. Nonetheless, it does not mean that there is no way for them to improve their knowledge about the rules of the financial institution of their host country. For that matter, this book points to the importance and utilization of ethnic social networks—here, the "MissyUSA" community—in obtaining information on the rules of the American social institutions. The same account is also applied in this chapter of the American financial institution that mainly focuses on the rules of its three broad but distinctive sectors, that is, banking, insurance, and taxation.

The "MissyUSA" community is one of the Korean-American women's online communities in which full members hold similar backgrounds or statuses in marriage (married in the past, or being married at present), gender (female), the country of birth (South Korea), the use of the same language online (Korean), the country of current residence (the United States or Canada), and so on. More importantly, the "MissyUSA" community is a specific type of online social network that has the potential to create social capital among its participating members. In approaching the "MissyUSA" community from the perspective of information seekers (inquirers), it becomes an important network and channel for assessing information that has been regarded, in this book, as one form of social capital (social resources). In other words, some of its members seek a wide range of information about the rules of the American financial institution by posting their inquiry messages on the basis of their personal interests or concerns. For example, in the credit card business of the American banking sector, some of the "MissyUSA" members posted their messages requesting information on pay methods (online, mail), monthly payment amount (exactly or over the minimum, or the full payment), interest rates, outstanding balance, credit card fraud, access to an online account or statement, late, annual, or transaction fees, balance transfer, and the like. As another example, some of its members expressed their interests in a wide array of rules of the American insurance sector by posting their messages requesting information about the selection or the recommendation of insurance companies, agents, hospitals, or clinics, benefits or coverage, copayment, deductible, and so forth. Furthermore, there were also some members seeking information about the American tax system at federal, state, or local levels. In the case of individual income tax, for example, the widely requested inquiries from some of its members include such topics as the report methods (joint or individual, mail or electronic), required documents (W-2, receipts), the preparation of the report forms (a certified public accountant or their own), the period of tax report (deadline, extension), and tax refund, among others.

So far, then, still little is known about patterns of money management (assets, capital expenses), general and specific financial plans, and the decision-making process in the allocation of family financial resources in Korean-American families. In one sense, the handling of each of these family financial issues in Korean-American, husband-wife families appears to be influenced by their personal thoughts on family finances, attitudes to gender role or equity, division of labor (the care of the home or for the family, participation at work), socio-economic status, different degrees of their knowledge about financial portfolios, marital satisfaction, their level of English proficiency, their accessibility to ethnic financial sectors in or outside the Korean-American community, and so on. Likewise, another important point that remains unanswered in this chapter is also about the personal reasons why some "MissyUSA" members seek information on the specific matters directly or indirectly related to the rules of the American financial institution; however, it seems clear that most of them attempt to resolve their own or family's financial issues, and in the long run, to reach their good financial standing. Despite no further investigation of these two research topics in this chapter, there is no doubt that the transmission of financial information through the "MissyUSA" community will help its information seekers improve their knowledge of the financial matters that are difficult or often vague to comprehend on their own. Instead, there are two areas of concern in this chapter. First, a wide range of information on each of the three sectors of the American financial institution—banking, insurance, and taxation—will be introduced in great detail below to ensure the point that in the standpoint of its information seekers, the "MissyUSA" community functions as the important source of social resources (information).

Second, social support is another form of social capital. In the "MissyUSA" community, information providers (or respondents) are social supporters for its information seekers. In turn, the "MissyUSA" community can also be understood for them as the kind of social network oriented to support its information seekers. In this book, all the social supporters—information providers (respondents)—are largely classified into two broad groups according to the contents of their messages in response to the inquiry messages: instrumental guiders (information describers, analysts, confirmers, and advisors) and emotional supporters (companions, encouragers, and critics). Besides, it is this book's premise that their response messages are mostly subject to their personal experiences, expertise, judgment, or based on hearsay. Below, some specific cases of their messages in response to the posts seeking information are in detail illustrated and discussed under the setting of these two broad social support groups.

This chapter begins by introducing the brief history and general character of each of three U.S. financial institutional sectors (banking, insurance, and taxation). Second, Korean-Americans' familiarity with each of these three U.S. financial institutional sectors is discussed in the nexus between social capital and their ethnic community. Lastly, this chapter focuses on the analysis of some inquiry messages and their accompanying response messages in the framework of two forms of social capital (social resources and social support).

THE AMERICAN FINANCIAL INSTITUTION: HISTORY, LAWS, AND ORGANIZATIONS

The American financial institution is, in this chapter, defined as the collectivity of all the private (commercial banks, savings and loans associations, credit unions, investment banks, insurance companies) and public (all the finance, insurance, and taxation departments, and regulatory agencies attached to federal, state, or local governments) organizations that emerge from (or vanish after) the enactment (or revocation) of certain financial laws, rules, and policies to realize its own institution-wide goals, and operate at national, state, and local levels. Simply stated, one of the underlying goals of its private financial sectors is to raise their profits more by investing in lucrative businesses and contrarily, by reducing their business risks to be as low as possible. On the other hand, some clear goals of public financial sectors like financial regulatory agencies are to monitor and regulate unlawful competition in business, to prevent the potential conflicts of interest among financial companies—but in some cases, to promote safe and sound environments in their business activities, to protect consumers from those financial companies violating the laws (i.e., fraudulent charges, discriminatory lending practices), or to generate revenues through various tax codes designed to collect the resources for public budgets. Below is the general overview on the brief history of major laws, policies, programs, and key governance structures for each of the three American financial institutional sectors, namely, banking (deposits, transaction services, lending, and savings), insurance (life, health, and property), and taxation (personal income tax and other taxes).[2]

Banking

The banking sector, as one important segment of the American financial institution, is a very complicated one in the context of both business areas and regulatory systems. The key reason for the complexity of the U.S. banking sector, first of all, comes from the varying range of financial products or services offered by different types of banking companies over time, as the results of the enactments and amendments of the federal and state financial laws.[3] As to banking products or services, for example, the Banking Act of 1933, also known as the Glass-Steagall Act, was an early financial landmark law under which commercial banks and savings and loan associations, called "thrifts," could raise their capital by offering deposit accounts (checking and savings) and credit lending (loans and credit cards) to their customers, but their participation in the investment banking business was completely forbidden for the purpose of avoiding their potential conflicts of interest with investment banks in the financial market.[4] In contrast, this legislation also prohibited investment banks from offering checking and savings accounts, and it further set them to raise capital only through their issuances of securities (stocks, notes, and bonds) and the sales in the stock market or the money markets (any investors' markets). However, this 1933 Glass-Steagall Act was repealed by the Gramm-Leach-Bliley Act of 1999, also called the Financial Services Modernization Act, which is still effective today. The main provisions of this 1999 financial law were that banks or any financial companies in possession of a bank or more—namely, financial holding companies—are allowed to consolidate all resources and operate in a wide range of financial services, including both commercial and investment banking, investment in real estate, and insurance underwriting.[5]

Another major reason for the complication in the U.S. banking sector is because various public regulators in federal or state jurisdictions have different legal authorities to permit banking business licenses only to certain types of financial companies, and to oversee their operations to ensure their safe and sound banking practices and compliance with banking laws and regulations.[6] Of a wide variety of financial companies, for example, national banks are charted and regulated by the Office of the Comptroller of the Currency (OCC) at the Department of Treasury, while state banks are licensed and supervised by either the Federal Reserve System (or the Federal Reserve), also known as the central banking system of the United States, or the Federal Deposit Insurance Company (FDIC) as an independent agency of the federal government.[7] Other federally chartered financial companies such as savings banks and savings and loan associations are under the supervision of the Office of Thrift Supervision (OTS) as a bureau of the Department of Treasury.[8] Moreover, state finance departments also supervise and regulate both state-charted banks and thrifts. For example, the Office of Depositories with the Office of Consumer Finance in the New Jersey State Department of Banking and Insurance supervises all state-chartered commercial banks, savings banks, and savings and loan associations, regulating them in accordance with federal and state banking laws.[9]

In the early history of the U.S. banking industry, all banks and thrifts were state-chartered prior to the National Bank Act of 1864 that established the banking system for the chartering of banks at the national level (national banks).[10] Despite this 1864 financial law, the majority of U.S. federal and state banks and thrifts, until the late twentieth century, were relatively small in bank assets and size, and operated in geographically limited areas within their home states. In bank assets, for example, almost 96 percent of chartered commercial banks—14,078 out of 14,438—by 1980 held less than $1 billion much of which amount was derived from their businesses in local communities.[11] As their main business, these community banks were mainly concentrated on those financial areas of capital deposit (savings), transactions services, and lending (home, car, educational, personal or commercial loans) by targeting their local customers and households.[12] More broadly, the geographical restrictedness of banking businesses and the restricted business scopes of these small asset-holding banks were for a long period of time in effect due to the McFadden Act of 1927 that prohibited interstate branch banking, and the Bank Holding Company Act of 1956 that prohibited banks from the acquisition of other banks located outside of their home states or their merger or consolidation with banks in another state.[13] However, eventually, a long-time dominance of community banks in the U.S. banking business came to an end with the enactment of the Riegle-Neal Interstate Banking and Branching Efficiency Act (IBBEA) of 1994 that allowed interstate banking and also permitted a bank in the home state to acquire or consolidate banks in other states.[14] In addition to the effect of the Gramm-Leach-Bliley Act of 1999, the modern-day ascendancy of those banks holding large-scale assets over community banks in the banking industry appears to come up with this 1994 banking law that provided them an opportunity to increase the number of their branch banks (affiliates) across state lines.

In the stance of national, state, and community banks being established for the business of commercial banking, not only do they make revenues through deposit gathering and consumer finance (loans, credit cards), but also through their offering of a variety of transactions services to customers. For the latter, the typical way these banks make revenues is to charge fees on some transactions services to their checking account holders. In this case, some fees for their transactions services are named under monthly service fees, overdraft fees, return (bounded) check fees, and bank wire transfer fees.[15] Many commercial banks, especially national banks, also make profits through their bank-issuing credit card businesses by imposing a set of service charges to the credit card holders, as well as to those merchants accepting either of both payment cards—credit cards and debit cards.[16] For example, most of these service charges to their credit card cardholders come from monthly interest rates, annual fees, late payment fees, cash advance fees, balance transfer fees, and over limit fees.[17]

Above all, higher credit card interest rates often bore financial burden to many cardholders. Prior to the 1978 Supreme Court's decision, also known as the *Marquette* ruling, many states, under their state banking laws, imposed ceilings on the interest rates charged by credit card issuers to protect state cardholders.[18] At that time, a strong compliance to home state and out-of-state credit card issuers was a legal requirement on them under state banking laws that regulated higher credit card interest rates. However, the state regulators had no legal power in the matter of credit card interest rates after the decision of the *Marquette* ruling, and thereafter, any credit card issuers have acquired legal powers in applying the same interest rates of their home states to their out-of-state cardholders. In the years that followed after its legislation, the *Marquette* ruling brought out the relocation of some large-scale credit card issuers across states, the expansion of their credit card business sector, and as a consequence, the growing increase in consumer credit card debts.[19] Despite this really strong, substantial anti-consumer protection law, to some extent, cardholders have been also protected under some other federal laws, for example, such laws that prohibited "the unsolicited issuance of credit cards" by the Truth in Lending Act of 1968, required card issuers the correction of any error in credit card bills by the Fair Credit Billing Act of 1974, required credit card issuers the disclosure of their customers' credit terms and charges by the Fair Credit and Charge Card Disclosure Act of 1988, established the protection of identity theft in consumer credit by the Fair and Accurate Credit Transactions Act of 2003, and that placed existing accounts limits on the increase in interest rates and finance charges by the Credit CARD Act of 2009.[20]

Insurance

Insurance is the principal financial instrument of the insurance industry—especially, insurance companies and their agents and brokers, and by one or more purchases of their products, the policyholders can be insured, guaranteed, or indemnified "against loss, harm, damage, disability, or death," or build their cash up, in return for the premium paid in one lump sum or payable periodically—monthly, quarterly, semiannually, or annually.[21] Upon this point the insurance sector of the American financial institution can be generally classified into three major segments: life/annuities, accident (workers' compensation) and health (medical, dental), and property/casualty (auto, home).[22] Furthermore, diverse kinds of insurance products are available within these respective

American insurance segments. In the case of the home insurance business, for example, there is an array of insurance products, such as those for homeowners, landlords, and renters, flood insurance, and condominium insurance, among others. Then, the fact that selling insurance products is a very lucrative business for insurance companies has always had the potential to produce inhospitable competition against each other and to harm the rights and interests of consumers.

In response, legal regulations for stabilizing the U.S. insurance market and protecting consumers from the unlawful business conducts of insurance companies were in effect over time under some federal and state financial (banking and insurance) laws and their amendments. In the early periods in the history of the U.S. insurance industry, to insurance companies the insurance business was a highly protected and separate financial market for them under the Banking Act of 1933 and the Bank Holding Company Act of 1956 that prohibited banks (commercial banks and thrifts) and other financial sectors (investment banks and brokerage firms) from engaging in the underwriting of insurance and the transaction of its products in their business.[23] As an exception, the Bank Holding Company Act of 1956 allowed insurance companies to be owned by one-bank holding companies—not holding companies with two banks or more.[24] Besides, this 1956 banking law also upheld the provisions of the National Bank Act in 1916 and 1918, which permitted the insurance companies affiliated to one-bank holding companies to sell insurance products to people in a local community where the population is fewer than 5,000.[25] Since the mid-1980s, however, the insurance business was no longer the business area exclusively permitted to independent insurance companies or those insurance companies affiliated to banks. This new legal status for non-insurance companies—e.g., commercial banks or thrifts holding companies—to sell some insurance products came into effect after the Office of the Comptroller of the Currency (OCC) supervising national-chartered banks had authorized them to participate themselves directly in a few selected insurance businesses—i.e., the selling of variable and fixed-rate annuities.[26]

It was the Gramm-Leach-Bliley Act of 1999 that made it possible for bank or thrift holding companies to sell the full array of insurance products, under the legal provisions to permit them to be consolidated with insurance companies and a financial holding company owning banks as its subsidiaries (affiliates or branches).[27] This 1999 banking legislation further granted the legal right to state insurance departments—i.e., the New York State Department of Financial Service—for supervising and regulating insurance companies in their states.[28] This provision of the 1999 banking law was really in compliance with the McCarran-Ferguson Act of 1945, in which within the state, the business activities of insurance companies are under the supervision of its regulatory agency.[29] Upon the enactment of these legislations, for example, state insurance departments have had the legal power to determine company licensing to sell insurance products or its suspension or revocation, producer licensing (insurance agents and brokers), the approval of sellable products or the terms of each insurance product (policy premiums, coverage, or benefits), and the oversight of accounting or marketing practices to certain insurance companies with those aims to promote fair competition among them and to protect consumers.[30] Thus, until now, the business of insurance is to a great extent subject to state regulations. It also implies that state insurance laws usually supersede comparable federal laws (antitrust laws) in regulating the business of insurance that ultimately emphasizes the relationship between an insurer and the policyholder.[31] Otherwise, federal antitrust laws are mostly applicable to the out-of-state business activities of the insurer (an insurance company), or any of its businesses beyond the scope of the insurance business—i.e., company mergers or joint ventures, its provider arrangements (pharmacies), or unreasonable fee charges or fraudulent benefit payments to its policyholders.[32]

Taxation

Tax revenues are a financial lifeline for the planning, management, and operation of all the U.S. federal, state, and local governments and their affiliated organizations. For the U.S. federal and state governments—especially the federal government, tax revenues have also been its major source of finance to achieve its social goals for the general public, for example, by investing them for improvements of social infrastructure services (roads, ports, electric power facilities, water service and sewerage), new job creations, and for public social programs (education, health, housing, unemployment, or welfare).[33] In the long history of the U.S. tax system, however, such federal government's policies on wealth redistributions through investment in infrastructure and social programs funded by tax revenues were not always successful. For it is because certain social groups (i.e., the rich, entrepreneurs) often expressed their strong support to the tax legislations favoring the economic stimulus package and heavy government spending cuts that ultimately involve lowering tax rates on various tax bases.[34] Thus, the shifting power dynamics among social groups with different interests over time have been the crux of the matter in the U.S. tax history.

The current U.S. federal tax system, known as the Internal Revenue Code (IRC), covers four main tax sources: income taxes on individuals and corporations, employment taxes on employers, estate or gift taxes, and excise taxes on selected goods and services.[35] For example, the taxable income of a corporation (the corporate income tax) is calculated through all gross incomes (profits, dividends, rents, loyalties, and other gains), deductions or liabilities (wages, expenses, debts, losses, and other expenses), and credits (investment, research, or employment).[36] On this basis, federal income tax rates for corporations vary from 15 percent to 35 percent.[37] The employment (or payroll) taxes are levied from both employers and employees to provide social security benefits and Medicare benefits to their employees. In fiscal year 2013, each party should have paid for 6.2 percent of social security tax (earnings up to $113,700) and 1.45 percent of Medicare tax (all earnings), respectively.[38] Since 2010, the gift tax was combined with the estate tax; for example, the gift and estate tax exemption is up to $5 million so that a 35 percent tax rate is imposed on any amount over that.[39] Some goods and services on excise taxes are alcoholic beverages, tobacco products, firearms, certain medical devices, the annual fee for health insurance providers, and so on.[40]

Above all, personal income tax is of great concern to most taxpayers. In 1913, the Sixteenth Amendment to the U.S. Constitution gave Congress the power to tax income.[41] From then until now, federal tax laws on personal income have been many times revised in those sections of income bases (wages, salaries, loyalties, dividends, and other income sources), the number of income brackets and tax rates, deductions (or exemptions), and credits. For example, the Tax Reform Act of 1986 excluded unemployment compensation and long-term capital gains (i.e., the sale of stocks or paintings held for over a year) from the sources of taxable income, both of which were taxable in the fiscal year 2013.[42] As taxpayers' annual income increases, so do their tax rates. In the fiscal year 2013, for instance, taxpayers in the highest income bracket ($400,000 for single filers, or $450,000 for married filing jointly) had a 39.6 percent tax rate.[43] But, the Economic Growth and Tax Relief Reconciliation Act of 2001 (EGTRRA) that was repealed this time allowed taxpayers in the same highest income bracket to pay a 35 percent tax rate.[44] These days, taxpayers can reduce their tax liability by deducting their expenses in moving, tuition, student loan interest, alimony, self-employed health insurance, retirement savings plan, and home mortgage interest, among others.[45]

Moreover, the amount of their personal taxable income can be further reduced with their tax credits subject to their income, age, filing status, and the number of dependent children. For example, the Taxpayer Relief Act of 1997 provided for a $500 tax credit for each qualifying child under the age of 17, while the 2001 EGTRRA doubled per child tax credit into $1,000, still the same amount in fiscal year 2013.[46] This same 2001 EGTRRA also introduced a measure of the standard deduction in which the amount is twice for couples filing jointly, compared with singles or couples filing separately, and that ratio was the same in fiscal year 2013.[47] From the outset, the Internal Revenue Services (IRS), as a bureau of the Department of the Treasury, is responsible for the collection of all federal taxes, and it also has the legal power to investigate various tax law violations (tax frauds, false claims, and tax schemes).[48]

State and many local governments (cities, counties, or municipalities) also have their own tax laws or codes to collect income taxes on individuals and corporations, employment taxes on employers, estate or gift taxes, and excise taxes on selected goods and services.[49] For example, in New York State, personal income tax rates in the fiscal year 2012 varied from 4 percent to 8.82 percent according to income (earnings) and filing status.[50] Similar to the federal income tax return, the taxable income of New York residents or non-residents having the New York source of income is also calculated after the subtraction of their deductions or credits, such as college tuition expenses, child credit, resident credit, volunteer firefighters and ambulance workers credit, and so on.[51] The corporations in New York State are also obliged to pay the corporate income tax to New York State up to a rate of 7.1 percent.[52] Besides, New York State imposes a 4 percent sales tax on the sale of most goods and services, having excise taxes on certain goods (cigarette and tobacco products, alcoholic beverages, highway diesel motor fuel).[53] Furthermore, local governments in New York State, like those in other states, are primarily in charge of collecting property taxes on real property.[54]

FINANCE AND SOCIAL CAPITAL IN THE KOREAN-AMERICAN COMMUNITY

Among the Korean immigrant families that arrived in the United States during their childhood or adulthood, more than 75 percent of them in the years of 2006–2008 were married-couple families; for the same period, approximately 13 percent of them constituted female-headed households.[55] In either case, so far little is known about their short- and long-term family financial plans. Also, much remains unknown about the general financial managements, decision-making, and behaviors especially among the married couples of Korean immigrant, or Korean-American, families whose home financial arrangements often correlated with their personal attitudes to their own and family finances, their work status, their gender-based division of labor in the family, their marital relationship, their family structure with or without other adults or children, their stage in life, and so forth. As for the sources of information about and advice on family finances in their new land, the questions of who their key informants are and what social networks they participate in are also mostly left unanswered. Nonetheless, one thing that is clear here is that their residence in one of larger Korean-American gateway cities or communities provides them a great opportunity to make use of a larger pool of ethnic social networks in times of their needs to improve their knowledge or understanding about the rules of various American financial sectors and, in particular, to assess information about a wide array of products and services to be now implemented by each of these three afore-mentioned American financial sectors.

For instance, the family members or friends settled earlier in a large Korean-American gateway must be a great source of social resources for their newly arrived Korean families or friends being inhabited in the same area. Indeed, the dissemination of all sorts of information about the rules of the American financial institution can be considered one type of their social support to these newcomers. In the banking sector of the American financial institution, for example, some of these earlier settled family members or friends become important guiders or advisors to their newcomers who seek to open up new bank checking accounts to deposit or withdraw money, or manage various transactions such as wire transfer and bill payments, to open up their debit or credit card accounts to purchase goods and services and pay for those bills, or to understand their bank or card statements. Moreover, their important roles goes beyond such banking sector because some of them also used to become guiders or advisors to their newcomers who seek to obtain information on some products and services offered by other financial sectors—e.g., insurance and taxation. In addition, another important role some of them typically take on is the role of informants through which they introduce some co-ethnic financial experts to their newcomers suffering from certain kinds of financial matters. On the whole, the general list of these co-ethnic financial experts includes bank managers or clerks, insurance agents or brokers, certified public accounts (CPAs), and financial advisors or planners (retirement and other investments). At this juncture, the roles of Korean-American churches and their members should not be underestimated in Korean immigrants' financial lives in American society. Regardless of where Korean immigrants live—in or outside Korean immigrant gateway metropolitan areas, their participation in Korean-American churches provides some of them an opportunity to learn information necessary to tackle certain financial matters they have faced, or to improve their overall financial well-being, through interactions with their other church members.

Interestingly enough, in the case of the larger Korean immigrant gateway metropolitan areas, the improvement of Korean immigrants' knowledge about the rules of the American financial institution is also in close connection with a growing number of Korean financial sectors, most of which are targeting Korean-Americans as their major customer base, along with the growth of their Korean-speaking staffs who provide services to their co-ethnic customers with or without a limited proficiency in English. As a matter of fact, Korean- or Korean-American owned banks and their branches, also under the supervision of federal or state regulatory agencies, have grown from 30 in 1990 and 74 in 2000 to 138 in 2006, in the three larger Korean immigrant gateway metropolitan areas (their central cities and suburbs)—e.g., Los Angeles, New York, and Washington, DC.[56] This time, though not much specific data is available yet, many non-Korean (mainstream) banks and branches in these areas and other larger Korean immigrant gateways—i.e., Chicago, Atlanta, San Francisco, Philadelphia, or Houston—are also likely to hire Korean-speaking bank managers or tellers more as a way to attract more local Korean-speaking customers. In these same Korean-American gateways, many Korean-speaking people are also working as insurance agents who deal with a certain or wide range of insurance products or services—i.e., life, annuities, children's education, accident, health, or property and casualty—or as tax accounts (all the tax-related matters) and/or financial advisors—i.e., any monetary, retirement, or investment plans and managements. According to a recent Korean business directory that covers New York and New Jersey metropolitan areas, for example, there were more than 300 large- or mostly small-scale insurance agencies owned by Koreans, or worked by Koreans who are working at either Korean-owned or mainstream insurance companies.[57] In these same Korean or Korean-American concentrated gateways, the number of financial advisors and mostly, certified public accounts in Korean names also exceeded 300.[58]

When Korean immigrants settle in one of the largest Korean immigrant metropolitan gateways, there are also other routes for them to improve their knowledge about their personal or family financial issues in American society, and to gain information about recent trends in the U.S. financial markets or in the U.S. financial or taxation laws. First of all, American financial information and updated news on it are generally well covered by various local Korean language media, such as locally aired Korean television or radio stations, locally issued daily Korean newspapers, and dozens of Korean magazines or periodicals issued on a monthly or weekly basis. For example, two major Korean language daily newspapers—*The Korea Times* and *The Korea Daily*—give heavy coverage to a broad range of financial topics that include the currency of national financial markets and their individual sectors, any updates or revisions in American financial or taxation laws or systems at the national, state, and local levels, and their resulting general or specific impacts on the financial lives of Korean-Americans. Second, one-day seminars or lectures on many financial topics are frequently organized by regional- or local-level Korean-American associations or non-profit organizations in such larger Korean immigrant gateways. These forums especially are highly valuable to some local Korean-American residents who are interested in enhancing their understanding of certain financial issues—i.e., financial plans for investment, retirement, or children's education, the self-employment tax report, and the annual tax report of foreign-asset holders, among others.

As stated in previous chapters, the residential location of Korean-Americans becomes less and less important in this new age of computer and information technologies. Their direct link to the online websites of these local Korean-language newspapers now makes them easily accessible to American financial news and recent trends in American federal and local financial markets. Even the acquisition of information or advice about their personal financial matters is now much easier for them by posting their inquiry messages seeking information on such a well-known Korean-American online website as the "MissyUSA" community.

THE AMERICAN FINANCIAL INSTITUTION ON THE "MISSYUSA" COMMUNITY

The homepage of the "MissyUSA" website offers a list of links for its members of married Korean-American women, such as talk lounge, health and beauty, home and food, motherhood, life information, commerce, missy writer, and missy shopping. The message board called "Life Q&A" within its talk lounge page was selected in this book in an attempt to demonstrate that the messages posted on it generally embrace the two distinctive forms of social capital—that is, social resources (information) in the perspective of information seekers (inquirers) and social support for information seekers in the perspective of respondents (or information providers). As stressed earlier, the latter was further classified into two broad groups: instrumental guiders (information describers, analysts, confirmers, and advisors), and emotional supporters (companions, encouragers, and critics). Below, some text messages on the three broadly classified American financial sectors—banking (deposits, transaction services, lending, and savings), insurance (life, health, and property), and taxation (personal income tax and other taxes)—are in detail illustrated, and then, discussed in the framework of these two forms of social capital.

Banking

Many members of the "MissyUSA" community requested a wide range of information about the rules of the U.S. banking business sector. Their frequent inquiries in this broad category can be largely divided into three parts: checking bank accounts, the other services of commercial banks, and credit cards. At first, the major topics of its members' inquiries, in the category of checking bank accounts, are on the opening or closing of a checking account at a bank, bank deposit, money withdrawal, the usage of a bank ATM, the usage of a debit card or a personal check, overdraft or bounced check fees, monthly maintenance fees, and so on.[59] Three specific cases for it are in detail introduced here. On April 2, 2012, one member posted a message requesting information about the deposit of a large amount of cash at the bank after which post there were five response messages:

Q: I am planning to purchase my house soon. I am now holding myself $30,000 in cash as part of its down payment cost. Then, I have heard earlier that if more than $10,000 in cash is deposited in a bank, I should prepare a document reporting its source to the IRS [Internal Revenue Service]. Does its amount limit mean the money written in a personal check or the total money deposited for a certain period of time like per month? What are the best ways to deposit $30,000 safely?
A1: Your bank will handle any matter so that you can deposit it all together. There is no problem in your bank deposit if you didn't obtain that money illegally. Hold the record that the money deposited at the bank was used for a down payment on a house. In my case, I didn't have any problem with the deposit of almost $70,000 in cash at the bank.
A2: There is an automatic reporting system to the IRS when the deposited money is linked to money laundering, drug trafficking, tax evasion, and other illegal sources. You don't have to worry about your bank deposit if your money was legitimately obtained.
A3: If your cash wasn't unlawfully obtained, just deposit it. Your bank will fill in a form for you. Why do you worry about it? There is no tax for your deposit. You will get a suspicion from your bank in case you deposit that money three times.
A4: When you purchase a house, your mortgage lender will request you its legal source. . . . Keep in mind that your deposit over $10,000 will be reported to the IRS.
A5: Deposit it at your bank in four times. . . . Each time, try to deposit $8,000 or $9,000.

In the early history of the Korean-American community, there has been an unidentified anecdote that depositing a large amount of cash at the bank would bring some negative outcomes, such as increasing income tax, disqualification for some public services due to a high income, or the IRS investigation on the sources of the cash and a tax fraud. Clearly, the worry of this inquirer came from the third reason. In this series of messages, all five respondents belong to the subgroup of information advisors to the inquirer. Both roles of information analysts and emotional encouragers for the inquirer are also revealed in the messages of three respondents (A1, A2, and A3) among whom Respondent 1 (A1) shared her experience (companionship) on the issue raised by the inquirer.

An information inquiry about the balance on a bank account was posted on January 7, 2012. Three members responded to this post:

Q: Now the balance of my bank account falls below zero. Can I still use my debit card to buy some items at the grocery store?
A1: It differs across banks. In my case, it didn't work. At that time, I felt how tough life is.
A2: I worked at a bank before. You cannot use your debit card, and there will even be a charge of $20 or $30 from your bank when you attempt to use it. The best way is to use your personal check for the

> purchase of any product, and then deposit money to your bank as early as possible . . .
> A3: There are two options in your case. The first is that you can use it in your agreement to pay for that charge. But you should make your bank balance positive by depositing some money to your bank on the same day. Otherwise, you cannot make use of this option next time. The second is your agreement not to use it in case your balance falls below zero. For more information, visit or call your bank.

Overall, two respondents (A2 and A3) belong to the subgroup of information analysts, as well as the subgroup of information advisors, for the inquirer. Besides, companionship to the inquirer is contained in the message of Respondent 1 (A1) who is also considered to be the information describer to her.

On December 5, 2012, one member posted a message requesting information about banks' policies on monthly maintenance fees. There were seven response messages, the first five of which are stated here:

> Q: I have been holding a checking account at Wells Fargo [a nationwide provider of banking services] over the last 20 years. Until recently, I didn't pay any monthly maintenance fee, despite the fact that the balance of my bank account was below $1,000. But, this time, there is a $10 monthly maintenance fee. When I contacted the bank to find out the reason for this new charge, the response from my bank was that I should maintain my monthly balance of at least $1,500 for no fee. How about the other banks?
> A1: It depends on what kinds of checking accounts you hold. There is no requirement of a minimum balance in my checking account.
> A2: That's why I changed my bank from Wells Fargo to Chase . . .
> A3: It also happened to me. I pay $12 or $15 as a monthly maintenance fee if my monthly minimum balance falls below $2,000. There seems to be relatively high charges for other services as well . . .
> A4: Other banks, such as Bank of American and Sun Trust, are the same. Request the waiving of your monthly charge by visiting your bank.
> A5: It really depends on the types of checking accounts. I am holding two checking accounts from two different banks, one of which is Wells Fargo. I am satisfied with the services provided from it. I advise you to change your policy within which no monthly maintenance fee is offered.

As usual, most American banks impose monthly maintenance fees to their checking account holders. Then, the amount of monthly maintenance fees for checking accounts generally differs across banks that set out their own terms and conditions of the checking account. Here, two respondents (A4 and A5) are positioned to take on the role of information advisors to the inquirer. Like Respondent 5 (A5), Respondent 1 (A1) generally belongs to the subgroup of information analysts for the inquirer. In addition, strong companionship to the inquirer is revealed in the posts of two respondents (A2 and A3).

In the category of the other services of commercial banks, some major topics of information inquiry are on various sorts of services from banks, such as the offerings of bank loans, credit lines, or bank saving accounts, as well as such services as bill payments, cashier's check, wire transfer, and money order. Illustrated below are three specific cases in this category. First, information about a line of credit was requested by one member's message posted on August 8, 2012. Three members replied to this post:

> Q: Today I went to my bank and its manager, after reviewing my bank and credit card statements, who explained me good things about a line of credit. Still I don't understand what that is. Is there anyone who can have a right answer for this?
> A1: In Korean, it can be translated *Mainus Tongjang*.
> A2: There is an interest rate for it.
> A3: This is the amount of money you can borrow from your bank. If your bank sends you a check, you can use it in your credit limit or deposit it at a bank. Interest rates for credit lines are usually lower than those on credit cards. Your available credit line is often determined by your bank on the basis of your home equity. It is also well known to those who run their own businesses. I also received it from Bank of America by which I purchased a car and paid off credit card debt.

The first two respondents (A1 and A2) belong to the subgroup of information describers to the inquirer. But, Respondent 3 (A3) fulfills the multiple roles for her, as an information analyst, an advisor, and an encourager.

On September 4, 2012, one member posted a message requesting information on the fee for the money order.[60] It was followed by three response messages:

> Q: How much is the fee for the money order?
> A1: It differs across banks. You should go ask banks to figure it out.
> A2: Fees for the money orders at banks are expensive. Instead, use *Western Union* or *Stater Bros. Markets* through which the fee for the money order of less than $500 is only $1.00 or below. You can make several money orders in case your fund to send is more than $500.
> A3: Fees differ across regions. The public market in my community imposes a $1.00 fee on the money order of less than $500. Nearly a $2.00 fee is paid in making a money order in the post office in my community.

Money orders are a payment method frequently used to secure some types of transactions. For example, on the date of closing for home contract, the homebuyers are often required to bring a money order, not a personal check, for their down payment. In analyzing these three response messages, one observation is that two respondents (A1 and A2) take on the role of information advisors for the inquirer, and that Respondent 1 (A1) also belongs to the information describer to her. As another finding, Respondent 3 (A3) takes on her role as an information expositor for the inquirer.

On December 10, 2012, an information inquiry about the payment of bills was posted by one member, and then, two members responded to it, along with the postings of two additional messages from the inquirer:

> Q: I don't know how to use online banking for bill payments . . .
> A1: You need to set up your online bank account. Then, you can pay any bills like your rent by putting all necessary information (the name and address of your homeowner or your home management company, and the due day for its payment) on its pay section. If these steps are not easy for you to understand, try to call your bank for further assistance . . .
> A2: Put all the information on the pay section of your online bank account. Then, the convenience of online banking is that its system pays your bills automatically on designated days.
> Q: Thank you for providing this information. Let me suppose that I put all the information on the pay section of my online bank account, how are my bills paid, automatically or after responses from the receivers of my bills?
> A1: Your bills are automatically paid regardless of payees' responses. Your bank will pay by either wire transfer or its bank checks.
> Q: Thanks once again.

Both respondents (A1 and A2) belong to the subgroup of information analysts, as well as the subgroup of information advisors, to the inquirer. Several times, this inquirer expressed her appreciation to both respondents regarding their postings of the information that was requested from her.

There were many messages requesting information about credit cards. They cover a wide range of topics, such as services (the opening of a credit card, balance transfer, bill payments), interest rates, payments (late, minimum, the due date), fees (late, annual, cash advance), credit card debts or settlement, credit scores, fraud, and statements, among others. Of them, three specific examples are illustrated here. First, one member posted a message requesting information on the opening of a credit card on December 10, 2012. There were five response messages that followed this post:

> Q: At present, I am using my husband's credit cards by adding up my name. I tried to open up my own credit card, but my applications were rejected twice. The main reason of their rejection was that there was no history of my bank accounts and my transactions with banks. I didn't put my social security number when I first opened a checking account at the bank. Does this absence of my social security number in my

checking account affect my credit history? In my case, what should I do to open a new credit card account?
A1: *Sears* and *Macy's* issue credit cards to people with no or weak credit histories. If you have a good payment record for over a year, other credit card companies will offer you credit cards by mail.
A2: Some credit history is needed to open a *Sears* card.
A3: It is strange that you don't have any credit history. For your name has been already added in your husband's credit cards. Try to apply to those credit card companies like *Capital One, Citibank,* and *U.S. Bank.* If it doesn't work, try to open a secured card.[61]
A4: If you have a social security number, add it into your husband's credit cards. It can help you improve your credit history.
A5: You should include your social security number in your banks' checking accounts.

As usual, non-U.S. citizens with no Social Security number are required to provide other proof of their identification—e.g., passport, driver's license, employment ID—in order to open up a new bank account in the United States. After having their Social Security number, then it is important to report it to their banks to build their credit history. In these posts, all five respondents are regarded as the subgroup of information advisors to the inquirer. Besides, Respondent 3 (A3) gave great encouragement to her.

On January 3, 2012, information on a transaction fee for a cash advance from a credit card was requested by one member. Four response messages followed this inquiry message:

Q: I own a credit card at Bank of America. I want to take the cash advance of $1,000 from it. . . . How much is its transaction fee and interest rate?
A1: It depends on the level of your credit. You can find them from your credit card statements.
A2: I paid $80 as the transaction fee for the cash advance of $2,000. I didn't check its interest rate, but I felt that its transaction fee was too expensive.
A3: In my daughter's case, there was a $30 transaction fee on the cash advance of $50.
A4: Don't try to use cash advances from your credit card. It would rather borrow that amount of money from your bank . . .

By and large, the role of information describers to the inquirer is performed by three respondents (A1, A2, and A3) who posted their short response messages. Besides, two respondents (A1 and A4) take on the role of information advisors for the inquirer.

On June 4, 2012, there was a post requesting information about the relation between minimum payments and a credit score. Thereafter, there were six response messages and an additional message from the inquirer:

Q: I am using credit cards with minimum monthly payments for over a year. . . . Does this practice have a negative impact on my credit score?
A1: If you use them for over 30 percent of your total credit limits, your credit score will fall.
Q: Is my credit score expected to drop even if I pay off the amount used per month?
A2: A credit card issuer told me that it is fine to use my credit card up to 50 percent of my credit line. The most damaging thing for your credit score is your late payments. Try to pay your credit card bills on time.
A3: I didn't pay $70 of my bill over three months. The result was from 780 to 630 in my credit score . . .
A4: It is wise to use them below 30 percent of your total credit limit. Don't ignore their interest rates.
A5: You should take into consideration higher interest rates from them. Try to pay off your credit card balances.
A6: Increasing debts will make your credit score become lower. . . . Your pattern of paying the minimum amount every month will affect your credit score negatively. The best solution is to pay them off.

In the United States, a good management of credit cards can build a good credit history. Otherwise, its opposite damages one's credit record. In this series of messages, all six respondents belong to the subgroup of information advisors to the inquirer. Four of them (A1, A2, A4, and A6) are also to some extent considered as the subgroup of information analysts for the inquirer.

Insurance

On the "Life Q&A" message board of the "MissyUSA" community, there were many inquiry messages on the rules of the American insurance sector, which generally consists of those business units in health (medical, dental), property/casualty (auto, home) and accident (workers' compensation), and life/annuities. Interestingly, what is common among these three different insurance business units is that the inquirers expressed their interests in the acquisition of information about insurance providers (companies or agents), programs or products, the terms and conditions of coverage or benefits, payments or costs (copayment, deductible), or claims (procedures, compensation). Introduced below are the five specific cases selected among these topics. At first, on February 6, 2012, there was a message requesting information about health insurance coverage. Four response messages followed this initial post:

Q: I am covered by a health insurance program recommended by an insurance agent. Recently I had a surgery at a hospital. Then, I realized that my insurance company would cover only 80 percent of my medical bill. I thought that all of my medical expenses, in my contract, would be covered from my health insurance policy. When I contacted my insurance agent, what I was heard is that; a) there is no insurance covering 100 percent in any medical bill; b) in my insurance, my insurance company is responsible for 80 percent of that bill; and c) my responsibility is 20 percent ($20,000). From my agent's remarks, I was totally shocked and very angry. Is it really true that there is no health insurance program covering 100 percent of the medical bills?

A1: Most health insurance companies hold a co-payment agreement with their policyholders at their visits to hospitals or their doctors' offices, but there are many health insurances covering 100 percent of the medical bills . . .

A2: Most health insurances provide this 80/20 rule. . . . There are the full insurance coverages offered by insurance companies, but your monthly payment to your insurance company [premium] is its high cost.

A3: I think that you hold a policy with a 80/20 and a very high deductible. If your insurance had 100 percent coinsurance, you might have had no additional payment after your deductible. Unfortunately, it was too late . . . [62]

A4: You signed your insurance policy without checking it carefully. Your agent has no legal responsibility for it. It's completely in your fault.

By and large, the role of information analyst for the inquirer is conducted by the first three respondents (A1, A2, and A3) who explained the general terms and conditions on private health insurance. But, all four respondents belong to the subgroup of information advisors to the inquirer. As a critic, Respondent 4 (A4) pointed out the inquirer's carelessness in the review of her health policy plan.

On December 2, 2012, a member posted a message requesting information about her currently covered car insurance plan. There were seven response messages, the first five of which are here introduced, including an additional message from the inquirer:

Q: The table below shows the summary of my current car insurance policy:

BODILY INJURY & PROPERTY DAMAGE LIABILITY: BI $25,000 EACH PERSON— $50,000 EACH ACCIDENT PROPERTY DAMAGE LIABILITY— $10,000 EACH ACCIDENT	$253.00
MEDICAL PAYMENTS $1,000 EACH PERSON	$10.00
COMPREHENSIVE ACV LESS $500 DEDUCTIBLE	$43.00
COLLISION ACV LESS $500 DEDUCTIBLE	$285.00
UNINSURED/UNDERINSURED MOTORIST: $25,000 EACH PERSON - $50,000 EACH ACCIDENT	$20.00

> I am not willing to pay any extra cost of my car insurance, but want to know the extent of my current coverage.
> A1: The coverage for bodily injury should be at least $100,000 per person. Your insurance coverage is generally low.
> A2: You are not much covered when a car accident occurred. Try to raise the coverage of bodily injury into a range of $100,000 and $300,000.
> A3: Your coverage is limited only to a minor car accident.
> Q: Thank you. I am annually paying $1,200 for this car insurance plan. Anyhow, I will change the coverage for bodily injury into $100,000. What is $1,000 in medical payments per person?
> A4: It is for the amount of your medical expenses caused by a car accident. If you don't have any health insurance, you need to raise its coverage in the range of $2,500 and $5,000.
> A5: If you have changed Bodily Injury & Property Damage Liability into $100,000/$300,000, the same change should be appeared in Uninsured/Underinsured Motorist.

The first three respondents (A1, A2, and A3) and Respondent 4 (A4) belong to the subgroup of information advisors to the inquirer, while Respondent 4 (A4) also takes on the role of an information analyst for the inquirer.

On July 10, 2012, an information inquiry about the cost of home insurance was posted by one member. Four members responded to it:

> Q: The market value of my house is $675,000. The annual cost of my home insurance plan for it is $1,400 from AAA [the American Automobile Associate]. I was surprised to hear that one of my friends is paying $400 only. How much do you pay for your home insurance?
> A1: Home insurance costs vary across regions.
> A2: The range of its costs is between $515 and $1,050 per year.
> A3: In the State of California, its costs range from $500 to $1,000 per year.
> A4: In *Travelers* [an insurance company], the cost of home insurance is $2,000 on the condition of $500 deductible for the house value of $2,000,000.

In the United States, the costs of home insurance vary with the market value and the regional location of the property, the portion of homeowner's deductible (the amount of money homeowners should pay on their own from a loss due to fire, accidental damage, or storm), the extent of other coverages (personal property such as furniture and appliances, personal injury, water back-up), and so on. In the perspective of social support, the first three respondents (A1, A2, and A3) can be generally put into the subgroup of information describers to the inquirer. By explaining a specific case, Respondent 4 (A4) takes on the role of an information analyst to the inquirer.

On June 5, 2012, a message requesting information about workers' compensation insurance was posted. Thereafter, there were three response messages and two additional messages from the same inquirer:

> Q: I run a small business. There was a severe cut in one foot of my employee that caused twenty one stitches in a hospital. In addition to medical bills, what other benefits are covered by workers' compensation insurance? I remember signing its coverage that includes temporary disability payments to the employee . . .
> A1: I laid off one of my employees. Then, that person received almost $100,000 worth of workers' compensation benefits by appealing to the neck and back pains related to the job. I was so upset because that person worked only four months at my store . . .
> Q: I fully understand your feeling. . . . My business is not so good. To make matters worse, this incidence happened to me.
> A2: Your injured worker will receive two thirds (66.6%) of the worker's weekly average pay.
> Q: That's really good news to me. I worried about the burden of my dual payments—weekly wages to my injured worker and workers' compensation insurance premiums . . .
> A3: To find the level of coverage in your insurance policy, you need to contact your insurance agent.

Respondent 1 (A1) expressed some companionship to the inquirer by posting the case similar to the inquirer's. Respondent 2 (A2) generally takes on the role of an information describer to the inquirer, whereas Respondent 3 (A3) becomes the information advisor to the inquirer.

On April 10, 2012, one member posted a message requesting information about a pension plan for retirement and a life insurance policy for savings. There were six response messages, the first four of which are introduced below:

> Q: My husband and I are now in our late 30s. We have no child, no house, and no savings for our old ages. Now we are thinking about a preparation for our future by having either a pension plan for retirement like an IRA [individual retirement account] or a life insurance policy for savings [whole life insurance]. The insurance agent I contacted recommended me to buy a life insurance policy for savings . . . I need your advice.
> A1: There is no relationship between a pension plan for retirement and a life insurance. A life insurance is not fit for the purpose of savings, but it is a kind of a guarantee for future risk. . . . There is a heavy termination penalty in most life insurances for savings.
> A2: Life insurances for savings have a commission to salesman and the cost of fund management. . . . They are not good for a long-term investment.
> A3: It is not a good idea to hold a life insurance account for your savings. Try to buy a cheap life insurance plan like a term life insurance plan and put your remaining money in your IRA.

A4: I am now regretting holding a life insurance account for saving . . . I can only put small amounts of money in my 401 (k) and IRA accounts. If you want to buy a house, don't buy any life insurance plan for savings.

There are three customary retirement plans (or accounts): a 401(k) plan, a traditional IRA (individual retirement account), and a Roth IRA. A 401 (k) plan is an employer-sponsored retirement savings plan, while both IRA plans accounts are set up through insurance agents or advisors working at financial companies. There are many other differences between a 401(k) plan and both IRAs in terms of contribution limits, taxation, withdrawal penalty, and other benefits.[63] In this series of messages, all four respondents belong to the subgroup of information advisors to the inquirer. The role of an information analyst for the inquirer is also taken on by Respondent 1 (A1).

Taxation

Many members of the "MissyUSA" community requested information about a wide range of rules of the U.S. individual income tax. Some of the most frequently posted inquiries on it include such topics as filing status (married filing jointly or separately, single), tax report (forms, cost, methods, refund), tax credits/exemptions/deductions (dependents, child credit, moving, educational, or medical expenses, retirement savings, contributions to the church), or others (the extension for filing a tax return, tax penalty or IRS inspection, a tax level after credit card settlement, inheritance tax, taxes on foreign remittances tax transcript).[64] Of them, this section introduces five specific examples among these topics. First, one member posted a message requesting information about tax filing status on March 1, 2012. There were eight response posts, the first five of which are cited below:

Q: My husband and I live in different states. In our case, is it illegal to file tax returns separately?
A1: Each of you can file tax returns separately. But, your tax credit will be reduced.
A2: It's not illegal. There will be some reduction in your tax credit.
A3: It's not illegal. . . . But, both of you will have less deductions in your taxable income.
A4: Both of you should pay more taxes, compared to a joint tax return. Check tax brackets for the year 2011.
A5: You can select yourself a tax filing status. As usual, a joint tax return will lower the income tax charge.

Generally, all five respondents belong to the subgroup of information advisors to the inquirer. Besides, in a greater or lesser degree, all of them are also in the subgroup of information analysts for her because they all briefly pointed to some disadvantages in filing tax returns separately.

On May 3, 2012, there was a message requesting information about the possibility of a tax return in a state of unlawful immigration status. There were ten response messages, the first five of which are cited below:

> Q: Someone told me that undocumented immigrants can file their income tax returns. Is it true? If this is true, does it mean that they have their own social security numbers?
> A1: Go to a CPA [certified public accountant] office to make your taxpayer identification number, and then you can file your income tax return.
> A2: I received my taxpayer identification number by sending all necessary documents (copies of my visa and other materials) [to the IRS] . . .
> A3: It's possible. I did too.
> A4: I live in New York State. I did file my tax returns in my undocumented immigration status.
> A5: There is nothing to do with your immigration visa. In the state of my undocumented immigration status, I did file tax returns with my social security number and received tax refunds during the last six years.

The U.S. Social Security Administration grants a Social Security number to those foreigners with a lawful immigration status (permanent resident status, work-authorized status) or a non-immigration visa for temporary stay (international students, scholars, workers, and their family members), and American citizens.[65] Nonetheless, unlawful immigrants in the United States can file their annual tax return to the IRS after obtaining an individual taxpayer identification number. In this message thread, the role of information confirmers to the inquirer is conducted by three respondents (A3, A4, and A5). Here, Respondent 1 (A1) can be identified as the information advisor to the inquirer, whereas Respondent 2 (A2) takes on the role of an information analyst for her. And four respondents (A2, A3, A4, and A5) belong to the group of emotional supports as either or both subgroups of companions and encouragers to the inquirer.

Information about a tax deduction for medical expenses was requested in a message posted on February 1, 2012. It was followed by five response messages and three other messages from the inquirer:

> Q: My medical expenses to hospitals and my insurance company were a lot last year. Can I receive a tax credit for this? If that is the case, I would like to ask copies of my bills to hospitals and my insurance company.
> A1: That's helpful, but you should have had a lot of medical expenses. Even if you gave birth to a baby at a hospital, you might not be eligible to get a tax credit from it.
> Q: Does childbirth in a hospital cause a high medical expense?
> A2: It means that your medical expenses were above 10 percent of your annual gross income . . .

A3: A tax credit from medical expenses is determined by your total family income. I think that its payment out of your own pocket should be more than $5,000.
Q: The total medical expenses from last year were less than $5,000.
A4: Your total medical expenses should be more than 7.5 percent of your AGI [adjusted gross income] . . .
A5: I got a tax credit for the medical expenses of almost $15,000 out of my pocket . . .

In general, both respondents (A1 and A5) belong to the subgroup of information describers to the inquirer. Three other respondents (A2, A3 and A4) take on both roles of information analysts and information advisors to the inquirer.

On April 3, 2012, a member requested information about the possibility of an extension of time to file an income tax return. After the posting of this message, there were three response messages and an additional post from the inquirer:

Q: The tax I owed is approximately $3,000. Is it possible to extend the time for filing my income tax return?
A1: Yes, it's possible. But, you should pay it back with interest.
A2: Your tax should be paid with interest. It is unfair that [the IRS] does not add up the interest rate for the income tax refund.
Q: Can I know the interest rate for the extension of a $3,000 tax?
A3: The extension of filing your tax return is of little significance. Just hurry up to report your tax return and then, try to complete an installment agreement form for your tax repayments. For more information for this option, see the IRS website—http://www.irs.gov/individuals/article/0,,id=243335,00.html.

To those expected to pay some taxes owed to the IRS (the U.S. Internal Revenue Service), filing their annual tax return by the designated date can cause discomfort, like the case of this inquirer. By and large, all three respondents belong to the subgroup of information advisors to the inquirer. Besides, the first two respondents also belong to the subgroup of information confirmers to the inquirer.

On March 2, 2012, a member posted a message requesting information on a tax charge on a remittance from abroad. Three were ten response messages, the first five of which are cited here:

Q: Sooner or later, $30,000 will be sent to me, through my bank checking account here, by my parent in Korea. . . . Do I have to pay the tax for this remittance?
A1: You don't have to pay the tax on it.
A2: I received $100,000 from Korea, but I didn't pay any tax for it.
A3: There is no tax for it.
A4: That's no problem.

A5: There is no problem to you; however, your parent may pay some tax on that remittance to the NTS [the Korean National Tax Service]. Also, there is some basic service charge from your bank.

To some Korean-Americans, remittances sent to them by their families in Korea are an important part of supporting their lives in the United States. In this series of messages, all five members belong to the subgroup of information advisors, and four respondents, except for Respondent 5 (A5), can also be classified into the subgroup of information describers to the inquirer. Here, Respondent 5 (A5) also becomes the information analyst for the inquirer.

SUMMARY

Many messages about the rules of the American financial institution were posted on the "Life Q&A" message board of the "MissyUSA" community. In this chapter, some of these posts introduced above have been discretely evaluated in the context of two forms of social capital—social resources (information) and social support. In approaching the "MissyUSA" community as the source of social resources (information), many of its members posted their messages requesting information about a wide range of rules of the American financial institution. In general, its members looked for information on its various legal regulations, guidelines, and procedures. In the U.S. banking sector, a broad set of its rules and procedures were, for example, concerning the opening or closing of bank accounts, deposits, loans, transactions, and fees. In the U.S. insurance sector, the rules some members looked for were usually involved with some formal insurance terms and the related procedures to qualify for access to certain levels of benefits (coverage, profit, or compensation) and to pay for certain amounts of costs (premium, deductible, or penalty) over the insurance products offered by different insurance companies. In the case of the U.S. tax system, its formal rules requested by some inquirers included some stated (or written) tax provisions for personal income tax, such as filing status, tax credits or/and deductions, tax return, and so forth.

Social support to those seekers (inquirers) of information on the rules of the American financial institution is the other form of social capital that is created among some members of the "MissyUSA" community. Otherwise, its development begins with the posting of the messages in response to the messages seeking information. Thus, the revelation of social support is never possible without the appearance of posts requesting information about the rules of the American financial institution. This also means that patterns of social support are constrained in the types of information its members were looking for. However, there exists a great diversity in the contents and types of social support. In this chapter, this has been fully scrutinized according to the classification of the groups of social supporters: instrumental guiders (information describers, analysts, confirmers, and advisors) and emotional supporters (companions, encouragers, and critics). In response to information inquiries on the rules of the American financial institution, some "MissyUSA" members took on the role of information describers to the inquirers by posting their messages that only include facts, comments, or straight answers without making any further explanation, suggestion, or advice. In fact, the most prevailing roles of instrumental guiders were both roles of information analysts and advisors to the inquirers. In the messages in response form, information analysts usually wrote the texts that explain the backgrounds, conditions, essential issues or major features, reasons, processes, or even outcomes.

In comparison, information advisors posted their messages that give advice, suggest some general or specific ideas or options, or provide their thoughts regarding what to do now or what will happen next, sometimes based on their past experiences, expertise, hearsay, or guesswork. Even some response messages in this subgroup have often included such instructions as necessary steps, procedures, or specific ways to tackle the issues posted by the inquirers. Taken together, in this broad group of instrumental guiders, some respondents took on a single role, but some others took on multiple roles across its four subgroups. Relative to the roles of instrumental guiders—especially, those of information analysts and information advisors, however, the roles of emotional supporters have been weak. Nonetheless, some respondents expressed their companionship to the inquirers by sharing the experiences of their own similar to the inquirers'. Likewise, in some messages in response to the inquiry posts, the role of encouragers to the inquirers also appeared in such expressive words as praise about the past efforts of the inquirers, or as encouragement for their further efforts. Interestingly enough, there were also some respondents who conducted the joint roles as both instrumental guiders and emotional supporters for the inquirers. In short, it is obvious that the "MissyUSA" community is a unique kind of online social network for its members as the inquirers or respondents to post their messages embracing social capital.

NOTES

1. Una Osili and Anna Paulson, "What Can We Learn about Financial Access from U.S. Immigrants? The Role of Country of Origin Institutions and Immigrant Beliefs," *The Word Bank Economic Review* 22 (2008): 431–455; and Sherrie L.W. Rhine and William H. Greene, "The Determinants of Being Unbanked for Immigrants," *Journal of Consumer Affairs* 40 (2006): 21–40.

2. In my earlier analysis, there was my recognition that the great majority of postings requesting financial information on the "Life Q&A" message board of "MissyU-

SA" website are those inquiries directly or indirectly related to one of these three financial institutional sectors.

3. In chronological order, the major U.S. banking laws and their important provisions are available under the title of important banking laws at one section of the FDIC website. Sources: https://www.fdic.gov/regulations/laws/important/index.html.

4. Jonathan R. Macey, "The Business of Banking: Before and After Gramm-Leach-Bliley," *Faculty Scholarship Series* (Paper 1412, 2000); and Ken B. Cyree, "The Erosion of the Glass-Steagall Act: Winners and Losers in the Banking Industry," *Journal of Economics and Business* 52 (2000): 343–363.

5. Ibid.

6. As to different federal and state supervisory authorities over a wide range of financial institutions, check the website link: http://www.federalreserve.gov/pf/pdf/pf_5.pdf.

7. For more information about the missions, policies, and organizational structures of both federal authorities, check the following two website links: http://www.federalreserve.gov/ and http://www.fdic.gov/.

8. Besides, the Federal Reserve System and the Federal Deposit Insurance Company (FDIC) were established by the Federal Reserve Act of 1913 and two banking laws of 1933 and 1935, respectively.

9. For further information about the mission, policies, and organizational structure of the OTS, check the website link: http://www.occ.gov/.

10. For detailed information, check the website link: http://www.state.nj.us/dobi/division_banking/depositories/bnkdep_menu.htm.

11. Mark Furletti, *The Debate Over the National Bank Act and the Preemption of State Efforts to Regulate Credit Cards* (Report of Federal Reserve Board of Philadelphia, March 2004).

12. Robert DeYoung, William C. Hunter, and Gregory F. Udell, "The Past, Present, and Probable Future for Community Banks," *Journal of Financial Services Research* 25 (2004): 88.

13. In chapter 6, major laws and regulatory authorizes for home finance were already discussed.

14. For further details, check the website link: https://www.fdic.gov/regulations/laws/important/index.html.

15. DeYoung et al., "The Past, Present, and Probable Future for Community Banks," 104.

16. An overdraft fee is a bank's financial charge to customers who processed transactions over the funds in their checking accounts.

17. Those merchants must pay a certain portion of each purchase (1.7 percent to 2 percent) to credit card issuers (banks, Visa, MasterCard, American Express, Discover) and debit card issuers (mostly, banks). Here, bank customers can purchase products and services with their debit cards from merchants receiving their bank debit cards, and then, their debit card issuers deduct the exact amount of the purchase from their bank checking accounts. See David S. Evans and Richard Schmalensee, *Paying with Plastic: The Digital Revolution in Buying and Borrowing* (Cambridge: The MIT Press, 2005).

18. To credit card holders, their over limit fees occurs when their outstanding credit card balances go over their credit limits.

19. Mark Furletti, *The Debate Over the National Bank Act and the Preemption of State Efforts to Regulate Credit Cards*; and Laurence M. Ausubel, "The Failure of Competition in the Credit Card Market," *The American Economic Review* 81 (1991): 50–81.

20. For general information about the list of consumer credit protection laws and their major provisions at the federal level, check those two website links: http://www.federalreserve.gov/creditcard/regs.html and http://www.flofr.com/PDFs/mbl.pdf.

21. See the category of *ENGAGING IN ACTIVITIES THAT ARE FINANCIAL IN NATURE* in Section 4 of the Bank Holding Company Act of 1956, Compilation of Basic Banking Laws within the Jurisdiction of the Committee on Financial Services (May

2001), Committee on Financial Services, U.S. House of Representatives (Sources: http://financialservices.house.gov/media/pdf/bankcomp.pdf). An annuity, as one form of insurance products, provides its policyholders opportunities to build cash up for their or their family's future use (tax-deferred savings), and it is issued by the life insurance companies. For example, individual life insurance, as one sector of life insurance, provides various insurances products, such as term, whole life, universal life, variable life, or variable-universal life insurance. These five insurance products in individual life insurance differ in terms of the period of coverage, the amount of the premium, or the amount of benefits. For more information, see *Life Insurers Fact Book 2013* by American Council of Life Insurers by checking the website link: https://www.acli.com/Tools/Industry%20Facts/Life%20Insurers%20Fact%20Book/Documents/Life_Insurers_Fact_Book_2013_All.pdf.

22. Ibid.

23. James R. Barth, R. Dan Brumbauch, Jr., and James A. Wilcox, "Policy Watch: The Repeal of Glass-Steagall and the Advent of Broad Banking," *Journal of Economic Perspectives* 14 (2001): 191–204. In a bank holding company, company means "any corporation, partnership, business trust, association, or similar organization, or any other trust" according to the Bank Holding Company Act of 1956, 12 U.S.C. 2 (1941).

24. James R. Barth et al. "Policy Watch"; and Faith R. Neale and Pamela P. Peterson, "The Effect of Gramm-Leach-Bliley on the Insurance Industry," *Journal of Economics and Business* 57 (2005): 317–338.

25. Kenneth A. Carow, "The Wealth Effects of Allowing Bank Entry into the Insurance Industry," *The Journal of Risk and Insurance* 68 (2001): 129–150.

26. Kenneth A. Carow, "The Wealth Effects of Allowing Bank Entry into the Insurance Industry." There are two broad types of annuities: variable and fixed-rate annuities. The major difference between them is whether policyholders have guaranteed savings or not. As usual, the policyholders' money in variable annuities is not guaranteed to grow because it is based upon stock market performance. By contrast, the policyholders' capital in fixed rate annuities grows because the contracts with their insurers set a guaranteed minimum (fixed) interest rate. For a specific comparison between them, see the section of life insurance and annuities on the website of Liberal Mutual Insurance company: http://www.libertymutual.com/life-insurance/annuities/answers.

27. James R. Barth et al. "Policy Watch."

28. Ibid.

29. Alan M. Anderson, "Insurance and Antitrust Law: The McCarran-Ferguson Act and Beyond," *William and Mary Law Review* 81 (1983): 81–130.

30. For more information, see the section of state insurance regulation prepared by the National Association of Insurance Commissioners (NAIC) that is an advisory body and service provider for state insurance departments. Sources: http://www.naic.org/documents/topics_white_paper_hist_ins_reg.pdf.

31. Alan M. Anderson, "Insurance and Antitrust Law."

32. For a brief summary of three major federal antitrust laws – the Sherman Act, the Federal Trade Commission Act, and the Clayton Act, also see the section of antitrust law at the website of Federal Trade Commission (FTC): http://www.ftc.gov/tips-advice/competition-guidance/guide-antitrust-laws/antitrust-laws.

33. W. Elliot Brownlee, *Federal Taxation in America: A Short History* (New York: Cambridge University Press, 1996).

34. Ibid.

35. For detailed information, see Report on Present Law and Historical Overview of the Federal Tax System prepared by Joint Committee of the House and Senate on Taxation (2011): http://www.taxpolicycenter.org/legislation/upload/x-1-11.pdf.

36. Ibid.

37. See 2013 instruction for U.S. Corporate Income Tax Return: http://www.irs.gov/pub/irs-pdf/i1120.pdf.

38. See a released document of the United States Social Security Administration (SSA): http://www.ssa.gov/pubs/EN-05-10003.pdf.

39. See Joint Committee of the House and Senate on Taxation (2011).

40. For excise tax rates for beer, wine, tobacco products, and firearms and ammunition, see the website link: http://www.ttb.gov/tax_audit/atftaxes.shtml.

41. See the section of Income Tax Law: An Overview on the website of Legal Information Institute at the Cornell Law School: http://www.law.cornell.edu/wex/income_tax.

42. C. Eugene Steuerle, *Contemporary U.S. Tax Policy* (Washington, DC: The Urban Institute Press, 2004).

43. There are seven tax rate schedules (10, 15, 25, 28, 33, 35, and 39.6 percent) across annual income and taxpayers' filing status (single filers, couples filing jointly or separately, and head of a household). For more information, see the 2013 Tax Table: http://www.irs.gov/pub/irs-pdf/i1040tt.pdf.

44. Alex M. Brill, "Individual Income Taxes After 2010: Post-Permanance-ism," *National Tax Journal* 60 (2009): 347–369.

45. See the section of Credits and Deductions at the website of the Internal Revenue Services (IRS): http://www.irs.gov/Credits-&-Deductions.

46. C. Eugene Steuerle, *Contemporary U.S. Tax Policy*.

47. C. Eugene Steuerle, *Contemporary U.S. Tax Policy*. In the fiscal year of 2013, couples filing jointly have the standard deduction of a $12,200, while singles or couples filing separately have its half, $6,100 for their standard deduction. Sources: http://www.irs.gov/Credits-&-Deductions.

48. Franziska Hertel, "Qui Tam for Tax: Lessons from the States," *Columbia Law Review* 113 (2013): 1897–1937.

49. A state income tax for individuals is exempted in nine states: Alaska, Florida, Nevada, New Hampshire, South Dakota, Texas, Tennessee, Washington, and Wyoming. Sources: http://www.irs.gov/uac/States-Without-a-State-Income-Tax.

50. For more information, see Handbook of New York State and Local Taxes (October 2012): http://www.tax.ny.gov/pdf/stats/policy_special/handbook_of_new_york_state_and_local_taxes_october_2012.pdf.

51. Ibid.

52. Ibid.

53. Ibid.

54. Ibid.

55. For detailed information about the marital status of Korean Americans who came to the United States at their childhood (1.5 generation immigrants) or adulthood (first-generation immigrants), see Min and Kim's "Statistics on Korean-Americans' Marriage and the Family."

56. Michela M. Zonta, "The Continuing Significance of Ethnic Resources: Korean-Owned Banks in Los Angeles, New York, and Washington, DC," *Journal of Ethnic and Migration* Studies 38 (2012): 475.

57. *The 2012 New York Business Directory* (The Korea Times New York, 2013).

58. Ibid.

59. An overdraft or bounced check fee from your bank is imposed when the amount written in our check or the amount of your transaction exceeds the balance (or fund) in your checking bank account.

60. According to the description on the dictionary section of one website known as Investopedia, money order is "a certificate that allows the stated payee to receive cash on-demand, usually issued by governments and banking institutions." For more information, check the website link: http://www.investopedia.com/terms/m/money-order.asp.

61. A secured card is the kind of credit card that requires you to have collateral (the certain amount of deposit in your checking account or your credit card-issuing bank) to receive credit. For more information, see https://www.wellsfargo.com/credit-cards/secured/.

62. A deductible is the dollar amount you should pay for health care services during each policy year before your health insurance company begins to pay. Coinsurance is your share of the costs of a health care service in your plan. For example, if your deductible is $10,000, your plan won't pay anything until the amount you paid reaches $10,000. Thus, you are responsible for the payment of your medical expenses that are below $10,000. Suppose that you have already paid out your deductible and your copayment is 20 percent. You would pay $400 for your $2,000 medical bill and the remaining $1,600 (80 percent) would be paid by your insurance company. For more information, see the website link of a health insurance provider: http://www.empireblue.com/home-providers.html.

63. For more information about their differences, see the website link: http://money.usnews.com/money/blogs/the-smarter-mutual-fund-investor/2013/02/06/retirement-basics-ira-or-401k. There are also some differences between a traditional IRA and a Roth IRA (see http://www.rothira.com/traditional-ira-vs-roth-ira). In life insurance plans, basically, term life insurance is designed to provide life insurance coverage only for a certain period of time (one year, 10 years, 20 years or even up to 30 years). With life insurance coverage, savings services are also available from whole life insurance.

64. In classifying all the messages about taxation, there were no inquiries about income taxes on corporations, employment taxes on employers, and excise taxes on selected goods and services. But, there were some messages requesting information about estate taxes; one specific case was introduced in chapter 6 (housing).

65. For more information, see the website of the U.S. Social Security Administration: http://www.ssa.gov/ssnumber/.

SEVEN

Conclusion: Overview and Implications

In this book, the message board of "Life Q&A," a subsection of the website "MissyUSA" was assessed to examine a great number of both inquiry and response messages about the rules of American social institutions with the aim of evaluating them in the framework of two distinctive forms of social capital (social resources, identified here as information, and social support). To that end, the underlying premise that was set at the outset has been that this online "MissyUSA" network of married Korean-American women would serve as a new kind of community—namely, a Korean-American women's online community. This assertion needs to provide a clear rationale to further the concept of "community." First, many definitions of community put great emphasis on community members' shared places within geographic propinquity—e.g., neighborhoods, villages, towns, cities, or metropolitan areas.[1] The requirement of territorial boundaries in the concept of community is not fully met for the "MissyUSA" community that is not limited to one locality. Despite this fact, however, the "MissyUSA" community is not in total disregard of the necessity of space within the concept of "community" because a condition of its membership is that it is only for married Korean women living in the United States or Canada.

Second, building up social relationships is characteristic of most kinds of communities; usually, such communities rely on face-to-face interaction and communication among their participating members.[2] This is not true of the "MissyUSA" community. Both types of communities differ substantially in the size of their membership and their individual members' knowledge about, and personal closeness to, other members participating in their communities. Typically, communities' membership is relatively small, consisting of people from families, friends, coworkers, neighbors, or acquaintances. On the contrary, the "MissyUSA" community is very large in the size and features their members' identities in anonymity so that they are mostly unknown to each other. So what to expect next is that these two types of communities—here the "MissyUSA" community versus the traditional conception of community—are also not the same in the scope, intensity, intimacy, and duration of social relationships among their own members. Since the members of the community are mostly comprised of those that can be easily identified, social relationships among them are often close-knit, intimate, predictable, and lasting. However, this is not the case in the social relationships of "MissyUSA" members. Indeed, "MissyUSA" members make social relationships/connections with each other in the form of posting the messages of inquiry and response for the sake of acquiring or transmitting information or advice. When there is no message in response to a message seeking information, this type of social relationship among certain "MissyUSA" members ends suddenly and naturally. Therefore, in appearance, their relationships with each other are rather loosely knit, often superficial, very unpredictable, and temporary, due to its large membership, online connectivity, and anonymity.

Third, a sense of we-ness is central to the concept of "community." In turn, a sense of we-ness among its members is what makes the "MissyUSA" community become a community. The root of its members' sense of we-ness comes basically from their common backgrounds (their births in South Korea, their use of the Korean language, their knowledge about Korean history, culture, and society), and their shared experiences and statuses (immigration, their residence in the United States or Canada, marriage, and gender). To become a true community, its members need "the communal sharing of culture" in history, identity, experiences, and rituals.[3] After immigrating to the United States, many Korean-American women maintain vivid memories about their past lives in their home country (Korea), a nation that is highly homogeneous racially and very group orientated in culture (collective values, norms, and identity). Another important point about the "MissyUSA" community is the fact that almost all postings on the "MissyUSA" community are written in Korean. Indeed, the shared language in Korean enables members to have a better understanding of their ethnic history, ideologies, activities, which makes themselves socially distant from outsiders,[4] just as it helps to create and maintain their national identity or what the international studies scholar Benedict Anderson called "the nationally imagined community."[5] More importantly, the sharing of a common language contributes to "the mental similarity of people" that ultimately causes even unidentified members of the same linguistic community to feel a sense of weness to each other.[6] In other words, a sense of we-ness among the "MissyUSA" members has evolved after they, as people from the same linguistic culture, constructed a very similar mental world in ways to share their values, norms, emotions, and behaviors.

Furthermore, many "MissyUSA" members have similar statuses and life experiences in their new country, which can also be regarded as a strong basis for their sense of we-ness. As stated above, members of the "MissyUSA" community immigrated to the United States (or Canada) and were married with or without children, and many of them are now full-time homemakers, have the primary responsibility for child rearing and children's education, suffer from relatively poor English language skills, and also attend Korean-American churches on a regular basis. As a result, they have a predisposition to feel connected to each other. In other words, they are predisposed to have a sense of we-ness with other members who are from similar backgrounds and life circumstances. In one sense, "MissyUSA" members' sense of we-ness can be a specific mode of "bounded solidarity," also known as the sentiments of in-group solidarity that are really grounded on their national identity and continuous cultural practices learned from their origin country (Korea), and that also arise when their immigrant community—e.g., the Korean-American community—is in confrontation with the host society's racism or discrimination.[7] Overall, the "MissyUSA" community can be identified as a collective entity of their members' commonly shared identity, mother tongue (Korean), culture, birth country (Korea), positions in the family (a housewife and/or mother), and life experiences in their new country (immigration status). What is interesting here is the fact that two distinctive forms of social capital (social resources and social support) will emerge from the "MissyUSA" community.

THE TWO FORMS OF ONLINE SOCIAL CAPITAL

Social networks produce social capital as a result of their members' sense of we-ness or group identity. The "MissyUSA" community, as a particular type of online social network, sets inquiry- and response-based interactions among its members. In its "Life Q&A" message board, for example, the total number of posts from January 1, 2012 to December 31, 2012 was 121,297 (inquiry messages only), averaging 332 inquiry messages and 5 response messages per inquiry on a daily basis. Although some members participate less actively in many daily postings, the average number of daily participants, as either inquirers or respondents or both, is generally quite large. Such large-scale, inquiry- and response-based daily interactions among its members have been made possible by their sense of we-ness that springs mostly from their shared nationality, culture, memories, similar statuses and life experiences, and so on. In essence, a sense of we-ness or group identity promotes online-level trust among in-group members, or what Psychologist Tom Tyler called "social trust."[8] In other words, caring attitudes or benevolent actions towards in-group members increase as social trust develops among them.[9] Therefore, it is not difficult to predict that such ethnic and cultural contexts of social trust among members of the "MissyUSA" community can offer them their comfort zone before their attempts to post their messages of inquiry and response on its "Life Q&A" message board. In the same context, individual members of the "MissyUSA" community are also inculcated with group norms of cooperation. For example, group norms of cooperation manifest at the very moment when its members post messages of detailed information or extremely valuable advice in response to the inquiry messages, without regard to any consideration for compensation or the time spent on their answers to the inquiry messages. It is also likely that group norms of cooperation are closely related to group norms of mutual support or reciprocity.[10] In the "MissyUSA" community, indeed, group norms of mutual support are quite strong among its members. One possible reason this inference makes sense is that the position of respondents can turn back anytime to that of inquirers across the topics. Thus, some "MissyUSA" members, as the respondents, share their knowledge or experiences with other members, but the same members, now positioned as the inquirers who seek information on certain matters, tend to post the messages requesting information or advice to other members, some of whose respondents might be inquirers earlier.

Social capital is the product of a social network that nurtures its members within a sense of we-ness and its related effects (social trust, and norms of cooperation and mutual support). Two distinctive forms of social capital stressed in this book have been social resources (information) and social support. In addition to the observation of social capital in these two forms, what is of great importance in this book has been to associate the roles of the "MissyUSA" members with one of these two forms of social capital. A rationale for this is that the "MissyUSA" community, as the unique kind of social network, functions quite differently for its inquirers (information seekers) and respondents (information providers). In approaching this point from the perspective of inquirers, the "MissyUSA" community becomes a source of social resources and in particular, an important source of information necessary for their new life in the United States. By accessing the "Life Q&A" message board, inquirers posted messages requesting information of various kinds—i.e., background, case, content, process, outcome, and/or advice. In so far as the American social institutions are concerned, they posted the messages seeking information on the rules of the American social institutions—formal or informal, general or specific. Sometimes, their posts might not receive a response from other members. In that case, the "MissyUSA" community loses its function of social capital for those inquirers. Thus, a social network like the "MissyUSA" community requires its other members to offer social support to information seekers. From the perspective of respondents, the "MissyUSA" community functions as a social support network for its anonymous members seeking certain kinds of information. As observed before, there have been two broad types of social support groups in the "MissyUSA" community: instrumental guiders (information describers, analysts, confirmers, and advisors) and emotional supporters (companions, encouragers, and critics).

INQUIRIES FOR INFORMATION ON THE RULES OF THE AMERICAN SOCIAL INSTITUTIONS

Some "MissyUSA" members, called inquirers or information seekers, have understood this online community as a network, a platform, and furthermore, as a valuable source to obtain social resources—in other words, as an important source of information about the rules of American immigration, welfare, education, housing, or financial institutions. As already argued in chapter 1, one commonality across these five American social institutions was their seeking of information about their formal or informal rules, such as formal laws, policies, procedures, or informal conventions or norms. Another important point here is that each of the five American social institutions explored in this book has been set up on two different but interconnected units (institution and its organizations), each of which has its own capacity to issue individually both formal and informal rules. Thus, these two different sources of rules are institution-wide rules and within-institution, organizational rules. In what followed, an assumption about the relationship between these two different sources of rules, in the case of an American social institution, was that its formal institution-wide rules would affect the emergence, content, or change of the formal organizational rules. However, one of the objectives of this book was to highlight the existence of both sources of rules across each of all the five American social institutions, without taking an interest in examining what specific legal clauses or provisions about institution-wide and organizational rules are related to each other. In other words, what I wanted to emphasize in previous chapters is that a group of "MissyUSA" members (inquirers or information seekers) tends to post messages seeking information on either institution-wide and/or within-institution organizational rules to be being enacted in each of the five American social institutions. Finally, there is some clear evidence about the presence of both sources of rules from each of the five American social institutions, briefly summed up below based upon the key findings of each chapter.

First, institution-wide rules of all five American social institutions are passed by the legislative or judicial branches of the government (U.S. Congress, state or local assemblies, or federal or state supreme courts), and administered, monitored, or enforced by the executive branches of the government (all the public departments and agencies at federal, state, or local levels). In the chapter of the American immigration institution, the focus was on lawful permanent residency or naturalization through citizenship. Some of "MissyUSA" inquirers' attention to formal institution-wide rules was focused on their pursuit of information about legal qualifications (immigration status, class of admission, sponsorship, marital status, age, criminal records, or duration of residence in the United States) and formal procedures (application package, fingerprinting, interviewing, or the English and civics tests). In the chapter on the American welfare institution, some "MissyUSA" members' concerns, as reflected in their inquiry messages, were focused on information about one of five social programs: the Unemployment Insurance (UI), Social Security, health care assistance programs (e.g., Medicaid), nutrition assistance programs (e.g., the Supplemental Nutrition Assistance Program), and housing assistance programs (e.g., the public housing program). For example, for both Social Security and nutrition assistance programs, many "MissyUSA" members requested information about eligibility standards—e.g., in Social Security, duration of work, wages, legal status, and age—and benefit guidelines (recipients, amounts, and duration) for each program. Just as the UI and health care assistance programs are typical federal and state partnership programs, housing assistance programs are largely regarded as federal, state, and local partnership programs. Here, some "MissyUSA" members' inquiries, similar to the cases of the first two public assistance programs, also sought information on their formal institution-wide rules, mostly regarding the legal rules of eligibility criteria for each social program—e.g., in the UI, legal status, employment period, working hours, the amount of wages, and benefit amount and period.

In the chapter of the American educational institution, as previously mentioned, the United States, federal, state, and local governments have their own legal right to authorize the laws involved in certain areas of education. Nonetheless, more broadly, the primary responsibility for public education in the United States is granted to individual states. Indeed, the state governor, the state legislature, and the state board of education have the legal powers to set state educational laws and policies regarding the establishment of schools and colleges, educational standards and assessment in public schools, teacher certification, and state educational budgets. Although there were not many posts seeking information on the formal institution-wide rules of the American educational institution, some of the information "MissyUSA" members sought in this social institution had to do with written policies or formal requirements for high school graduation, especially relating to course completion and class absence, student disciplines, in-state college tuition policy, eligibility criteria for state scholarship or loan programs, and financial aid through the FAFSA (the Free Application for Federal Student Aid), and so on. In the chapter on the American housing institution, the matter of its formal institution-wide rules was discussed under four broad categories: the financing of homeownership, the home-buying process, homeowners' options and burdens, and rental housing. The general findings from this chapter were that some "MissyUSA" members were inclined to request a wide range of information about formal institution-wide rules at the federal, state, and local levels. For instance, the focus of some information inquiries, in the section of the home-buying process, was on the hiring of a real estate attorney, home inspection, title insurance, and homeowners insurance. In the section of rental housing, some inquiry messages were about security deposit, late fees for rent, the management of rental units, and house foreclosures. Chapter 6 of this book addressed the rules of the American financial institution that is divided into three thematic sections: banking (deposits, transaction services, lending, and savings), insurance (life, health, and property), and taxation (personal income tax and other taxes). Many inquiries for information on institution-wide rules were especially concentrated in the section of taxation—e.g., filing status (married filing jointly or separately, single), tax report (forms, methods, refund), tax credits and deductions (dependents, child credit, moving, educational, or medical expenses, retirement savings), and so on.

Laws shape organizations.[11] Likewise, the formal institution-wide rules of a social institution have substantial effects on the creation, structural form or transformation, and extinction of its formal, within-institutional organizational rules. Then, their unidirectional relationship does not mean that the formal, intra-institutional organizational rules of a social institution stand out in the complete absence of their own particularities. In fact, a propensity to have a strong self-rule independent of institution-wide rules can be relatively stronger among private-sector organizations (mostly for-profit organizations) than among public-sector (government-sector) ones, both of whose formation and operation are to a greater or lesser extent under the influence of their institution-wide rules. Of course, by and large, it cannot be denied that the general nature of the formal, within-institution organizational rules in a social institution reflects their basic role and function of upholding the realization of their institution-wide rules. But, in both the chapters on American immigration and welfare institutions, there was little clarity on what are the actual forms and types of formal, within-institution organizational rules. One of the reasons is that in both of these American social institutions, their respective organizational rules are deeply engrained under the influence of their institution-wide rules. Some of their formal organizational rules were included in their guidelines to be publicly released for applications (required documents, methods to prepare application forms or submission) and the procedures relating to them—e.g., fingerprinting and interviewing for citizenship, weekly claims for unemployment insurance (UI).

Relative to these first two American social institutions (immigration and welfare), however, the overall influence of institution-wide rules on within-institution, organizational rules was less strong in the American educational institution. As stated earlier, a high degree of autonomy and legal authority in education is handed to school districts under the control of districts' boards of education, the individual public elementary and secondary schools, or to public and private colleges and universities. For example, some "MissyUSA" members sought information on organizational rules in public schools such as school registration, skipping a grade, dress code, course selection, gifted and talented programs (G&T), and extracurricular activities, among others. Some of their specific inquiries for information, in the domain of the organizational rules for colleges and universities, were about college classes, grading policies, health insurance, college scholarships or financial aid, college transfer, college club activities, dormitory life, and so forth. What's more, there were a great number of inquiries for information about the formal organizational rules in both the American housing and financial institutions. Under the shield of institution-wide rules, many private organizations—e.g., commercial banks, savings and loan associations, credit card companies, mortgage companies, and insurance companies (life and annuities, accident and health, and property and casualty)—have their own formal organizational rules. For example, in the chapter of the American housing institution, some "MissyUSA" members sought information about home financing, including certain mortgage lenders' own rules, such as mortgage types, the period of mortgage payments, the mortgage interest rates, the amount of down payment, and the ratio of income to debt for mortgage approval. As another example, in the chapter of the American financial institution, some "MissyUSA" members posted messages seeking information on the organizational rules and policies of insurance companies—e.g., those programs or products to be offered, the terms and conditions of coverage or benefits, payments or costs (copayment, deductible), and claims (procedures, compensation).

In any social institution, there might be some unwritten or informal rules at both the institution and within-institution organizational levels—e.g., conventions, norms, codes of behavior, customs, or practices—can sometimes be hardly detectable to people outside of the organization. Some "MissyUSA" members sought information about some of those unwritten or informal rules within one of the three American social institutions—immigration, education, and housing. Because distinguishing between institutional- and the within-institution, organizational-level informal rules is often difficult, some of their posts about them were understandably without such distinctions. For example, regarding the American immigration institution, messages seeking information about its informal or unwritten rules were related to such varied topics as the completion of an application form with integrity (ethics), the possibility of no interviewing for green card applicants holding an H1-B visa or through marriage to a U.S. citizen, the practices of fee payments by sponsors (employers) or applicants for employment-based immigration petitions, how to behave during the interview, and standard processing times for applications. The unwritten rules, particularly at the American educational institution's organizational levels (public schools or the district board of education), were about, for example, parents' volunteering in school or class, students' participation in the school band, chorus, or orchestra, school fund raising, school events for students (trips, SAT/ACT prep, a college fair), and so on. In the case of the American housing institution, some "MissyUSA" members requested information about organization-level conventions or practices such as the mortgage lenders' down payment requirement for the purchase of a house, citizenship or immigration status for the purchase of a house, check preparation in making an offer on a house, and the submission of mortgage applications with or without home inspection.

Today, the legal environments of the American social institutions—e.g., civil rights, minimum wages, employment or educational opportunities—make immigrants easier than ever before for immigrant assimilation into American society.[12] But, many immigrants and their family members in the United States are still facing huge challenges, making their settlement in American society difficult. On the whole, this book has shown that many "MissyUSA" members (inquirers or information seekers) expressed interest in seeking information about the rules of the American social institutions. One thing that is clear overall is that their actions to seek information about the rules of the American social institutions through the "MissyUSA" community can also be considered as one of their efforts to better adjust to their new life in the United States.[13]

TWO TYPES OF SOCIAL SUPPORT GROUPS

Another form of social capital is social support, which comes by participating in social networks. In this respect, the "MissyUSA" community has been also understood as a network or community of social supporters (respondents or information providers) for its inquirers (information seekers). In turn, social support for the inquirers seeking information on the rules of the American social institution is the other aspect of social capital that is inherent in, and attainable through, the "MissyUSA" community. As addressed earlier, message threads on the "Life Q&A" message board of the "MissyUSA" community embrace various kinds of social support created from its respondents, who post their messages in response to those inquirers seeking information or advice. Social support would never take place if none of the "MissyUSA" members responded to inquiry messages.[14] At the same time, the patterns of social support displayed by "MissyUSA" respondents are highly constrained by the content of the inquiry messages themselves. In both matters, an approach that is vital in this book has been the creation and classification of two social support groups: instrumental guiders and emotional supporters.

Instrumental guiders post information in their responses to inquirers' messages. For that reason, this type of social support group can be further divided into four subgroups: information describers, analysts, confirmers, and advisors. As illustrated and discussed in the previous chapters of the five American social institutions, instrumental guiders' supportive roles for the "MissyUSA" inquirers (or information seekers) have been similar or otherwise very different, in type and extent. More specifically, in their messages that respond to messages seeking information on the rules of the American social institutions, information describers, as one of its subgroups, usually post messages that only include short phrases (simple facts), one or two short sentences (straight answers), or comments out of context, with or without disclosing information from their own cases, as well as without making any further explanation, confirmation, correction, or suggestion. This subgroup of instrumental guiders is in stark contrast to information analysts whose response messages usually included relatively detailed comments and reasonable explanations, likewise with or without making connections with their own experiences. Thus, what makes them a unique subgroup of information guiders comes from the fact that many response messages of these information analysts put a greater focus on analysis of the key issues within the inquiry messages; they develop their analyses under the expressions of backgrounds or origins, character, processes, or outcomes on those issues. In general, as previously demonstrated, this second subgroup of instrument guiders attested to a pervasive, strong social support group for many "MissyUSA" inquirers seeking information on the rules of the five American social institutions.

Information confirmers are the third subgroup of instrumental guiders. The main role of these information confirmers is to confirm or reassure the "MissyUSA" inquirers that the information they wrote in the text is accurate or proper on the issue, or that they are on the right track. Of the four subgroups of instrumental guiders, this social support group was least likely to emerge in response to posts seeking information about the rules of the five American social institutions. The fourth and last subgroup of instrumental guiders is that of information advisors. Their main tasks focus on advice, correction, or suggestions. Thus, those information advisors of the "MissyUSA" community were inclined to post response messages that give advice, suggest some ideas or options, correct misinformation, or project what would happen on the basis of their past experiences or expertise in the field. Some information advisors even had a tendency to post messages that included such specific instructions as necessary steps, procedures, or ways to tackle the issues raised by their inquirers. Like information analysts, this subgroup of instrumental guides was also another core subgroup of social support for the "MissyUSA" members seeking information on the rules of the five American social institutions. Notably, some "MissyUSA" respondents took on only a single role, but some others took on multiple roles across these four subgroups of instrumental guiders.

Overall, informational support, that is, support in the way of information dissemination, is an important common interest among the "MissyUSA" instrumental guiders who responded to inquiry messages in their own way, regardless of whether they were offering description, explanation or analysis, confirmation, and/or advice.[15] In other words, they generally provided comprehensive, accurate, and/or in-depth information on the rules of the American social institutions, which is often not easily obtainable from members of their personal or small-scale networks usually made up of co-ethnic families, friends, or workers in the workplace. For the "MissyUSA" inquirers, such possibility to obtain so much rich information through the online community is indeed attributed to its other members' (here, respondents) diverse backgrounds in occupation and expertise, and more importantly, their direct or indirect participation in the American social institutions as immigration lawyers, social workers, educators, or housing or financial experts. On the one hand, online post-based interactions between the "MissyUSA" instrumental guiders and their inquirers are, in the context of information diffusion, a mode that reflects a sort of "bridging social capital" or "weak ties." This is because most of the "MissyUSA" instrumental guiders transmitted a wide range of valuable information to their anonymous co-ethnic members seeking information.[16] In fact, some "MissyUSA" members who responded to inquiries cited their own professional credential or personal experiences to certify the credibility of information they posted. On the other hand, some "MissyUSA" instrumental guiders, such as professionals, people who have knowledge, or people with experience, also became such important agents as they take on the role of co-ethnic institutional middlemen for their information-seeking members in quest of the knowledge about the American social institutions. Thus, their middleman position here points to their brokerage role—e.g., the conveyance of various types and contents of information—for their co-ethnic members (the "MissyUSA" inquirers) who seek information on the rules of the American social institutions. However, it has nothing to do with their ability to compare one social institution to another in American society, or to compare similarities and differences between the social institutions of the United States and those of their home country (Korea).

The other social support group for the "MissyUSA" inquirers is respondents who act as emotional supporters.[17] Needless to say, some emotional supporters are also instrumental guiders. However, the main concern of emotional supporters is to present their inner feelings or emotions in the texts of their response messages. Since the quest for information is the main reason for most inquirers' post on the "Life Q&A" message board, the emotional expressions of the "MissyUSA" respondents occur less frequently. Nonetheless, the contents and type of their emotions stated in their response messages were very similar in some cases, but very different in other cases. In this book, this sort of social support group was, previously, divided into three subgroups: companions, encouragers, and critics. First, companions are those who express their sympathy or closeness (intimacy or empathy) to the inquirers. In the "MissyUSA" online community, their close companionship with the inquirers was often demonstrated in their postings of their own past or current experiences or stories similar, or identical, to the inquirers'. Second, encouragers are those who encourage the inquirers with low self-worth or less self-confidence. Their role of offering encouragement, in the "MissyUSA" community, was demonstrated in their messages to inquirers, urging them to change their attitudes or approach their goals differently, or simply to do their best. The third subgroup of emotional supporters has been called critics who admonish some inquirers with poor knowledge, misjudgment, or carelessness, in an attempt to point them in the right direction. Relative to the first two subgroups of emotional supporters, however, the presence of this social support group has happened very rarely in this book's study of the five American social institutions.

One of the strengths of small-scale, personal networks is a great opportunity for their members to express sympathy, encouragement, or positive criticism as ways to support other members facing difficult circumstances. Despite the fact that the "MissyUSA" community is a large-scale, online social network, one of this book's important findings is that such signs of "bonding social capital" or "strong ties"—e.g., social and psychological or emotional support—appeared among its anonymous members in some response messages.[18] It is uncommon that these expression of emotional support, especially companionship and encouragement, would appear in such a large-scale, anonymous network.[19] This must be partly due to a sense of we-ness among the anonymous members who share similar backgrounds and experiences, as addressed above. In a social psychological perspective, some "MissyUSA" members, acting as emotional supporters for inquirers, can also be considered to have taken on the role of psychological counseling for those who expressed their worry, frustration, stress, or hopelessness in their messages of inquiry, albeit temporarily.

In conclusion, this book has demonstrated, even in this age of social media and the growing geographical dispersion of Korean-Americans from one area to another in the United States, the two forms of online social capital, in the case of the "MissyUSA" community, are still accessible and obtainable, on the basis of the sense of we-ness and its related ramifications (social trust, and norms of cooperation and mutual support) among members who have had similar or shared backgrounds, positions, or experiences—e.g., language (Korean), culture, past experiences in Korea, positions in the family (a housewife and/or mother), and life experiences in their new country. In short, this book, under the chapters of the five American institutions, has approached and proven the "MissyUSA" community to be a unique online network where its members, as either information seekers or respondents, post messages constituting social capital.

NOTES

1. Robyn B. Driskell and Larry Lyon, "Are Virtual Communities True Communities? Examining the Environments and Elements of Community," *City & Community* 1 (2002): 375; and Barry Wellman, "The Community Question: The Intimate Networks of East Yorkers," *American Journal of Sociology* 84 (1979): 120–231.
2. Robyn B. Driskell and Larry Lyon, "Are Virtual Communities True Communities?"
3. Amitai Etzioni and Oren Etzioni, "Can Virtual Communities Be Real?" in *The Monochrome Society*, ed. Amitai Etzioni (Princeton, New Jersey: Princeton University Press, 2001), 93.
4. Sarah B. Benor, "Ethnolinguistic Repertoire: Shifting the Analytic Focus in Language and Ethnicity," *Journal of Sociolinguistics* 14 (2010): 159–183.
5. Benedict Anderson, *Imagined Communities*, 44–46.
6. Mary Chayko, *Connecting*, 28–29.
7. Alejandro Portes and Julia Sensenbrenner, "Embeddedness and Immigration: Notes on the Social Determinants of Economic Behavior."
8. Tom R. Tyler, "Why Do People Rely on Others? Social Identity and Social Aspects of Trust," in *Trust in Society*, ed. Karen S. Cook (New York: Russell Sage Foundation, 203), 285–306.
9. Tom R. Tyler, "Why Do People Rely on Others?" 288–289.
10. Robert Putnam, *Bowling Alone*, 136.
11. Frank Dobbin, John R. Sutton, John W. Meyer, and Richard Scott, "Equal Opportunity Law and the Construction of Internal Labor Markets," *American Journal of Sociology* 99 (1993): 396–427; Lauren B. Edelman and Mark C. Suchman, "The Legal Environments of Organizations," *Annual Review of Sociology* 23 (1997): 479–515; Mark C. Suchman and Lauren B. Edelman, "Legal Rational Myths: The New Institutionalism and the Law and Society Tradition," *Law & Social Inquiry* 21 (1996): 903–941; and Pamela S. Tolbert and Lynne G. Zucker, "Institutional Sources of Change in the Formal Structure of Organizations: The Diffusion of Civil Service Reform, 1880–1935," *Administrative Science Quarterly* 28 (1983): 22–39.
12. Richard Alba and Victor Nee, *Remaking the American Mainstream*, 52–54.
13. Then, one question that remains unanswered in this book was the issue of how the "MissyUSA" inquirers would deal with the response messages to their posts, such as their re-evaluations of the information obtained. Thus, little was known about general patterns of inquirers' feedbacks—e.g., their expressions of knowledge acquisition, better understanding, confirmation, confusion, appreciation, or their anticipated plan or action. As an exception, some few of "MissyUSA" inquirers who re-responded to the response messages to their initial posts often wrote, "Thank you," "I appreciate your replies," "Thank you for responding to my post," or "Thank you for posting your advice."

14. Regardless of different types of social networks, it is our misperception that all the people in need would receive some support from their network members. Their support is quite dependent upon their givers' conditions and definitions of "the situation of need." (See Leonard I. Pearlin's "Social Structure and Processes of Social Support," in *Social Support and Health*, eds. Sheldon Cohen and S. Leonard Syme (New York: Academic Press, 1985), 49.

15. In Alan Vaux's *Social Support* and Nan Lin and his associates' *Social Support, Life Events, and Depression,* the concept of social support was systemically reviewed and there, information support was regarded as a component of social support.

16. Robert Putnam, *Bowling Alone,* 22–23; and Mark Granovetter, "The Strength of Weak Ties."

17. In both books – Alan Vaux's *Social Support* and Nan Lin and his associates' *Social Support, Life Events, and Depression,* emotional support was also reviewed as another prevailing component of social support.

18. Robert Putnam, *Bowling Alone,* 22; and Mark Granovetter, "The Strength of Weak Ties."

19. John A. Bargh and Katelyn Y. A. McKenna, "The Internet and Social Life," *Annual Review of Psychology* 55 (2004): 573–590; and Patricia Radin, "To Me, It's My Life: Medical Communication, Trust, and Activism in Cyberspace," *Social Science and Medicine* 62 (2006): 591–601. In some cases, comfort, sympathy, and mutual encouragement are often expressed among members of certain large-scale online networks with anonymity. For example, these are such online networks whose members suffer from the same illness (cancer, AIDS), or the same stigma (sexual orientations, political beliefs).

References

ACADEMIC AND GOVERNMENTAL SOURCES

Abramovitz, Mimi. 1989. *Regulating the Lives of Women: Social Welfare Policy from Colonial Times to the Present*. Boston, MA: South End Press.

Alba, Richard, and Victor Nee. 1997. "Rethinking Assimilation Theory for a New Era of Immigration." *International Migration Review* 31 (4): 826–874.

______. 2003. *Remaking the American Mainstream: Assimilation and Contemporary Immigration*. Cambridge, MA: Harvard University Press.

Anderson, Alan M. 1983. "Insurance and Antitrust Law: The McCarran-Ferguson Act and Beyond." *William and Mary Law Review* 81: 81–130.

Anderson, Benedict. 1991. *Imagined Communities: Reflections on the Origin and Spread of Nationalism*, Revised Edition. New York: Verso.

Ausubel, Laurence M. 1991. "The Failure of Competition in the Credit Card Market," *The American Economic Review* 81: 50–81.

Bargh, John A., and Katelyn Y. A. McKenna. 2004. "The Internet and Social Life." *Annual Review of Psychology* 55: 573–590.

Barth, James R., R. Dan Brumbauch, Jr., and James A. Wilcox. 2001. "Policy Watch: The Repeal of Glass-Steagall and the Advent of Broad Banking." *Journal of Economic Perspectives* 14: 191–204.

Benor, Sarah B. 2010. "Ethnolinguistic Repertoire: Shifting the Analytic Focus in Language and Ethnicity." *Journal of Sociolinguistics* 14 (2): 159–183.

Blau, Joel, and Mimi Abramovitz. 2004. *The Dynamics of Social Welfare Policy*. New York: Oxford University Press.

Bloemraad, Irene. 2006. *Becoming a Citizen: Incorporating Immigrants and Refugees in the United States and Canada*. Berkeley: University of California Press.

Borjas, George J. 2002. "Homeownership in the Immigrant Population." *Journal of Urban Economics* 52: 448–476.

Bourdieu, Pierre. 1986. "The Forms of Capital." In *The Handbook of Theory and Research for the Sociology of Education*, edited by John Richardson, 241–258. New York: Greenwood.

Brassil, Margaret M. 2010. *The Creation of a Federal Partnership: The Role of the States in Affordable Housing*. Albany: State University of New York Press.

Brill, Alex M. 2009. "Individual Income Taxes After 2010: Post-Permanance-ism." *National Tax Journal* 60: 347–369.

Brouwer, Lenie. 2006. "Dutch Moroccan Websites: A Transnational Imagery?" *Journal of Ethnic and Migration Studies* 32 (7): 1153–1168.

Brownlee, W. Elliot. 1996. *Federal Taxation in America: A Short History*. New York, NY: Cambridge University Press.

Byun, Soo-yong, and Hyunjoon Park. 2012. "The Academic Success of East Asian American Youth: The Role of Shadow Education." *Sociology of Education* 85: 40–60.

California Department of Consumer Affairs. 2011. *California Tenants: A Guide to Residential Tenants' and Landlords' Rights and Responsibilities*. http://www.dca.ca.gov/publications/landlordbook/catenant.pdf.

Carow, Kenneth A. 2001. "The Wealth Effects of Allowing Bank Entry into the Insurance Industry." *The Journal of Risk and Insurance* 68: 129–150.

Castells, Manuel. 2001. *The Internet Galaxy*. New York: Oxford University Press.

Chayko, Mary. 2002. *Connecting: How We Form Social Bonds and Communities in the Internet Age*. New York: State University of New York Press.

Clark, William A. V., Marinus Deurloo, and Frans Dieleman. 2006. "Residential Mobility and Neighbourhood Outcomes." *Housing Studies* 21 (3): 323–342.

Clauretie, Terrence M., and Nasser Daneshvary. 2011. "The Optimal Choice for Lenders Facing Defaults: Short Sale, Foreclose, or REO." *The Journal of Real Estate Finance and Economics* 42 (4): 504–521.

Cohen, Sheldon, and S. Leonard Syme, eds. 1985. *Social Support and Health*. New York: Academic Press.

Coleman, James. 1994. *Foundations of Social Theory*. Cambridge, MA: Harvard University Press.

Coleman, Mathew. 2009. "What Counts as the Politics and Practice of Security, and Where? Devolution and Immigrant Insecurity after 9/11." *Annals of the Association of American Geographers* 99 (5): 904– 913.

Cutrona, Carolyn E. and Julie A. Suhr. 1992. "Controllability of Stressful Events and Satisfaction with Spouse Support Behaviors." *Communication Research* 19: 154–174.

Cyree, Ken B. 2000. "The Erosion of the Glass-Steagall Act: Winners and Losers in the Banking Industry." *Journal of Economics and Business* 52: 343–363.

De Genova, Nicholas P. 2002. "Migrant 'Illegality' and Deportability in Everyday Life." *Annual Review of Anthropology* 31: 419–447.

DeLaet, Debra L. 2000. *U.S. Immigration Policy in an Age of Rights*. Westport, CT: Praeger.

DeYoung, Robert, William C. Hunter, and Gregory F. Udell. 2004. "The Past, Present, and Probable Future for Community Banks." *Journal of Financial Services Research* 25 (2): 85–133.

DiMaggio, Paul, and Water Powell. 1983. "The Iron Cage Revisited: Institutional Isomorphism and Collective Rationality in Organizational Fields." *American Sociological Review* 48:147–160.

Dobbin, Frank, and John R. Sutton. 1998. "The Strength of a Weak State: The Rights Revolution and the Rise of Human Resources Management Divisions." *American Journal of Sociology* 104: 441–476.

Domina, Thurston. 2005. "Leveling the Home Advantage: Assessing the Effectiveness of Parental Involvement in Elementary School." *Sociology of Education* 78: 233–249.

Driskell, Robyn B., and Larry Lyon. 2002. "Are Virtual Communities True Communities? Examining the Environments and Elements of Community." *City & Community* 1(4): 373–390.

Edelman, Lauren B. 1992. "Legal Ambiguity and Symbolic Structures: Organizational Mediation of Civil Rights Law." *American Journal of Sociology* 97: 1531–1576.

Edelman, Lauren B., and Mark C. Suchman. 1997. "The Legal Environments of Organizations." Annual Review of Sociology 23: 479–515.

Edelman, Lauren B., Christopher Uggen, and Howard S. Erlanger. 1999. "The Endogeneity of Legal Regulation: Grievance Procedures as Rational Myth." *American Journal of Sociology* 105: 406–454.

Eskridge, William N. 1984. "One Hundred Years of Ineptitude: The Need for Mortgage Rules Consonant with the Economic and Psychological Dynamics of the Home Sale and Loan Transaction." *Virginia Law Review* 70 (6): 1083–1218.

Etzioni, Amitai, and Oren Etzioni. 2001. "Can Virtual Communities Be Real?" In *The Monochrome Society*, edited by Amitai Etzioni, 77–101. Princeton, NJ: Princeton University Press.

Evans, David S., and Richard Schmalensee. 2005. *Paying with Plastic: The Digital Revolution in Buying and Borrowing*. Cambridge, MA: The MIT Press.

Fremstad, Shawn, and Laura Cox. 2004. *Covering New Americans: A Review of Federal and State Policies Related to Immigrants' Eligibility and Access to Publicly Funded Health Insurance*. Washington, DC: Center on Budget and Policy Priorities.

Furletti, Mark. 2004. *The Debate over the National Bank Act and the Preemption of State Efforts to Regulate Credit Cards. Report of Federal Reserve Board of Philadelphia, March 2004*. Philadelphia: Federal Reserve Board of Philadelphia.

Furletti, Mark., and Laurence M. Ausubel. 1991. "The Failure of Competition in the Credit Card Market." *The American Economic Review* 81: 50–81.

Gilbert, Liette. 2009. "Immigration as Local Politics: Re-Bordering Immigration and Multiculturalism through Deterrence and Incapacitation." *International Journal of Urban and Regional Research* 33 (1): 26–42.

Gilbertson, Greta, and Audrey Singer. 2003. "The Emergence of Protective Citizenship in the USA: Naturalization among Dominican Immigrants in the Post-1996 Welfare Reform Era." *Ethnic and Racial Studies* 26 (1): 25–51.

Gleeson, Shannon, and Roberto Z. Gonzales. 2012. "When Do Papers Matter? An Institutional Analysis of Undocumented Life in the United States." *International Migration* 50 (4): 1–19.

Gordon, Adam. 2005. "The Creation of Homeownership: How New Deal Changes in Banking Regulation Simultaneously Made Homeownership Accessible to Whites and Out of Reach for Blacks." *The Yale Law Review* 115 (1): 186–226.

Gordon, Milton M. 1964. *Assimilation in American Life: The Role of Race, Religion, and National Origins*. New York: Oxford University Press.

Granovetter, Mark S. 1973. "The Strength of Weak Ties." *American Journal of Sociology* 78 (6): 1360–1380.

_________. 1985. "Economic Action and Social Structure: The Problem of Embeddedness." *American Journal of Sociology* 91 (3): 481–510.

Green, Richard K., and Stephen Malpezzi. 2003. *A Primer on U.S. Housing Markets and Housing Policy*. Washington, DC: The Urban Institute Press.

Green, Richard K., and Susan M. Wachter. 2005. "The American Mortgage in Historical and International Context." *The Journal of Economic Perspectives* 19 (4): 93–114.

Hann, Michael. 2007. "The Homeownership Hierarchies of Canada and the United States: The Housing Patterns of White and Non-White Immigrants of the Past Thirty Years." *International Migration Review* 41 (2): 433–465.

Hareven, Tamara K. 1991. "The Home and the Family in Historical Perspective." *Social Research* 58 (1): 253–285.

Hertel, Franziska. 2013. "Qui Tam for Tax: Lessons from the States." *Columbia Law Review* 113: 1897–1937.

Hirsch, Barton J. 1980. "Natural Support Systems and Coping with Major Life Changes." *American Journal of Community Psychology* 8: 159–172.

House, James S. 1981. *Work Stress and Social Support*. Reading, MA: Addison-Wesley.

Institute for Educational Leadership. 2001. Leadership for Student Learning: Recognizing the State's Role in Public Education. A Report of the Task Force on State Leadership, May 2001. Washington, DC: Institute for Educational Leadership.

Kane, Pearl Rock. 2000. "The Difference between Charter Schools and Charterlike Schools." In *City Schools: Lessons from New York*, edited by Diane Ravitch and Joseph P. Viteritti, 65–68. Baltimore: The Johns Hopkins University Press.

Katz, Michael B. 2001. *The Price of Citizenship: Redefining the American Welfare State*. New York: Henry Holt and Company.

Kelly, Erin L. 2003. "The Strange History of Employer-Sponsored Child Care: Interested Actors, Uncertainty, and the Transformation of Law in Organizational Fields." *American Journal of Sociology* 109: 606– 649.

Kibria, Nazli. 2002. *Becoming Asian American: Second-Generation Chinese and Korean American Identities*. Baltimore: The Johns Hopkins University.

Kim, ChangHwan. 2013. "The Generational Differences in Socioeconomic Attainments of Korean Americans." Paper presented at The Research Center for Korean Community at Queens College, April 7, 2013.

Kim, Pyungho. 2006. "Is Korea a Strong Internet Nation?" *The Information Society* 22: 41–44.

Labaree, David F. 1997. "Public Goods, Private Goods: The American Struggle over Educational Goals." *American Educational Research Journal* 34 (1): 39–81.

________. 2010. *Someone Has To Fail: The Zero-Sum Game of Public Schooling*. Cambridge, MA: Harvard University Press.

________. 2011. "Consuming the Public School." *Educational Theory* 61 (4): 381–394.

Lareau, Annette. 1987. "School Class Differences in Family-School Relationships: The Importance of Cultural Capital." *Sociology of Education* 60: 73–85.

Lee, Hakyoon. 2010. "I am a *Kirogi* Mother: Education Exodus and Life Transformation Among Korean Transnational Women." *Journal of Language, Identity, and Education* 9: 250–264.

Legal Services of New Jersey. 2007. *Tenants' Rights in New Jersey: Legal Manual for Tenants in New Jersey*. http://www.lsnjlaw.org/Publications/Pages/Manuals/TenantsRights.pdf.

Lew, Jamie. 2004. "The 'Other' Story of Model Minorities: Korean American High School Dropouts in an Urban Context." *Anthropology & Education Quarterly* 35 (3): 303–323.

Lin, Nan. 1982. "Social Resources and Instrumental Action." In *Social Structure and Network Analysis*, edited by Peter V. Marsden and Nan Lin, 131–145. Beverly Hills, CA: Sage.

________. 2001. *Social Capital: A Theory of Social Structure and Action*. Port Chester, NY: Cambridge University Press.

Lin, Nan, Alfred Dean, and Walter Ensel. 1986. *Social Support, Life Events, and Depression*. New York: Academic Press, Inc.

Lobo, Arun P., and Joseph J. Salvo. 1998. "Changing U.S. Immigration Law and the Occupational Selectivity of Asian Immigrants." *International Migration Review* 32 (3): 737–760.

Macey, Jonathan R. 2000. *The Business of Banking: Before and After Gramm-Leach-Bliley. Faculty Scholarship Series*. Yale, CT: Yale Law School.

Madianou, Mirca. 2005. "Contested Communicative Spaces: Rethinking Identities, Boundaries and the Role of the Media among Turkish Speakers in Greece." *Journal of Ethnic and Migration Studies* 31 (3): 521–541.

Madigan, Ruth, Moira Munro, and Susan J. Smith. 1990. "Gender and the Meaning of the Home." *International Journal of Urban and Regional Research* 14 (4): 625–647.

Martin, Susan F. 2011. *A Nation of Immigrants*. New York: Cambridge University Press.

Menjívar, Cecilia. 2006. "Liminal Legality: Salvadoran and Guatemalan Immigrants' Lives in the United States." *American Journal of Sociology* 111 (4): 999–1037.

Merton, Robert K. 1972. "Insiders and Outsiders: A Chapter in the Sociology of Knowledge." *American Journal of Sociology* 70 (1): 9–47.

Meyer, John W., and Brian Rowan. 1983. "Institutionalized Organizations: Formal Structure as Myth and Ceremony." *American Journal of Sociology* 83 (2): 340–363.

Michaelides, Marios, and Peter R. Mueser. 2012. "Recent Trends in the Characteristics of Unemployment Insurance Recipients." *Monthly Labor Review* July: 28–47.

Min, Pyong Gap. 1996. *Caught in the Middle: Korean Communities in New York and Los Angeles*. Berkeley and Los Angeles: University of California Press.

________. 2006. "Korean Americans." In *Asian Americans: Contemporary Trends and Issues*, edited by Pyong Gap Min, 199–259. Thousand Oaks, CA: Pine Forge Press.

________. 2011. "The Immigration of Koreans to the United States: A Review of 45 Year (1965-2009) Trends." *Development and Society* 40 (2): 195–223.

________. 2012. *Growth and Settlement Patterns of Korean Americans*. Research Report No. 4: The Research Center for Korean Community Queens College of CUNY.

Min, Pyong Gap, and Chigon Kim. 2012. "Statistics on Korean-Americans' Marriage and the Family." In *Ethnic Families in America: Patterns and Variations*, edited by Roosevelt Wright, Jr., Charles Mindel, Thanh Van Tran, and Robert Habenstein, 174–198. New York: Pearson.

Mink, Gwendolyn, and Rickie Solinger. 2003. *Welfare: A Documentary History of U.S. Policy and Politics*. New York: New York University Press.

Moon, Seungsook. 2003. "Immigration and Mothering: Case Studies from Two Generations of Korean Immigrant Women." *Gender and Society* 17 (6): 840–860.

National Center for Educational Statistics. 2011. *Digest of Educational Statistics: 2011.* Washington, DC: Institute of Education Sciences.

Neale, Faith R., and Pamela P. Peterson. 2005. "The Effect of Gramm-Leach-Bliley on the Insurance Industry." *Journal of Economics and Business* 57: 317–338.

Ngai, Mae M. 2004. *Impossible Subjects: Illegal Aliens and the Making of Modern America.* Princeton, NJ: Princeton University Press.

North, Douglas C. 1990. *Institutions, Institutional Change and Economic Performance.* New York: Cambridge University Press.

Office of Communications and Outreach, 2010. *Overview of the U.S. Department of Education.* Washington, DC: U.S. Department of Education.

Osili, Una Okonkwo, and Anna Paulson. 2008. "What Can We Learn about Financial Access from U.S. Immigrants? The Role of Country of Origin Institutions and Immigrant Beliefs." *The Word Bank Economic Review* 22: 431–455.

Painter, Gary, Lihong Yang, and ZhouYu. 2004. "Homeownership Determinants for Chinese Americans: Assimilation, Ethnic Concentration, and Nativity." *Real Estate Economics* 32: 509–539.

Painter, Gary, and ZhouYu. 2008. "Leaving Gateway Metropolitan Areas in the United States: Immigrants and the Housing Market." *Urban Studies* 45: 1163–1191.

_________. 2010. "Immigrants and Housing Markets in Mid-Size Metropolitan Areas." *International Migration Review* 44 (2): 442–476.

Panagakos, Anastasia N. 2003. "Downloading New Identities: Ethnicity, Technology, and Media in the Global Greek Village." *Identities: Global Studies in Culture and Power* 10: 201–219.

Park, Kyeyoung. 1997. *The Korean American Dream: Immigrants and Small Businesses in New York City.* Ithaca, NY: Cornell University Press.

Park, Sangmoon, and Soo-Hyeon Yoon. 2005. "Separating Early-Adopters from the Majority: The Case of Broadband Internet Access in Korea." *Technological Forecasting & Social Change* 72: 301–325.

Pencer, Karen M. 2006. "Foreclosing on Opportunity: State Laws and Mortgage Credit." *The Review of Economics and Statistics* 88 (1): 177–182.

Pew Research Center. 2013. *The Rise of Asian Americans.* http://www.pewresearch.org.

Portes, Alejandro, and Julia Sensenbrenner. 1993. "Embeddedness and Immigration: Notes on the Social Determinants of Economic Behavior." *American Journal of Sociology* 98 (6): 1320–1350.

Putnam, Robert D. 1995. "Bowling Alone: America's Declining Social Capital." *Journal of Democracy* 6 (1): 65–78.

_________. 2000. *Bowling Alone: The Collapse and Revival of American Community.* New York: Simon & Schuster.

Radin, Patricia. 2006. "To Me, It's My Life: Medical Communication, Trust, and Activism in Cyberspace." *Social Science and Medicine* 62: 591–601.

Ravitch, Diane, and Joseph P. Viteritti. 2000. *City Schools: Lessons from New York.* Baltimore: The Johns Hopkins University Press.

Reeves, Terrance J., and Claudette E. Bennett. 2004. *We the People: Asians in the United States. Census 2000 Special Reports.* Washington, DC: U.S. Census Bureau.

Rheingold, Howard. 2000. *The Virtual Community.* Cambridge, MA: The MIT Press.

Rhine, Sherrie L.W., and William H. Greene. 2006. "The Determinants of Being Unbanked for Immigrants." *Journal of Consumer Affairs* 40: 21–40.

Rudolph, Christopher. 2006. *National Security and Immigration: Policy Development in the United States and Western Europe Since 1945.* Stanford, CA: Stanford University Press.

Ruth, Madigan, Moira Munro, and Susan J. Smith. 1990. "Gender and the Meaning of the Home." *International Journal of Urban and Regional Research* 14: 625–647.

Salins, Peters D. 1997. *Assimilation, American Style: An Impassioned Defense of Immigration and Assimilation as the Foundation of American Greatness and the American Dream.* New York: Basic Books.

Schwartz, Alex F. 2006. *Housing Policy in the United States: An Introduction*. New York: Routledge.

Scott, Richard W. 2008. *Institutions and Organizations: Ideas and Interests*. Los Angeles: Sage, 3rd Edition.

Sidel, Ruth 1998. *Keeping Women and Children Last: America's War on the Poor*. New York: Penguin Books Ltd.

Skop, Emily, and Paul C. Adams. 2009. "Creating and Inhabiting Virtual Places: Indian Immigrants in Cyberspace." *National Identities* 11 (2): 127–147.

Steensland, Brian. 2006. "Cultural Categories and the American Welfare State: The Case of Guaranteed Income Policy." *American Journal of Sociology* 111 (5): 1273–1326.

Steuerle, C. Eugene. 2004. *Contemporary U.S. Tax Policy*. Washington, DC: The Urban Institute Press.

Suchman, Mark C., and Lauren B. Edelman. 1996. "Legal Rational Myths: The New Institutionalism and the Law and Society Tradition." *Law and Social Inquiry* 21: 903–941.

Sun, Yongmin. 1998. "The Academic Success of East-Asian-American Students: An Investment Model." *Social Science Research* 27: 432–456.

Teixeira, Carlos. 1998. "Cultural Resources and Ethnic Entrepreneurship: A Case Study of the Portuguese Real Estate Industry in Toronto." *The Canadian Geographer* 42 (3): 267–281.

The Chosun Ilbo. 2003. "Social Bonds among Korean-American Mothers." 23 July, 2003.

________. 2013. "MissyUSA as a Reliable Source of Information?" 10 May 2013.

The Congress of the United States. 2010. *Immigration Policy in the United States: An Update*. Washington, DC: Congressional Budget Office.

The Korea Times. 2005. "The Popularity of the "MissyUSA.com" among Korean-American Women." 20 March 2005.

The Korea Times New York. 2012. *The 2012 New York Business Directory*.

The State of Tennessee, 2012. *Tennessee Code Annotated*. http://tn.gov/consumer/documents/UniformResidentialLandlordandTenantAct7.12.12.pdf.

Tolbert, Pamela S., and Lynne G. Zucker. 1983. "Institutional Sources of Change in the Formal Structure of Organizations: The Diffusion of Civil Service Reform, 1880-1935." *Administrative Science Quarterly* 28: 22–39.

Tyler, Tom R. 2001. "Why Do People Rely on Others? Social Identity and Social Aspects of Trust." In *Trust in Society*, edited by Karen S. Cook, 285–306. New York: Russell Sage Foundation.

Van Hook, Jennifer, Susan K. Brown, and Frank D. Bean. 2006. "For Love or Money? Welfare Reform and Immigrant Naturalization." *Social Forces* 85 (2): 643–666.

Varsanyi, Monica W. 2008. "Rescaling the 'Alien,' Rescaling Personhood: Neoliberalism, Immigration, and the State." *Annals of the Association of American Geographers* 98 (4): 877–896.

________. 2011. "Neoliberalism and Nativism: Local Anti-Immigrant Policy Activism and an Emerging Politics of Scale." *International Journal of Urban and Regional Research* 35 (2): 295–311.

Vaux, Alan. 1988. *Social Support: Theory, Research, and Intervention*. New York: Praeger.

Wasserman, Stanley, and Katherine Faust. 1994. *Social Network Analysis: Methods and Applications*. New York: Cambridge University Press.

Wellman, Barry, Janet Salaff, Dimitrina Dimitrova, Laura Garton, Milena Gulia, and Caroline Haythornthwaite. 1996. "Computer Networks as Social Networks: Collaborative Work, Telework, and Virtual Community." *Annual Review of Sociology* 22: 213–238.

Wellman, Barry, and Scot Wortley. 1990. "Different Strokes from Different Folks: Community Ties and Social Support." *American Journal of Sociology* 96 (3): 558–588.

Wellman, Berry. 1979. "The Community Question: The Intimate Networks of East Yorkers." *American Journal of Sociology* 78: 1201–1231.

_______. 2001. "Physical Place and Cyber-Place." *International Journal for Urban and Regional Research* 25: 227–252.

Wells, Miriam J. 2004. "The Grassroots Reconfiguration of U.S. Immigration Policy." *International Migration Review* 38 (4): 1308–1347.

Wilson, Samuel M., and Leighton C. Peterson. 2002. "The Anthropology of Online Communities." *Annual Review of Anthropology* 31: 449–467.

Yinger, John. 1995. *Closed Doors, Opportunity Lost: The Continuing Costs of Housing Discrimination*. New York: Russell Sage Foundation.

Zhou, Min, and Susan S. Kim. 2006. "Community Forces, Social Capital, and Educational Achievement: The Case of Supplementary Education in the Chinese and Korean Immigrant Communities." *Harvard Educational Review* 76: 1–29.

Zonta, Michela M. 2012. "The Continuing Significance of Ethnic Resources: Korean-Owned Banks in Los Angeles, New York, and Washington, DC." *Journal of Ethnic and Migration Studies* 38: 463–484.

Additional Resources

ON-LINE SOURCES

ABC News Network: www.abcnews.com
American Council of Life Insurers (ACLI): www.acli.com/Tools/Industry%20Facts/Life%20Insurers%20Fact%20Book/Documents/Life_Insurers_Fact_Book_2013_All.pdf
A School District in the State of New Jersey: www.wearenorwood.org
Banks: www.banks.com/articles/understanding-escrow-accounts
Board of Governors of the Federal Reserve System:

- www.federalreserve.gov/
- www.federalreserve.gov/boarddocs/supmanual/supervision_cch.htm
- www.federalreserve.gov/boarddocs/supmanual/cch/respa.pdf
- www.federalreserve.gov/pf/pdf/pf_5.pdf
- www.federalreserve.gov/creditcard/regs.html
- www.flofr.com/PDFs/mbl.pdf

Center for New York City Affairs at the New School: insideschools.org/districts/manhattan/district-5
Florida Office of Financial Regulation: www.flofr.com/PDFs/mbl.pdf
Investopedia: www.investopedia.com/terms/m/money-order.asp
Legal Information Institute at the Cornell Law School: www.law.cornell.edu/wex/income_tax
Legal Services of New Jersey: www.lsnjlaw.org/Publications/Pages/Manuals/TenantsRights.pdf
Liberal Mutual Insurance Company: www.libertymutual.com/life-insurance/annuities/answers
Office of Immigration Statistics in the U.S. Department of Homeland Security: www.dhs.gov/xlibrary/assets/statistics/publications/lpr_fr_2011.pdf
Pew Research Center: www.pewresearch.org
Public.Resource.Org: ftp://ftp.resource.org/gao.gov/89-329/00004C57.pdf
Retirement Online LLC: www.rothira.com/traditional-ira-vs-roth-ira

The American Council of Life Insurers: https://www.acli.com/Tools/Industry%20Facts/Life%20Insurers%20Fact%20Book/Documents/Life_Insurers_Fact_Book_2013_All.pdf

The Centers for Medicare & Medicaid Services: www.medicaid.gov/; www.medicaid.gov/CHIP

The Consumer Financial Protection Bureau (CFPB): files.consumerfinance.gov/f/201305_compliance-guide_home-ownership-and-equity-protection-act-rule.pdf

The Empire Health Choice: www.empireblue.com/home-providers.html

The Federal Deposit Insurance Corporation (FDIC): www.fdic.gov/

- www.fdic.gov/regulations/laws/rules/6500-3030.html
- https://www.fdic.gov/regulations/laws/important/index.html
- www.fdic.gov/regulations/compliance/manual/pdf/V-1.1.pdf
- https://www.fdic.gov/regulations/laws/important/index.html

The Federal Financial Institutions Examination Council (FFIEC): www.ffiec.gov/cra/

The Federal Housing Finance Agency Office of Inspector General:fhfaoig.gov/LearnMore/History

The Federal Reserve Board:

- www.federalreserve.gov/
- www.federalreserve.gov/pf/pdf/pf_5.pdf
- www.federalreserve.gov/boarddocs/supmanual/supervision_cch.htm
- www.federalreserve.gov/creditcard/regs.html

The Federal Trade Commission (FTC):

- www.ftc.gov/tips-advice/competition-guidance/guide-antitrust-laws/antitrust-laws
- www.federalreserve.gov/boarddocs/supmanual/cch/respa.pdf

The Financial Services Committee of the United States House of Representatives: financialservices.house.gov/media/pdf/bankcomp.pdf

The Internal Revenue Service (IRS):

- www.irs.gov/pub/irs-pdf/i1120.pdf
- www.irs.gov/pub/irs-pdf/i1040tt.pdf
- www.irs.gov/Credits-&-Deductions
- www.irs.gov/uac/States-Without-a-State-Income-Tax

The National Association of Insurance Commissioners (NAIC): www.naic.org/documents/topics_white_paper_hist_ins_reg.pdf

The National Conference of Commissioners on Uniform State Laws: uniformlaws.org/ActSummary.aspx?title=Residential+Landlord+and+Tenant+Act

The New Jersey Department of Banking and Insurance (DOBI): www.state.nj.us/dobi/division_banking/depositories/bnkdep_menu.htm

The New York City Department of Education:

- schools.nyc.gov/default.htm
- www.schools.nyc.gov/Academics/GiftedandTalented
- schools.nyc.gov/SchoolPortals/10/X141/EducationalSupport/Guidance/hs+guidance.htm
- schools.nyc.gov/documents/d75/district/attendance/home_schooling/HOMESCHOOLING_PROCEDURES_bb.pdf
- csd3.nycdoe.org/

The New York City Housing Authority (NYCHA): www.nyc.gov/nycha

The New York City Human Resources Administration's Office of Citywide Health Insurance Access (OCHIA): www.nyc.gov/public_insurance

The New York State Department of Health (NYSDOC): health.ny.gov/family_health_plus

The New York State Department of Labor: www.labor.ny.gov

The New York State Department of Taxation and Finance: www.tax.ny.gov/pdf/stats/policy_special/handbook_of_new_york_state_and_local_taxes_october_2012.pdf

The New York State Education Department:

- usny.nysed.gov/about
- www.highered.nysed.gov/ocue/lrp/rules.htm
- www.p12.nysed.gov/psc

The New York State Homes and Community Revival: www.nyshcr.org/Topics/Home/Buyers/SONYMA/SONYMAProductsforFirstTimeHomebuyers.htm

The Office of Comptroller of the Currency (OCC): www.occ.gov/

The Tennessee Division of Consumer Affairs (TDCA): tn.gov/consumer/documents/UniformResidentialLandlordandTenantAct7.12.12.pdf

The United State Bureau of Census: www.census.gov/hhes/www/housing/census/historic/owner.html

The United States Congressional Budget Office (CBO): www.cbo.gov/sites/default/files/cbofiles/ftpdocs/119xx/doc11959/12-03-immigration_chartbook.pdf

The United State Department of Agriculture:

- www.fns.usda.gov
- www.fns.usda.gov/snap
- www.fns.usda.gov/wic
- www.fns.usda.gov/slp

The United States Department of Justice: www.justice.gov/crt/about/hce/housing_ecoa.php

The United States Department of Labor: www.foreignlaborcert.doleta.gov/reg.cfm

The United States Government Printing Office:

- www.gpo.gov/fdsys/pkg/PLAW-111publ148/pdf/PLAW-111publ148.pdf
- www.gpo.gov/fdsys/pkg/USCODE-2011-title15/

The United State House of Representatives:

- ftp://ftp.resource.org/gao.gov/89-329/00004C57.pdf
- financialservices.house.gov/media/pdf/bankcomp.pdf

The United States Joint Committee of the House and Senate: www.taxpolicycenter.org/legislation/upload/x-1-11.pdf

The United States Social Security Administration: www.ssa.gov/pubs/EN-05-10003.pdf

The U.S. Alcohol and Tobacco Tax and Trade Bureau (TTB): www.ttb.gov/tax_audit/atftaxes.shtml

The U.S. Citizenship and Immigration Services (USCIS):

- www.uscis.gov/about-us/our-history
- www.uscis.gov/humanitarian/refugees-asylum/refugees
- www.uscis.gov/sites/default/files/USCIS/Resources/A1en.pdf
- www.uscis.gov/sites/default/files/USCIS/Resources/B1en.pdf
- www.uscis.gov/green-card/green-card-processes-and-procedures/consular-processing
- www.uscis.gov/sites/default/files/files/article/chapter5.pdf

The U.S. Department of Education:

- www2.ed.gov/about/overview/mission/mission.html
- www2.ed.gov/about/offices/list/ocr/docs/hq43e4.html
- www2.ed.gov/policy/elsec/leg/esea02/pg1.html
- www2.ed.gov/programs/magnet/index.html
- studentaid.ed.gov/about

The U.S. Department of Homeland Security: https://www.dhs.gov/xlibrary/assets/statistics/publications/lpr_fr_2011.pdf

The U.S. Department of Housing and Urban Development:

- www.huduser.gov

- portal.hud.gov/hudportal/HUD?src=/program_offices/housing/mfh/mfinfo/sec202ptl
- portal.hud.gov/hudportal/HUD?src=/program_offices/public_indian_housing/programs/hcv
- www.hud.gov/rental_assistance
- portal.hud.gov/hudportal/HUD?src=/program_offices/housing/sfh/ins/203b--df

The U.S. Department of State's Office of the Historian: history.state.gov/milestones/1945-1952/immigration-act.

The U.S. Departments of the Treasury: www.occ.gov/

The U.S. Departments of the Treasury & Housing and Urban Development:

- www.makinghomeaffordable.gov/programs/lower-rates/Pages/harp.aspx
- www.makinghomeaffordable.gov/programs/lower-payments/Pages/hamp.aspx

U.S News and World Report: money.usnews.com/money/blogs/the-smarter-mutual-fund-investor/2013/02/06/retirement-basics-ira-or-401k

Wells Fargo: www.wellsfargo.com/credit-cards/secured/

Index

About the Author

Joong-Hwan Oh is an associate professor of sociology at Hunter College of the City University of New York.

www.ingramcontent.com/pod-product-compliance
Ingram Content Group UK Ltd.
Pitfield, Milton Keynes, MK11 3LW, UK
UKHW040909190926
475560UK00008B/55

9 781498 519267